Experimental Philosophy

Experimental Philosophy

A Critical Study

Nikil Mukerji

London • New York

Published by Rowman & Littlefield International Ltd
6 Tinworth Street, London, SE11 5AL
www.rowmaninternational.com

Rowman & Littlefield International Ltd. is an affiliate of Rowman & Littlefield
4501 Forbes Boulevard, Suite 200, Lanham, Maryland 20706, USA
With additional offices in Boulder, New York, Toronto (Canada), and Plymouth (UK)
www.rowman.com

Translation copyright © 2019 by Nikil Mukerji

Originally published in German as *Einführung in die experimentelle Philosophie*
Copyright © Verlag Wilhelm Fink, Paderborn, 2016
Wilhelm Fink is an imprint of Brill Deutschland GmbH
All rights reserved by and controlled through Verlag Wilhelm Fink, Paderborn, Brill Deutschland DmbH.

All rights reserved. No part of this book may be reproduced in any form or by any electronic or mechanical means, including information storage and retrieval systems, without written permission from the publisher, except by a reviewer who may quote passages in a review.

British Library Cataloguing in Publication Data
A catalogue record for this book is available from the British Library

ISBN: HB 978-1-78661-123-9
       PB 978-1-78661-125-3

Library of Congress Cataloging-in-Publication Data
Names: Mukerji, Nikil, author.
Title: Experimental philosophy : a critical study / Nikil Mukerji.
Other titles: Einführung in die experimentelle Philosophie. English
Description: London ; New York : Rowman & Littlefield International, Ltd., [2019] | Includes bibliographical references and index.
Identifiers: LCCN 2018056826 | ISBN 9781786611239 (cloth : alk. paper) | ISBN 9781786611253 (pbk. : alk. paper) | ISBN 9781786611246 (ebk.)
Subjects: LCSH: Philosophy. | Methodology.
Classification: LCC B52 .M8513 2019 | DDC 101—dc23
LC record available at https://lccn.loc.gov/2018056826

∞™ The paper used in this publication meets the minimum requirements of American National Standard for Information Sciences – Permanence of Paper for Printed Library Materials, ANSI/NISO Z39.48–1992.

Printed in the United States of America

To my grandparents,
Katharina and Valentin Klass

Contents

Acknowledgements	ix
Abbreviations	xi
Preface to the English Edition	xiii
Foreword to the German Edition	xv
Introduction	xvii

1	**The Armchair and the Laboratory**	**1**
	1.1 Armchair Philosophy	1
	1.2 Analytic Philosophy	4
	1.3 The Cognitive Science View of Experimental Philosophy	8
	1.4 Empirically Informed Philosophy	12
	1.5 Positive Experimental Philosophy	15
	1.6 Negative Experimental Philosophy	19
	1.7 Philosophy, Metaphilosophy, and Metametaphilosophy	21
	1.8 Summary	26
2	**Experimentally Informed Arguments**	**31**
	2.1 Empirical Propositions	32
	2.2 Philosophical Propositions	34
	2.3 The Relevance of Experimental Data	36
	2.4 Bridging the Gap	41
	2.5 Relevant Questions	50
	2.6 Summary	54

3	Experimental Studies	59
	3.1 Knowledge	59
	3.2 Reference	76
	3.3 Intentional Action	87
	3.4 Free Will	103
	3.5 Summary	118
4	Objections	127
	4.1 The Scope of Objections	127
	4.2 Methodological Objections	131
	4.3 Philosophical Objections	145
	4.4 Summary	162
	Conclusion	169
References		173
Appendix A		191
Appendix B		197
Appendix C		203
Index		219
About the Author		227

Acknowledgements

Philosophical books tend, in a certain sense, to be joint projects. This one is no exception. I was fortunate enough to have the opportunity of discussing my ideas with colleagues, students, and friends. This helped me tremendously to clarify and correct my thoughts. Therefore, I would like to thank all those who have supported me in writing this book.

Unfortunately, I am unable to mention explicitly all of those who deserve to be mentioned. This, however, shall not keep me from acknowledging at least some persons who surely do deserve it. These are, first, Johanna Jauernig, Christoph Luetge, Julian Müller, Hannes Rusch, and Matthias Uhl of Technische Universität München, Jan Heilinger of the Munich Center for Ethics, and Michael von Grundherr as well as Martin Rechenauer of Ludwig-Maximilians-Universität München. I was fortunate enough to be able to discuss my ideas about experimental ethics with them.

In recent years, I also had the opportunity to discuss experimental philosophy more broadly with Erik Angner, Monika Betzler, Sven Bernecker, Dieter Birnbacher, Andreas Brachmann, Christine Bratu, Miguel Egler, Eugen Fischer, Thomas Grundmann, Stephan Hartmann, Nora Heizelmann, Joachim Horvath, Christoph Jäger, Joshua Knobe, Martin Kocher, Édouard Machery, Adriano Mannino, Albert Newen, Niki Pfeiffer, Kevin Reuter, Alexander Reutlinger, Achim Stephan, Stephen Stich, and Sven Walter. For that, I owe them a great debt. The same is true in the case of Julian Nida-Rümelin who has encouraged me and supported my work throughout the past few years.

Furthermore, I would like to thank Nadine Albert, Christiane Bacher, Lisa Sauerwald, Ute Schnückel, Henning Siekmann, and Mechthild Vogt of Wilhelm Fink Verlag for supporting me in the planning and realisation of the German version of this monograph (*Einführung in die experimentelle Philosophie*, 2016) as well as Natalie Lihn Bolderston, Isobel Cowper-Coles, and Emily Eastridge of Rowman & Littlefield International, who supported and facilitated the publication of this English version. I also thank Boudewijn de Bruin for his helpful advice regarding the English book and, especially, for his encouragement. Furthermore, I am grateful to Victoria Schöffel and Georgios Karageorgoudis, who served me as test readers and gave me valuable suggestions for improving the manuscript. Above that, I thank three anonymous reviewers for Rowman & Littlefield International, whose circumspect and apt criticisms I found very valuable.

Moreover, I owe a great debt to my friends Ludwig Heider, Robert Hümmer, Thomas Kaczmarek, and Nikolai Kleinhammer as well as to my parents Maria und Kiran Mukerji for their valuable support over many years. Finally, and most importantly, I would like to thank, heartily, my grandparents Katharina and Valentin Klass. In their lifetime, they embarked upon numerous experiments, and what they accomplished is truly remarkable. For this reason, I dedicate this book to them.

Abbreviations

Abbreviation	Meaning
A-Phi	analytic philosophy
AC-Phi	armchair philosophy
C	Charles (thought experiment)
CEO	chief executive officer
D	Dave (thought experiment)
EA	Easter Asian person
E-Phi	empirically informed philosophy
FWNMW intuition	"free will no matter what" intuition
$intention_A$	intention in the action
$intention_M$	motivating intention
$intention_P$	prior intention
K	Karen (thought experiment)
MAP	method of analytic philosophy
R&D	research and development
S	Suzy (thought experiment)
SC	person from the Indian subcontinent
SES	socioeconomic status
T	thought experiment
x-phi	experimental philosophy
$X\text{-}Phi_C$	cognitive science view of experimental philosophy
$X\text{-}Phi_N$	negative experimental philosophy
$X\text{-}Phi_P$	positive experimental philosophy
XRP	x-phi replicability project
W	Westerner (i.e. American of European descent)
WEIRD	western, education, industrialised, rich, and democratic

Preface to the English Edition

In 2016, I published *Einführung in die experimentelle Philosophie* with Wilhelm Fink Verlag. It was the first German monograph about experimental philosophy (x-phi), and it was meant to serve as an introduction to the field, geared towards professional philosophers, philosophy students, and interested laypersons alike. In writing it, I aimed, above all, to provide a *systematic* account of experimental philosophy. I did so for two reasons. Firstly, I have a taste for systematicity. When I delve into a new topic, I try to get a systematic overview of it early on. I try to understand how things hang together and where lines can be drawn. Accordingly, I wanted to introduce my readers to x-phi using that same approach. Secondly, I noticed that many texts which are usually recommended as introductory and foundational readings on x-phi do not put a special emphasis on systematicity. Instead, they highlight specific aspects of experimental philosophy, for example, specific experimental findings, distinctive techniques used by experimental philosophers and critiques of traditional armchair philosophers and how to rebut them. Though such contributions are, of course, valuable, they leave room, I reasoned, for a text that brings a "big picture" approach to the x-phi debate.

Such a text, I believed, should address questions like the following: (1) What is x-phi? Which versions of x-phi exist? How do they differ from each other and more traditional views of philosophy (e.g. analytic philosophy)? Is x-phi incompatible with armchair philosophy and, if so, why, how, and to which extent? (2) What is the basic motivation for doing x-phi research, what are the arguments its protagonists use to support philosophical conclusions, and what are the commonalities and differences between the arguments used by different x-phi researchers? (3) What are the most important debates in x-phi? How did these develop out of traditional philosophical problems, and how have initial findings given rise to current x-phi debates?

(4) What are the main critiques of x-phi, which of these critiques target which versions of x-phi, which criticisms are justified, and where does this leave us in terms of an overall evaluation of x-phi as an approach to doing philosophy?

The German book, which addressed these questions, was received well, and many people who read it, especially colleagues working on x-phi, pointed out that the book was quite different from existing English texts. This encouraged me to publish an English version with Rowman & Littlefield International. It is the book you are reading right now. I should note, however, that it is more than a mere translation of the German original. Two years have passed since the publication of the German *Einführung*, and the x-phi debate has moved on since then. Accordingly, I have updated the main text, included additional references to recent works, and added passages where I felt that this was appropriate. I have also added three appendices that address aspects of x-phi that the main text does not cover or does not cover sufficiently. While chapter 3, which discusses important x-phi studies, focuses on experimental contributions to epistemology, the philosophy of language, action theory, and the philosophy of mind, appendix A gives additional information about further contributions to ethics (A.1), metaphysics (A.2), the philosophy of science (A.3), and logic and rationality (A.4). Appendix B points the reader to additional resources, specifically online material on x-phi (B.1), introductory texts (B.2), and important book publications (B.3). Appendix C supplements the discussion of experimental methods with further information about bibliometrics (C.1), formal methods (C.2), tools from economic (C.3), genealogical arguments (C.4), neuroscientific approaches (C.5), qualitative methods (C.6), and sting operations (C.7). The main text contains references to the appendices at the appropriate passages.

These changes and additions, many of which were requested by three anonymous reviewers for Rowman & Littlefield International, have in my view substantially improved the book. I hope that the readers will find them helpful.

Nikil Mukerji
Ludwig-Maximilians-Universität München, Munich
November 2018

Foreword to the German Edition

I am delighted to see the publication of Nikil Mukerji's *Einführung in die experimentelle Philosophie*. In a number of important respects, this new book both encourages and embodies the transformations that have been steadily occurring in the field over these past few decades.

First, the field of experimental philosophy has expanded in the topics and methods it embraces. Research in experimental philosophy was initially confined to a relatively narrowly circumscribed set of issues. Over the past fifteen years, however, the scope of the field has expanded radically. There are now serious experimental research programmes investigating issues in moral philosophy, philosophy of mind, epistemology, philosophy of language, and numerous other areas. Moreover, experimental philosophy has become increasingly intertwined with work in other disciplines. Experimental philosophers now frequently collaborate with psychologists and publish in psychology journals, and over the past couple of years, there has been a surge of interest in issues at the intersection of experimental philosophy and linguistics.

Mukerji's *Einführung* embodies this broadening of the field. It introduces the reader to a broad array of different types of experimental research, and also to a number of different metaphilosophical perspectives on the importance of experimental work.

Second, and perhaps more strikingly, the field has expanded geographically. Initially, work in experimental philosophy was almost completely confined to Anglophone countries, especially the United States. By now, however, the situation has changed completely. Many of the most exciting new discoveries over the past few years have actually come out of research conducted in continental Europe. These years have seen a flowering of important experimental philosophy research programmes in France, Poland, Portugal, the Baltics, the Netherlands, and, of course, Germany.

Mukerji's work is a perfect manifestation of this second expansion. As the first German-language monograph on experimental philosophy, it bears witness to the growing importance of experimental philosophy in the German-speaking world. Yet, at the same time, by offering a clear and powerful introduction to these ideas, it promises to encourage further research in this area from German philosophers.

In general, I am reluctant to speculate about empirical matters in the absence of systematic quantitative data, but let me now advance one speculative empirical hypothesis. My guess is that the years following the publication of Mukerji's book will be exciting ones for experimental philosophy in the German-speaking community.

Joshua Knobe
Yale University, New Haven
July 2016

Introduction

If you understand the notion of a dwarf, then you should understand why there cannot be such a thing as a *giant* dwarf. Similarly, if you understand the concept of a bachelor, you should be able to see that there is no such thing as a *married* bachelor. In like manner, if you are sufficiently familiar with the idea of philosophy, it seems obvious to you that there is no such thing as an *experimental* philosophy. This, at any rate, seems to be the implication of a widespread understanding of the nature of philosophy. According to this view, it is an *armchair discipline*, which does not draw on empirical evidence and can, for this reason, be pursued, quite literally, from the armchair. On this understanding of philosophy, its practitioners should not gather empirical data, they should not employ empirical testing procedures, and they should, under no circumstances, roll up their sleeves and conduct experiments! Proponents of a new movement within the philosophical community beg to differ. They believe that empirical methods can, in fact, be put to good use in philosophy and can help us to pursue the answers to its perennial questions. They believe in an experimental philosophy or x-phi, for short.

At first glance, this notion is rather implausible. Here is why. The empirical sciences seek to establish empirical facts. Their methods help them to understand our world and the way it is *as a matter of fact*. In contrast, philosophy seems to go after entirely different questions. Classical philosophical questions appear to be of a rather different kind. This gets clear once we consider some examples:

- Philosophers do not ask how we perceive the world. Instead, they ask, as did Kant, *what has to be the case* for us to be able to perceive the world in the first place.
- They do not ask how humans act but, rather, *how they should act*.

- They are not satisfied to learn that people think they have free will. What interests them is, rather, whether it can be ascertained that what they believe is true or, failing that, whether *it is even conceivable* that something like a free will can exist in what appears to be a causally ordered universe.

Since philosophical questions seem to be distinctly non-empirical, empirical methods appear to have no place in philosophy. This impression, however, is based on a confusion. Even if philosophical questions are not empirical questions, it does not follow that insights into empirical matters are always *irrelevant* to philosophy. There are numerous examples to disprove this idea.

Consider, for example, normative ethics. Its central problem is the question what we ought to do. Whatever the answer may be, it is not an empirical, but a normative proposition. Nevertheless, empirical facts obviously play a role in answering ethical questions. For example, I may justify myself doing an act, ϕ, by pointing out that I promised my friend to do it. Or I might justify it in view of its desirable consequences. In both cases, I would be using an *empirical* proposition to argue for a *normative* view, namely, that I should do ϕ. In the first case, it is the fact that I have promised to do ϕ. In the second case, it is the fact that ϕ would have good consequences. So, initial appearances notwithstanding, empirical facts can play a role in philosophy.

Of course, it could still be true that empirical facts are rather unimportant. At this point, I cannot disprove this. In this study of experimental philosophy, it is my goal, however, to show that this idea is also mistaken. I aim to convince you that experimental methods can enrich the philosophical debate and make important contributions to it. To that end, we will discuss influential experimental studies from various areas, and we will analyse what they add to the philosophical debate. Of course, I can only give you a very limited insight into the flourishing field of x-phi. I hope, however, that this is enough to encourage you to do your own research and start reading experimental studies for yourself. If I at least succeeded in awakening your interest in x-phi, I would consider this "mission accomplished."

Before we start, allow me to say a few words about the basic idea behind the book, which will also explain its contents and structure. I wanted to give those interested in x-phi, above all, an accessible introduction to the field. There are, of course, different ways of doing this. One is to select individual studies that seem interesting and report their findings selectively. Though this approach certainly holds merit and can make for an interesting read, it runs the risk of neglecting the "bigger picture" and the way things hang together. To avoid this risk, a second approach suggests itself. It is to ask, first of all, which distinctions are important and which ideas are fundamental and, then, to draw on these foundations at later points in the discussion. In other words, the second approach emphasises *systematicity*. I have always found systematic introductions more valuable and, hence, felt naturally inclined to write one myself. In addition, I found that many introductory and foundational texts on x-phi emphasised other aspects over systematicity. Accordingly, I believed that there would be a need for such a text.

In addition, I wanted the book to meet further criteria that seemed important to me. Firstly, traditional philosophers, who are often critical of x-phi, frequently perceive it as a monolith. I wanted to show that it is, instead, a diverse field in which researchers argue and disagree about important issues, just as they do in any area of philosophy. For this reason, I chose to start, in chapter 1, with a short investigation of the various opinions about the nature and method of philosophy. My aim in this part is, first and foremost, to delineate armchair philosophy and, more particularly, its analytical variant from empirically informed philosophy, on the one hand, and three different kinds of x-phi, on the other. These distinctions will lay the ground for the discussion in the ensuing chapters and, in particular, the discussion of various objections to x-phi.

Secondly, the philosophical motivation for x-phi is often denied, and it is suggested that x-phi literature should be banished to the psychology sections of libraries. This, too, is a mistake that I wanted to address head-on. In fact, I believe that the motivation for x-phi research has its root in the method of analytic philosophy (MAP). In chapter 2, I explain why. Here, I specifically argue for two claims. The first is that modern analytic philosophy provides a natural point of connection for experimental studies. My second claim is that experimental research can add to philosophy by clarifying how we should interpret its central questions. It can do so, I hold, by analysing how we should interpret them in the context of, as Wittgenstein might have put it, our "lifeworld."

Thirdly, I wanted to address the most influential contributions to x-phi because I believe that any field is best approached by focusing on the studies that researchers have most intensely discussed. These contributions lie in *epistemology*, the *philosophy of language*, *action theory*, and the *philosophy of mind*. I examine them in chapter 3.[1] Unsurprisingly, the most influential papers in x-phi tend to be the oldest. Accordingly, we will start with them and discuss initial results in light of subsequent findings. After that, we will selectively review recent developments in each of the four areas.

Fourthly, I wanted this to be a *critical study* of x-phi. To me, that meant two things. Firstly, I did not want to tell only one side of the story. Though I am, as you can easily tell, very sympathetic to x-phi, I also wanted to give a *fair hearing to the critics*. Therefore, I have devoted chapter 4 to influential objections. Secondly, I wanted my study to be critical in the sense of discriminative.[2] It was my aim to pinpoint which aspects critics attack and to which versions of x-phi their criticisms apply. Therefore, I repeatedly draw on the distinctions between the different forms of x-phi (introduced in chapter 1) and the various argumentation schemes that x-phi researchers employ (introduced in chapter 2).

Fifthly and finally, I wanted to dispense with the idea that the rise of x-phi diminishes the role of armchair theorising. Though proponents of x-phi may have given us reason to believe that they were in favour of burning all armchairs,[3] I think it would be a mistake to conclude, as I have argued elsewhere (Mukerji 2014), that x-phi leaves no room for traditional ways of philosophising. In the conclusion, I explain why. Somewhat surprisingly, perhaps, I will try to convince you that x-phi does not diminish the role of armchair reflection in philosophical inquiry. Rather, it adds further tasks for armchair theorising that traditionally minded philosophers, who have no interest in running any experiments of their own, can tackle going forward. Accordingly, x-phi can, I believe, enrich philosophical debate overall and should, therefore, be welcomed by all philosophers. I would be glad if the ensuing discussion would succeed in making this idea more plausible.

NOTES

1. Appendix A provides further information on other areas of x-phi research, namely, ethics, metaphysics, the philosophy of science, and logic and rationality.

2. The word "critical" derives from the Greek word "κρίνειν," which can be translated as "to separate" or "to distinguish."

3. The video of the experimental philosophy anthem shows a burning armchair: https://youtu.be/tt5Kxv8eCTA (accessed 31 Oct 2018).

Chapter 1

The Armchair and the Laboratory

The term "experimental philosophy" or "x-phi" is a term of art. Different authors use it in different ways to refer to different things. This can create confusions that make it hard to approach the debate about x-phi. In fact, it is not a problem that affects only laypersons. Rather, it also affects those of us who deal with philosophy professionally. For this reason, I believe that we should, first of all, take measures to circumnavigate these confusions. We can do this by discussing, right at the outside, what x-phi is and how its proponents understand it. In particular, we shall be concerned to delineate x-phi from some views about the nature of philosophy from which it is customarily distinguished.

To this end, we shall start with two views that discussants usually regard as x-phi's foils. These are *armchair philosophy* (AC-Phi), on the one hand, and *analytic philosophy* (A-Phi), on the other (sections 1.1 and 1.2, respectively). After that, we will discuss a view that may be called *empirically informed philosophy* (E-Phi) and three variants of x-phi that are often not sufficiently distinguished (especially by x-phi's critics). In doing that, we will, of course, analyse how these differ from armchair philosophy and, in particular, from its analytic version (sections 1.3–1.6). Finally, we will try to deepen our understanding of the different forms of x-phi further by analysing how they relate, logically, to other views of philosophy as well as to each other (section 1.7). At the end of the chapter, we will summarise our main findings.

1.1 ARMCHAIR PHILOSOPHY

Philosophers traditionally understand their subject as an "armchair discipline." Timothy Williamson, for example, writes the following:

> If anything can be pursued in an armchair, philosophy can. Its traditional method is thinking, *without observation or experiment*. If the pursuit is conceived as

social, rather than solely individual, then speaking must be added to thinking, and several armchairs are needed, but that still leaves philosophy looking methodologically very far from the natural sciences. Loosely speaking, their method is a posteriori, philosophy's a priori. (Williamson 2005, 1; emphasis added, NM)

In like manner, Russ Shafer-Landau writes:

Philosophy is not primarily an empirical discipline, but an a priori one. Its truths are ordinarily discoverable, when they are, not exclusively by appeal to what our senses can tell us. We don't bump into such things as universals, free will, or modalities; we can't see them, or hear or touch them. We may have reason to deny the existence of such things, but not because we aren't sure what they taste like. Dismissing such things from our ontology, or ratifying their inclusion in it, is something that no scientist is able to do. Such things are dealt with in an a priori way. (Shafer-Landau 2006, 216–17)

Williamson and Shafer-Landau describe what seems to me to be a rather widespread understanding of philosophical practice. It views the activity of philosophy as pure, a priori thinking that is, from a methodological viewpoint, far removed from the a posteriori procedure of the empirical sciences.

The terms "a priori" and "a posteriori" are, of course, key concepts. As such, we should clarify them. One way of doing this is as follows: a method, we may say, is a priori if the gathering of experiential data (e.g. through experiments) does not play a role in it. It is a posteriori if that is not the case. Let us illustrate the distinction using two examples.

- The method by which we test whether "$7+5=12$" is true is a priori. To ascertain that it is, in fact, true, we do not need to gather and assess any experiential data. It is entirely sufficient to check whether the equation is in line with the laws of arithmetic.
- In contrast, the sentence "All swans are white" can only be confirmed to be true using a posteriori methods. To check whether it is true, we need to resort to experience. We need to gather and assess empirical data.

We can also apply this distinction between the a priori and a posteriori to *questions*, namely, as follows: we think of a question as a priori if we can answer it without resorting to any form of experience. For example, we can answer the question "Is $7+5$ equal to 12?" in that manner. We cannot, however, answer the question "Are all swans white?" without recourse to any experience. To answer it, we need empirical data.

Now, x-phi is customarily delineated from armchair philosophy (AC-Phi). We can, therefore, take a first step towards understanding it – *ex negativo*, as it were – by clarifying the latter concept. To do this, we can deploy the distinction between the a priori and a posteriori that we have just spelt out.

Armchair Philosophy (AC-Phi)

Philosophical questions are to be answered using a priori methods only.[1]

This thesis contains a concept that has not been clarified, namely, the concept of a *philosophical question*. We should ask, therefore, what makes a question a philosophical one.

Admittedly, this question is hard to answer. There are, however, issues that surely pass as paradigm examples of philosophical questions and which we may thus call *classical philosophical questions*.[2] A list of such questions would contain problems about notions that are central to philosophical discourse, such as knowledge, meaning, intentional action, and freedom of will.[3]

To many philosophers, René Descartes seems to be a prime example of an armchair philosopher. In his perhaps most famous work – the *Meditationes de Prima Philosophia* (1641) – he deals with the problem of knowledge. He intends to reform all his beliefs. In quite a radical manner, he seeks to doubt everything that does not appear to be entirely certain. By doing that, his goal is to put all knowledge on a secure and unshakable foundation (lat.: "fundamentum inconcussum"). At the beginning of his Meditations, he writes:

> Some years ago I was struck by the large number of falsehoods that I had accepted as true in my childhood, and by the highly doubtful nature of the whole edifice that I had subsequently based them on. I realized that it was necessary, once in the course of my life, to demolish everything completely and start again right from the foundations if I wanted to establish anything at all in the sciences that was stable and likely to last. . . . So today I have expressly rid my mind of all worries and arranged for myself a clear stretch of free time. I am here quite alone, and at last I will devote myself sincerely and without reservation to the general demolition of my opinions. (Descartes 1641/1996, 12)

It is, thus, Descartes's intention to retreat into himself in order to overturn all of his beliefs. And as if that was not enough, he intends, furthermore, to reject any form of sensory experience as a source of knowledge.

> Whatever I have up till now accepted as most true I have acquired either from the senses or through the senses. But from time to time I have found that the senses deceive, and it is prudent never to trust completely those who have deceived us even once. (Descartes 1641/1996, 65)

In this passage, Descartes dismisses a posteriori methods as sources of justification from his subsequent philosophical investigations. And he does so categorically! Any insight that might come to him is regarded as unjustified if it relies on any form of experience. After all, the senses through which all experience passes may deceive us. Therefore, Descartes pursues an a priori train of thought that yields a *necessary* truth – a truth, that is, about which he cannot, possibly, be mistaken. He finds it in the second meditation. It is the famous principle that it is not possible for a thinking being to doubt its own existence:

> So after considering everything very thoroughly, I must finally conclude that this proposition, *I am, I exist*, is necessarily true whenever it is put forward by me or conceived in my mind. (Descartes 1641/1996, 17; emphasis in the original)

To Descartes, the fact that he exists can be known before and independently of any experience. This seems to be logically presupposed by the fact that he *doubts*. For if he doubts, there must be an entity that doubts, that is, he. Therefore, Descartes reasons, he may be able to doubt almost all propositions. However, the fact of his own existence he cannot doubt.

This train of thought would go down in the history of philosophy as the *cogito argument*. Because it seems to rely only on information that can be ascertained a priori and independently of any experience, many philosophers view Descartes as the textbook example of an armchair philosopher.

1.2 ANALYTIC PHILOSOPHY

The cogito argument relies on a particular type of a priori method. We can interpret it as a *transcendental* argument (Bardon 2005; Stern 2000). In such an argument, the conclusion gets its justification from the fact that it appears to be a necessary condition for the possibility of the truth of a given assumption. The assumption in question is "I doubt." A necessary condition for this assumption seems to be the fact that I exist. Hence, I can infer, following transcendental logic, that I necessarily exist.

The fact that a given argument is an a priori argument does not entail; however, that is also a transcendental one. In fact, in modern analytic philosophy, a different sort of a priori method has risen to prominence. It is the use of thought experiments that are employed as "intuition pumps," as Dennett (1984, 17–18) puts it.

> *Analytic Philosophy (A-Phi)*
>
> Philosophical questions are to be answered using a priori methods only. In particular, they should make methodical use of our intuitions about thought experiments.

Hence, A-Phi turns out to be a special version of AC-Phi. That means that it makes an even stronger claim. While AC-Phi only asserts that philosophers should rely only on a priori methods, A-Phi strengthens this thesis by *adding the requirement* that they employ, also, the method of thought experimentation. Often, this method is plainly called the *method of analytic philosophy*.[4] In stylised form, we may characterise it as follows:

Method of Analytic Philosophy

Step 1: Introduce a philosophical thesis.
Step 2: Describe a philosophically interesting scenario (= thought experiment).
Step 3: Examine which judgement follows from the thesis introduced in Step 1 in regard to the scenario introduced in Step 2.
Step 4: Check whether that judgement is intuitively plausible.
Step 5: If the judgement is intuitively plausible, take this to be a confirmation of the philosophical thesis in question. If it is not, take the thesis to be disconfirmed.

Before we examine how MAP is applied, I should mention that the characterisation of MAP that we are working with is far from uncontroversial. To be sure, some philosophers have pointed out that this method is so prominent in modern analytic philosophy that it deserves to be called the "standard justificatory practice" (Kornblith 2007, 29). However, not all authors who have written about analytic philosophy have taken MAP to be an essential feature of it. In an influential study, Glock (2008) makes two observations. Firstly, philosophers who are not customarily regarded as analytic philosophers have used MAP (e.g. the British empiricists). And, secondly, for some authors who are commonly viewed as analytic philosophers, MAP does not play any role at all (e.g. the early Wittgenstein).[5] In fact, there seems to be evidence for both points (see textbox 1.1). Nevertheless, it seems justified, in the context of the debate about x-phi, to interpret analytic philosophy as I have proposed. This is because the idea of analytic philosophy has commonly been understood in this (admittedly idiosyncratic) way.

TEXTBOX 1.1. IS THE APPEAL TO INTUITIONS IN PHILOSOPHY A NEW PHENOMENON?

Jaakko Hintikka believes that the methodical use of intuitions characteristic of analytic philosophy is a rather recent phenomenon. To quote him directly, he says: "Before the early 1960s, you could scarcely find any overt references, let alone appeals, to intuitions in the pages of philosophical journals and books in the analytical tradition. After the mid-1960s, you will find intuitions playing a major role in the philosophical argumentation of virtually every article or book" (Hintikka 1999, 127). Regarding the first point, Goldman (2007) thinks that there is evidence for the methodical use of intuitions about thought experiments in classical authors, who far predate analytic philosophy. In this connection, he refers to a passage in John Locke's *Essay Concerning Human Understanding* (1694) as an example: the famous "prince-cobbler case." Similarly, Levin (2005) opines that MAP is, in fact, a method that has been characteristic of philosophy all throughout its history. Stich (2001), too, traces it way back, namely, all the way back to Plato. Andow (2015) examines some relevant empirical evidence using bibliometrics (for more information on this method, see appendix C.1). According to him, there has been a significant increase in the methodical use of intuitions in philosophy in the twentieth century. However, this increase was not confined to the field of philosophy. Furthermore, within philosophy, it was not confined to the area of analytic philosophy. On this point, see also Ashton & Mizrahi (2018a). Cappelen (2012, 2014) and Deutsch (2009, 2010, 2015a, b, 2016, 2017), however, dispute that analytic philosophy relies, in any way, on appeals to intuitions. We will discuss this view in more detail in section 4.3.5.

To illustrate how MAP is applied, we shall resort to one of the classical philosophical problems, namely, the question "What is knowledge?" There is a traditional answer to this question which is commonly referred to as the "standard analysis of knowledge."

Standard Analysis of Knowledge

Knowledge is justified true belief.

To apply MAP, we decide, in Step 1, to examine this standard analysis of knowledge as a philosophical proposition. In Step 2, we introduce a scenario that appears to be suitable as a test case.

Thought Experiment 1

Anna wants to know what time it is. So she consults her watch, which displays 2:51 pm at the time. On that basis, Anna forms the belief that it is 2:51 pm. It is, in fact, 2:51 pm. Does Anna *know* that it is 2:51 pm?

In Step 3, we check which judgement follows from the standard analysis of knowledge about Thought Experiment 1. This analysis states that a person knows a proposition *p* if and only if all of the following conditions are fulfilled:

Condition 1 (Belief Condition)

The person *believes* that *p* is true.

Condition 2 (Truth Condition)

p is true.

Condition 3 (Justification Condition)

The person has a justification for believing that *p* is true.

Condition 1 is fulfilled in Thought Experiment 1 because Anna believes that it is 2:51 pm. Furthermore, Condition 2 is fulfilled because it is, in fact, 2:51 pm. Finally, Condition 3 is fulfilled as well because Anna has a justification for her belief that it is 2:51 pm. After all, she has just looked at her watch, and that watch displayed that time. Hence, all three conditions are fulfilled. Anna believes, justifiedly and truthfully, that it is 2:51. It follows, therefore, from the standard analysis of knowledge that Anna knows this.

Now we should, in Step 4 of MAP, examine whether this judgement matches our intuitive judgement about the case. We do this by checking which answer *appears* to be correct in this case. Does Anna seem to know? The answer seems to be that, yes, she does, indeed, appear to know. At any rate, it is not clear why we should deny that Anna knows that it is 2:51 pm.

Hence, we can conclude, in Step 5, that the standard analysis of knowledge is confirmed by Thought Experiment 1. This does not, of course, guarantee that it is correct. But, for the moment, we do not have reason to doubt it.

Things change, however, once we slightly modify the case. We are still interested in the standard analysis of knowledge (Step 1) and introduce a new scenario to test it (Step 2). It is the following:

Thought Experiment 2

Anna wants to know what time it is. So she consults her watch, which displays 2:51 pm at the time. On that basis, Anna forms the belief that it is 2:51 pm. It is, in fact, 2:51 pm. *However, the reason why the watch displays the correct time is that it stopped yesterday precisely at 2:51 pm.* Does Anna know that it is 2:51 pm?

Again we examine whether all conditions that the standard analysis of knowledge requires for the ascription of knowledge are fulfilled in this Thought Experiment 2 (Step 3). They obviously still are in this case because Anna still believes that it is 2:51 pm, it is true that it is 2:51 pm, and she still has the same justification for her belief. Hence, on the standard analysis of knowledge, we should continue to ascribe knowledge to Anna. We should still say that she knows that it is 2:51 pm.

Next, we should ask, in Step 4, whether this is still intuitively plausible. To this end, it seems to be important to observe that Anna's forming of a true belief is, in fact, only based on luck. Accordingly, Anna does *not* appear to know that it is 2:51 pm in Thought Experiment 2.

Therefore, we can conclude, in Step 5, that the standard analysis of knowledge is disconfirmed. In fact, this conclusion has largely been adopted by philosophers since the publication of an influential paper by Gettier (1963).

1.3 THE COGNITIVE SCIENCE VIEW OF EXPERIMENTAL PHILOSOPHY

In the two preceding sections, we discussed armchair philosophy (AC-Phi) and analytic philosophy (A-Phi). AC-Phi is the view that philosophical questions are to be answered using a priori methods only. A-Phi is, as we said, a special case of AC-Phi. It, too, relies only on a priori methods, and its paradigmatic method – the MAP – is the methodical use of intuitions about thought experiments. Towards the end of the previous section, we examined how it works.

Now, experimental philosophers take their views to be in critical opposition both to AC-Phi and to A-Phi. There are a number of reasons for this. One such reason is their belief that AC-Phi and, in particular, its narrower version A-Phi do not make enough room for interesting questions and methods in philosophy. At least some experimental philosophers have pointed out that even authors who nowadays count as pioneers of AC-Phi used a posteriori methods. Earlier, we considered the case of Descartes, and we recorded that he seemed to resort only to a priori methods in his famous *Meditations*. Justin Sytsma and Jonathan Livengood comment on this in their insightful introductory book *The Theory and Practice of Experimental Philosophy* (2016). They point out that Descartes did not, in fact, shy away from empirical methods:

> But even Descartes did not philosophize exclusively from the armchair. In fact, he did a good deal of empirical work, and such work is, in our opinion, as much a part of Descartes's philosophical legacy as are his meditations. (Sytsma & Livengood 2016, xviii)

In fact, even some of Descartes exegetes have pointed out that the French philosopher did not just speculate from the armchair and that he did, in fact, devote much of his time to empirical investigations. John Cottingham, for example, writes that

> Descartes has become a kind of philosophical icon, displayed in the textbooks and commentaries of the last hundred years or so in a confusing variety of guises. In a version of the history of ideas that was widely promoted some decades ago, he figured as the archetypal "rationalist" metaphysician, attempting to spin out a whole deductive system of philosophy and science *a priori*, from premises derived entirely from inner reflection.

Shortly after that, Cottingham proceeds to clarify that

> in reality, the "rationalist" image is belied by the importance Descartes himself gave to experimentation, and to empirical hypotheses tested against experience. (Cottingham 2011, 288)

What does this mean? Is Descartes not an armchair philosopher, after all? Could he even serve as a crown witness of x-phi?

Proponents of AC-Phi might try to circumvent that conclusion by making a distinction. They might split Descartes in half, as it were, namely, into a philosopher, on the one hand, and a natural scientist, on the other hand. Then, they might go on to claim that Descartes – *qua* philosopher – steered clear of a posteriori methods, while Descartes – *qua* scientist – did not necessarily do so. And the empirical questions that Descartes pursued are, they might add, of no philosophical significance. If this reasoning is sound, proponents of x-phi are unjustified in claiming Descartes – the philosopher – as one of their precursors. For their "philosophical" questions are of an a posteriori nature and are, hence, not genuinely philosophical – at least according to those who adhere to some version of AC-Phi.

Experimental philosophers who propose to use empirical methods with an avowedly philosophical interest have reacted to this type of argument with a "quizzical stare." At any rate, this is the phrase that Joshua Knobe and Shaun Nichols – two of the main exponents of x-phi – have used to describe their reaction. To them, the issues they investigate are evidently philosophical in nature. And hence they write:

> The questions addressed in this research program [experimental philosophy, NM] strike us as *so obviously philosophical* that we find it a little bit difficult to know how to respond. (Knobe & Nichols 2008, 13; emphasis added, NM)

This reply manifests an understanding of philosophy that is fundamentally different from the AC-Phi view, in general, and the A-Phi view, in particular.

Analytic armchair philosophers pursue what we have called classical philosophical questions. They ask, for example: What is the nature of knowledge, of meaning, of intentional action, or of free will? To address them, they resort to MAP as their method of choice. That is, they employ intuitions about thought experiments as premises in their philosophical arguments. They do not, however, take an interest in these intuitions for their own sake. To them, they are, rather, a means to an end. They are just the means to finding a justified answer to the classical philosophical questions we have discussed earlier. Experimental philosophers like Joshua Knobe and Shaun Nichols, however, take an interest in the intuitions themselves. And they do so *for their own sake*.[6] They want to know which intuitions we develop in response to philosophical thought experiments, and they want to know why we have them. To them, the experimental means that x-phi provides are primarily an instrument that they want to deploy to answer these questions (Knobe 2007a, 2016).

Experimental Philosophy as the Cognitive Science of Philosophy (X-Phi$_C$)

> Not all philosophical questions are classical philosophical questions. The issue which intuitions people form in response to philosophical thought experiments (and why) is also a genuine philosophical question. It should be answered through systematic experiments.

In a typical X-Phi$_C$ study, participants are confronted with a thought experiment and asked to answer a philosophically interesting question about it. The answers are then analysed statistically. This way, practitioners of X-Phi$_C$ seek to understand which intuitions philosophical thought experiments elicit and how uniform people's intuitions are. In addition, they want to find out which cognitive processes give rise to them and which factors affect them causally. Unlike the proponents of AC-Phi, the protagonists of X-Phi$_C$ believe that the answers to these questions are of genuine philosophical interest *in and of themselves*. They can, after all, tell us something about our human nature and the functioning of our minds. They can help us to understand better the way we think, and they can assist us in grasping why we view the world as we do.

  A paradigmatic instantiation of X-Phi$_C$ is a study by Joshua Knobe about the concept of intentional action (Knobe 2003).[7] He gave participants one of two case scenarios. In both of them, they were asked to assess whether a particular person had done a given act intentionally or not. This person was the chief executive officer (CEO) of a company who, according to their own testimony, only aimed at maximising their company's profits. The CEO decides to start a programme that will ensure this. In one scenario, this programme harms the environment. In the other scenario, it helps the environment. In both cases, the CEO knows about these side effects but does not care about them at all. Now, the question that Knobe asked his subjects was whether the CEO *harmed* the environment intentionally (in the first case) and whether he *helped* the environment intentionally (in the second case). The answers the participants gave showed an interesting asymmetry that has come to be known as the "side-effect effect" or, in homage to Knobe, the "Knobe effect." A large majority answered that the CEO did harm the environment intentionally (in the first case), while a similarly large majority denied that the CEO helped the environment intentionally (in the second case). This asymmetry may be taken to suggest that the moral quality of the side effect affects our inclination to view it as intentional. To champions of X-Phi$_C$, such a result is philosophically interesting in and of itself because it shows how humans ascribe intentions to others. According to them, the result's philosophical significance is not diminished by the fact that it does not yield any immediate implications for a classical philosophical question. Some philosophers have questioned, however, that X-Phi$_C$ is genuine philosophy (see textbox 1.2).

TEXTBOX 1.2. IS THE COGNITIVE SCIENCE OF PHILOSOPHY (X-PHI$_C$) PHILOSOPHY?

Some experimental philosophers reject the view that X-Phi$_C$ is genuine philosophy. Stephen Stich and Kevin Tobia write, for example, that this view of x-phi "invites an obvious challenge: Why is this work *philosophy*? Knobe's contention that it is pursuing philosophical questions in a genuinely new way is not likely to satisfy those who pose this challenge, since he has not told us what these questions are, or why they should be viewed as *philosophical* questions" (Stich & Tobia 2016, 18; emphasis in the original, NM). An anonymous reviewer for Rowman & Littlefield has voiced similar concerns, stating that Knobe's view of x-phi as cognitive science has "undermined experimental philosophy as a tool within philosophy" because it does not encourage philosophers to use empirical methods as a way to contribute to philosophy proper. Bickle (2018) has recently argued that the view of x-phi as X-Phi$_C$ could lead to its fall because it runs the risk of making it into a highly specialised and technical area within philosophy that is inaccessible to philosophers with a conventional training. At least some philosophers (other than Joshua Knobe) have expressed sympathies for X-Phi$_C$, however. Mortensen & Nagel (2016, 66), for example, write that "one of the great advantages of investigating the

> mechanisms that give rise to particular intuitive judgments for their own sake rather than for a predetermined philosophical purpose is that descriptions of the mechanisms can be worked out in isolation from the theories those descriptions might be evidence for or against." That is, findings of X-Phi$_C$ projects might provide the philosophical community with neutral data points that can then be used to adjudicate gridlocked philosophical debates.

1.4 EMPIRICALLY INFORMED PHILOSOPHY

Proponents of X-Phi$_C$ believe that there are some empirical questions which we can address *via* experiments and which are philosophically interesting in their own right. Armchair philosophers deny this. They believe that we should not accept the idea of philosophy put forward by proponents of X-Phi$_C$. To them, this is not genuine philosophy. Hence, they would prefer to have the writings of experimental philosophers banished from the bookshelves of our philosophical libraries. Naturally, those whose books they want to banish disagree with this. According to practitioners of X-Phi$_C$, they, too, are philosophers.

It looks as though we are faced here with a mere verbal and substance-free dispute about the use of the word "philosophy."[8] A proven strategy to deal with such disputes is to draw a conceptual distinction. William James explains how this strategy works using the example of a metaphysical problem. A squirrel is clinging to the trunk of a tree. A man, who is standing on the opposite side of the tree, is trying to catch a glimpse of the squirrel. So he starts walking around the tree. The squirrel, however, starts moving as well. It does so in a way that ensures that it is always on the side of the tree facing away from the man. If it were not for the trunk, the man would look the squirrel right in the face. However, he never catches a glimpse of it because when he moves around the tree, the squirrel moves as well and always stays on the side that the man cannot see. Now, the metaphysical question we may pose is the following: Does the man *move around* the squirrel, or does he not? James's answer is: it depends!

> If you mean passing from the north of him to the east, then to the south, then to the west, and then to the north of him again, obviously the man does go round him, for he occupies these successive positions. But if on the contrary you mean being first in front of him, then on the right of him, then behind him, then on his left, and finally in front again, it is quite as obvious that the man fails to go round him, for by the compensating movements the squirrel makes, he keeps his belly

turned towards the man all the time, and his back turned away. Make the distinction, and there is no occasion for any farther dispute. (James 1907/1921, 44)

James's point is, then, that once we distinguish between two different senses of "move around," the puzzle is dissolved, and the answer to our problem becomes evident. In like manner, we may distinguish between different meanings of the word "philosophy." Perhaps we should distinguish between philosophy$_{AC}$ and philosophy$_X$, where the former is intended to refer to the preferred, narrower understanding of armchair philosophers and the latter is meant to refer to the notion of philosophy favoured by experimental philosophers? All classical philosophical questions that belong to philosophy$_{AC}$ would also be part of the concept of philosophy$_X$. After all, proponents of x-phi do not deny that these questions are genuinely philosophical. They merely hold the view that there are additional problems that are also philosophical in nature, though armchair philosophers refuse to acknowledge them.[9] Philosophy$_L$ would then include all and only those philosophical questions that can be answered a priori, while philosophy$_X$ would also include questions that can be answered using a posteriori methods.

So far, so good. There is, however, a problem with this proposed solution to the problem: Descartes, who many armchair philosophers view as a textbook practitioner of their vision of philosophy, steps out of line once more. To be sure, it is true that he used a priori methods in his philosophy, and it is also true that he used a posteriori methods in his scientific investigations. There was, however, also a fair amount of crossover in his choice of methods. In particular, he deployed a posteriori methods in his philosophical works. As the German Descartes scholar Dominik Perler explains, Descartes only excluded a posteriori methods in his attempt to establish a secure foundation for knowledge. Regarding that problem, Descartes found it important to confine himself to the workings of pure reason. To him, this was necessary in order to achieve absolute certainty. As Perler goes on to explain, however, this does not mean that

> every time when we acquire knowledge or verify something that we purport to know, we need to restrict ourselves to the activity of the mind alone. We establish the foundation of all knowledge only once, as Descartes emphasises at the beginning of the Meditations. "Once in our lives" we have to question everything and look for an indubitable foundation of our knowledge. However, once we have established such an indubitable foundation and once we have found a guarantee for the reliability of our cognitive faculties ... we can and must draw on sensory experience to acquire knowledge of concrete facts. (Perler 1998, 85; translated from German, NM)

Evidently, then, AC-Phi's claim that philosophical questions are to be answered using only a priori methods is quite problematic, at least if we want to regard the problems Descartes dealt with as belonging to philosophy. It seems to me, however, that nobody should doubt the philosophical nature of these problems. To illustrate, let us consider an example.

Descartes was a metaphysical dualist. That is to say, he believed the world was made up of two substances, namely, *mind* and *body*. As humans, we are made up of both of these substances. We have an immaterial mind and a physical body. The two are, of course, not identical with one another and could, God willing, exist separately. At least, that was Descartes's view. Now, the distinctness and metaphysical independence of mind and body give rise to a problem: How can they interact? Surely, this question is a philosophical one if there is any. However, Descartes chose not to answer it entirely based on armchair reflection. To tackle it, he started looking, rather, for empirical evidence. He set out to find the place in the brain where mind and body interact. When he discovered a small gland in the middle of the brain, namely, the *pineal gland*, he believed that he had found it. This gland, Descartes reasoned, must be the primary residence of the soul (fr.: "le principal siege de l'âme"). Now comes the crucial part, that is, the question why it, rather than other parts of the brain, should be the place where mind and body interact. Descartes's argument may be sketched as follows: all our sense impressions and thoughts occur to us as single entities. This fact is remarkable because we have two eyes to see with, two ears to hear with, and two hemispheres of the brain that we use to think. But there is never more than one impression in the mind, and we never have more than one thought. Hence, there has to be one central organ in the body that integrates all impressions and thoughts. In Descartes own words:

> il faut de nécessité que les espèces qui entrent par les deux yeux, ou par les deux oreilles s'aillent unir en quelque partie du corps pour y être considérées par l'âme. (Descartes 1964–1974, III: 19)

The pineal gland, Descartes reasoned, is the ideal candidate. For it has all the attributes that seem necessary to unify our ideas and impressions. Firstly, there exists exactly one pineal gland in the brain. And, secondly, it possesses all the physical properties that would make it a suitable place for the soul. The details of the argument shall not concern us here. What counts is the observation that Descartes's a priori considerations about the nature of the soul led him to questions that, he believed, can only be answered using a posteriori methods. We can record, then, that Descartes was certainly no textbook example of an armchair philosopher – at least if we look beyond the *Meditations* and consider his philosophical works more broadly.

In fact, AC-Phi appears to be somewhat of a caricature of philosophy. The answers to many philosophical questions and, in particular, the classical ones obviously depend on the answers to certain empirical questions. Hence, it seems plausible to adopt a different understanding of philosophy. On that view, philosophical inquiry should be empirically informed, at least when it comes to investigating some of philosophy's questions.

> **Empirically Informed Philosophy (E-Phi)**
>
> Some philosophical questions – including some classical ones – are not to be answered using a priori methods only. Rather, the answers to those questions require additional a posteriori methods.

The problem of the *freedom of the will* is a suitable subject to make this picture of philosophical inquiry plausible. The problem consists, roughly speaking, in the fact that we, as human agents, live in what appears to be a causally ordered universe. On the one hand, we explain the behaviour of material entities in reference to natural laws and, especially, in reference to the laws of physics. These, we believe, govern the behaviour of bodies that exist in time and space. On the other hand, we regard ourselves as free, and we view our actions as largely undetermined and "up to us." We do so, even though we are material bodies that exist in time and space, such that our behaviour should, in principle, be determined by the laws of nature as well. The problem of free will lies, then, at the intersection of a number of disciplines. To address it, we obviously need to resort to the empirical natural sciences like physics, brain science, and psychology. But we also need philosophical reflection to attempt to reconcile our self-image and our idea of free agency with the scientific facts that appear to conflict with it. Hence, in the case of the free will problem, there is a deep entanglement of philosophical and empirical questions. It is not surprising, therefore, that outstanding scientists of the twentieth century (e.g. Libet 2002; Planck 1923) made an attempt to investigate it. The problem of free will, hence, illustrates that philosophy seems to be well advised, at least in regard to some questions, to draw on empirical evidence.[10] E-Phi makes precisely that claim.

1.5 POSITIVE EXPERIMENTAL PHILOSOPHY

We have already discussed one version of x-phi, namely, $X\text{-Phi}_C$. It construes x-phi as the cognitive science of philosophy. This variant of x-phi distinguishes itself from AC-Phi insofar as it regards as philosophical certain questions that can only be answered using a posteriori methods and, in particular, experiments. However, practitioners of $X\text{-Phi}_C$ do not, as it were, invade the space of those who do philosophy based on AC-Phi.

They do not claim, that is, that it is necessary to use a posteriori means to address classical philosophical questions. But in the previous section, we learnt that there are philosophers who do hold that view, namely, empirically informed philosophers. According to their favoured view of philosophy, E-Phi, there are, in fact, classical philosophical questions (e.g. the free will problem) that call for more than just a priori methods. According to E-Phi, these problems need to be addressed, rather, using a posteriori methods. Having introduced this view of philosophy, we can identify yet another version of x-phi, which is a subform of E-Phi. Note, however, that other authors have proposed different nomenclatures (see textbox 1.3).

Positive Experimental Philosophy as Philosophical Methodology (X-Phi$_p$)

Some philosophical questions – including some classical ones – are not to be answered using a priori methods only. Rather, the answers to those questions require additional a posteriori methods and, in particular, experimental ones.

Those who favour an empirically informed view of philosophy do not necessarily hold that philosophers should adopt an experimental methodology (Prinz 2008; Rose & Danks 2013).[11] Proponents of X-Phi$_p$, however, do hold exactly that view. They believe that there is a class of questions that we should address using systematic experiments. And they would include at least some classical philosophical questions into that class. Eddy Nahmias and his colleagues are among those philosophers who may be mentioned as instantiating that view. Nahmias et al. (2005, 2006) tried to find out whether one of the central premises in the debate about the free will problem was, in fact, correct. It is the assumption that a particular view of the relationship between determinism and free will is intuitively appealing. This view is called *incompatibilism*.

TEXTBOX 1.3. THERE ARE DIFFERENT NOMENCLATURES IN THE X-PHI DEBATE

In this study, we will be using the distinction between positive and negative experimental philosophy, following Alexander et al. (2014). Note, however, that different nomenclatures and distinctions have been proposed. Hales (2012), for example, differentiates between "ecumenicals" and "fundamentalists." The former, says Hales, believe that the new experimental techniques merely enlarge and enrich the toolbox of philosophers. The latter, however, think that the classic tools of philosophers and, in particular, their methodical use of thought experiments are untenable. Kauppinen (2007) distinguishes between the view of *Experimentalism (+)* and that of *Experimentalism (−)*. This distinction, too, is very much akin to the distinction between positive and negative x-phi. Rose & Danks (2013) distinguish between a broad and a narrow view of x-phi. On the former, "experimental philosophy involves philosophers conducting psychological experiments for which the primary target is intuitions or judgments" (Rose & Danks 2013, 514). On the latter, it is "the view that empirical data are relevant to certain philosophical questions" in conjunction with the idea of philosophers "actually conducting some of the relevant experiments" (Rose & Danks 2013, 515).

Incompatibilists believe that free will is impossible if the course of the world follows deterministic laws of nature. They routinely insist that this view is, as it were, the default position because it is so intuitively plausible. Their view, they say, has – in the words of Graham & Horgan (1994) – "squatter's rights".[12] That means that we can presume, in the absence of good reasons to the contrary, that incompatibilism will turn out to be the correct view. Accordingly, they regard their adversaries, namely, those who hold the contrary view, that is, *compatibilism*, as bearing the burden of proof (Nadelhoffer & Nahmias 2007, 126). They believe, in other words, that compatibilists face the task of demonstrating that incompatibilism is likely to be false rather than the other way around.

Nahmias et al. (2005, 2006) tested whether the assumption that underlies this line of argumentation is, in fact, empirically adequate. They investigated, that is, how intuitive incompatibilism actually is. To this end, they asked philosophical laypersons to judge a series of cases. Surprisingly, they found evidence which contradicted the incompatibilists' assessment that their view is more intuitive. In fact, a majority of their participants were inclined to ascribe free will to a person even though they were informed that the laws of nature fully determined that person's behaviour.

Now, what is the philosophical significance of this result? Proponents of X-Phi$_C$ would say that its significance consists in the fact that it is philosophically interesting in and of itself. Nahmias et al. (2005, 2006), however, seem to hold ideas that are in line with X-Phi$_p$. From their point of view, their result is interesting because it gives us information that is directly relevant to the debate about a classical philosophical question, namely, the free will problem. Many arguments that philosophers exchange in that debate presuppose that one view of the issue is more intuitively plausible than another. Nahmias et al. (2005, 2006), however, tested this assumption and drew from it an inference that pertains directly to the debate between incompatibilists and their critics.

Alexander et al. (2014) point out that proponents of positive x-phi (X-Phi$_p$) agree with proponents of analytic armchair philosophy (A-Phi) in one regard. Adherents of X-Phi$_p$, they observe, do not reject the MAP *tout court*. The example of Nahmias et al. (2005, 2006), in fact, illustrates this. These authors do not aim to defend an entirely new method of argumentation in philosophy. Rather, they accept the methodological principle of A-Phi that the intuitive plausibility of a thesis can be decisive in its philosophical assessment. In fact, it seems as though positive experimental philosophers diverge from the views of analytic armchair philosophers only with respect to Step 4 of MAP. This methodical step requires that we assess whether the judgement that follows from a philosophical claim in regard to a given case scenario is intuitively plausible. This requirement is ambiguous. The $64,000 question is then: What does it mean for a philosophical judgement to be "intuitively plausible"? Following Alexander & Weinberg (2007), we may distinguish three different interpretations.

Interpretation 1 (Solipsistic Position)

Only the intuitions of the philosopher evaluating the judgement in question are relevant.

Interpretation 2 (Elitist Position)

Only the intuitions of professional philosophers play a role.

Interpretation 3 (Populist Position)

Everybody's intuitions should be taken into consideration.

Analytic armchair philosophers have traditionally endorsed Interpretation 1 or Interpretation 2 (for some examples, see textbox 1.4). Nahmias et al. (2005, 2006), however, seem to base their argument on Interpretation 3. Their departure may be understood as a constructive, well-meaning critique of the traditional methodological view of A-Phi.[13]

TEXTBOX 1.4. SOLIPSISTIC, ELITIST, AND POPULIST VIEWS OF INTUITIVE PLAUSIBILITY

There is some evidence that David Lewis may be regarded as a supporter of Interpretation 1. He says: "One comes to philosophy already endowed

> with a stock of opinions. It is not the business of philosophy either to undermine or to justify these preexisting opinions, to any great extent, but only to try to discover ways of expanding them into an orderly system" (Lewis 1973/2001, 88). The moral philosopher John Rawls may pass as a supporter of Interpretation 2. To defend his conception of justice, which he calls "Justice as Fairness," he develops a famous contractualist thought experiment. In it, the representatives of various societal groups – Rawls calls them "parties" – negotiate the terms of their cooperation and coexistence. To Rawls, it is important to describe the situation in a way that will have intuitive appeal to his readers. Hence, he addresses them directly by saying: "Remember it is up to us, you and me, who are setting up justice as fairness to describe the parties . . . as best suits our aims in developing a political conception of justice" (Rawls 2003, 87). Frank Jackson is apparently one of the few analytically minded philosophers who dares to endorse Interpretation 3. Jackson says: "I am sometimes asked – in a tone that suggests that the question is a major objection – why, if conceptual analysis is concerned to elucidate what governs our classificatory practice, don't I advocate doing serious opinion polls on people's responses to various cases? My answer is that I do – when it is necessary" (Jackson 1998, 36–37). Harman (1999a) has made similar pronouncements.

1.6 NEGATIVE EXPERIMENTAL PHILOSOPHY

The so-called negative experimental philosophers dissociate themselves from the positive experimental philosophers whose methodological outlook we have just discussed. Unlike the latter, negative experimental philosophers do not intend to improve on the methodology of analytic armchair philosophers by making room for experimental methods. Rather, they intend to show, using experiments, that the MAP is "hopeless" (Weinberg 2007).[14]

Negative Experimental Philosophy as Metaphilosophical Critique (X-Phi$_N$)

> MAP is unsuited to address philosophy's questions, including its classical ones.

Now, how do negative experimental philosophers argue for X-Phi$_N$? As experimentalists, they seek to establish this, of course, using experiments. Some of the most well-known and influential examples of studies that fit the picture of X-Phi$_N$ are Weinberg et al. (2001) and Machery et al. (2004) that we will discuss in more detail in chapter 3.

Weinberg et al. (2001) tested, among other things, whether members of different ethnic and socioeconomic backgrounds would report different intuitions when faced with case scenarios that have played an important role in modern epistemology. They gave Western and East Asian subjects some classic thought experiments and then asked them to judge these. By doing that, they found out that the responses varied significantly between the two groups.

Machery et al. (2004) report a similar result about cases that they took from the philosophy of language, specifically the theory of reference. The scenarios they used are commonly employed to argue for (or against) particular theories. They came to the conclusion that subjects from different cultural backgrounds pass significantly different judgements about these scenarios.

What, then, can we conclude from such results? Sosa (2007) argues for a *selective* approach. He proposes to view as prima facie suspect the intuitions that were tested by Weinberg et al. (2001) and Machery et al. (2004) and advises us not to put any argumentative weight on them in our philosophical discussions. However, he does not regard it as problematic to use intuitions that practitioners of X-Phi$_N$ have hitherto not been able to discredit experimentally. To justify this view, he draws on an analogy between our faculty of intuition and our visual sense. To Sosa, it is uncontroversial that we can trust the latter in most cases. However, he does concede that in some cases our sense of vision is not trustworthy. We know, for example, that we cannot trust our eyes when there is insufficient light. In like manner, there are cases in which our intuitions are not trustworthy either. The findings reported by Weinberg et al. (2001) and Machery et al. (2004) show, for example, that we cannot trust particular intuitions in epistemology and the philosophy of language. This, argues Sosa, does not, however, discredit all intuitions. When there is, in a figurative sense, "sufficient light" for our faculty of intuition to function properly, our intuitions are trustworthy.

Negative experimental philosophers believe that the concessions that Sosa is willing to make are not far-reaching enough. They believe, rather, that results like those of Weinberg et al. (2001) and Machery et al. (2004) justify a more sweeping conclusion, namely, that we should place no trust in our intuitions about philosophical thought experiments. After all, they argue, we are not currently able to specify the conditions under which our intuitions are reliable and, hence, are not able to distinguish trustworthy intuitions from untrustworthy ones. Or, as Swain, Alexander, and Weinberg put it:

> At this time, we don't know what is the parallel for intuition of making sure that the light is on; that is, we do not know which are the circumstances that render intuition reliable or unreliable. (Swain et al. 2008, 148)

Certainly, the doubts that negative experimental philosophers raise about MAP do not seem unreasonable. In the case of an intuition, it does seem quite difficult to determine when the "light is on," metaphorically speaking. Unlike our visual impressions, our intuitions cannot, after all, be checked against other sources of knowledge that might confirm them independently (Cummins 1998).[15]

1.7 PHILOSOPHY, METAPHILOSOPHY, AND METAMETAPHILOSOPHY

As Nadelhoffer & Nahmias (2007) emphasise, the term "experimental philosophy" can refer to very different views. I hope that this has already become clear in our previous discussion, where we distinguished between X-Phi$_C$, X-Phi$_P$, and X-Phi$_N$. However, in this section, we will further elaborate on the distinctions between them. To this end, we will categorise them, first of all, against the background of two levels of analysis, namely, the philosophical and the metaphilosophical level. After that, we will investigate the logical relations between them and will finally introduce a further level, namely, that of metametaphilosophy, to clarify the status of X-Phi$_C$, X-Phi$_P$, and X-Phi$_N$ even further.

First, we should record that X-Phi$_C$, X-Phi$_P$, and X-Phi$_N$ are all interpretations or views of philosophy. As such, they are *metaphilosophical theses*. To explain what this means, we need to render the distinction between philosophy and metaphilosophy sufficiently clear.

It is hard to state precisely what philosophy is.[16] There are, however, some questions that are paradigmatically philosophical, such that the issue of the nature of philosophy can be answered at least by way of examples: What is knowledge? What is the meaning of linguistic terms? Is it possible to do something intentionally without intending to do it? Do we have free will? All of these questions are, as I already remarked in section 1.1, classical philosophical questions. So we might say that whenever we think about these questions or similar ones, we are doing philosophy.

When we engage in metaphilosophy, we, in a sense, also deal with philosophy. But we do not, in that case, try to answer a philosophical question. Rather, we pose a question about a philosophical question. We do not ask, for example: "What is knowledge?" We ask, rather: "What kind of question is the question 'What is knowledge?'?" Or, more generally: "What kinds of questions are philosophical questions?" These metaphilosophical issues are questions about the *nature of philosophy*. These, however, are not the only ones. From a metaphilosophical perspective, we may also ask "How should we proceed in order to answer the question 'What is knowledge?'?" Or, more generally: "How should we proceed in order to answer philosophical questions?" These are questions about the *methodology of philosophy*. Though there are further metaphilosophical problems, for the purpose of our subsequent discussion, these can be left aside. For this reason, we shall focus only on questions about the nature and methodology of philosophy.[17]

With the exception of X-Phi$_C$, all interpretations of philosophy that we have come across in this chapter have been, first and foremost, statements about philosophical methodology.

- Both adherents of AC-Phi and A-Phi state that we should answer philosophical questions using a priori methods only. A-Phi, which is a narrower view than AC-Phi, contains an endorsement of the methodical use of intuitions about thought experiments (i.e. MAP).
- In sharp contrast to these two interpretations of philosophy, advocates of E-Phi favour an empirically informed approach that makes room for the use of a posteriori methods in philosophy.
- X-Phi$_P$ is, as we learnt, a special version of E-Phi. Its proponents favour including experiments about intuitions into the toolbox of philosophy.
- X-Phi$_N$ is also a claim about philosophical methodology. It is, however, of a different kind than X-Phi$_P$. While the latter tells us something about the methods to be used in philosophy, X-Phi$_N$ tells us something about the methods we should *not* use. It claims that MAP is one of these.
- In contrast, X-Phi$_C$ is, first and foremost, a pronouncement on the *nature of philosophy*. It says that the discipline of philosophy does not only discuss classical philosophical questions, which may be solvable a priori. Rather, it also includes non-classical ones. The latter category comprises, in particular, the question how people judge philosophical thought experiments and how we may explain their judgements psychologically.

Having categorised the various views of philosophy as metaphilosophical theses, we can, in a next step, ask how they relate to each other logically. We can do this by asking which claims are compatible with one another, which are not, and which imply each other.

Because AC-Phi, A-Phi, E-Phi, X-Phi$_P$, and X-Phi$_N$ are all metaphilosophical theses about the methodology of philosophy and are, to that extent, *theses of the same type*, it should be possible, in principle, to establish how they are logically related. X-Phi$_C$, on the other hand, is, evidently, a claim of a different type, namely, one about the nature of philosophy. It might look, therefore, as though we commit a category error if we were to relate X-Phi$_C$ to the other views of philosophy.[18]

This, however, is only apparently so. It is possible, after all, to derive statements about the nature of philosophy from statements about its methodology (and vice versa). For example, AC-Phi, which says that philosophical problems should be answered using only a priori methods, seems to fit the view that philosophical problems are, by their very nature, of a kind that makes them amenable only to a priori methods. This, in turn, would contradict the view of X-Phi$_C$, which states, after all, that there do exist philosophical questions that can be examined using a posteriori means. For this reason, there are connections between all of the views of philosophy that we have considered in this chapter (table 1.1).

The above matrix shows how one view of philosophy (row) is related to another (column). The former might be compatible with the latter (◊), it might contradict it (¬), or it might imply it (□). Contradiction and compatibility are symmetric relationships. That is, if one view contradicts (is compatible with) another, the latter also contradicts (is compatible with) the former. The relation of implication is, however, not necessarily symmetric. In fact, there are asymmetries in the case of A-Phi and AC-Phi, on the one hand, and X-Phi$_P$ and E-Phi, on the other hand.[19] A-Phi implies AC-Phi, but the latter is only compatible with the former. Similarly, X-Phi$_P$ implies E-Phi, while E-Phi is merely compatible with X-Phi$_P$.

Now, two aspects of the matrix are of particular interest to us. They are the relation between A-Phi and E-Phi, X-Phi$_C$, X-Phi$_P$, and X-Phi$_N$, on the one hand, and the relation between E-Phi, X-Phi$_C$, X-Phi$_P$, and X-Phi$_N$, on the other hand. The former aspect is interesting because a large share of the debate about x-phi has been framed as a debate between the "new experimental paradigm" and the "old analytic paradigm." To be sure, this does seem somewhat justified. As the matrix makes clear, A-Phi is logically incompatible with all kinds of empirically informed philosophy and experimental philosophy. A-Phi states that we can answer all philosophical questions using only a priori methods and, in particular, MAP. In contrast, X-Phi$_C$ asserts that there are further non-classical philosophical questions that are not acknowledged by analytic armchair philosophers. We should tackle them, they believe, using experiments. E-Phi and X-Phi$_P$ maintain, contrary to A-Phi, that conducting experiments is a suitable method for addressing classical philosophical problems. Finally, X-Phi$_N$ directly negates MAP, that is, the method advocated by A-Phi.

Table 1.1. Logical Relations between Views of Philosophy

	AC-Phi	A-Phi	X-Phi$_C$	E-Phi	X-Phi$_P$	X-Phi$_N$
AC-Phi	□	◊	¬	¬	¬	◊
A-Phi	□	□	¬	¬	¬	¬
X-Phi$_C$	¬	¬	□	◊	◊	◊
E-Phi	¬	¬	◊	□	◊	◊
X-Phi$_P$	¬	¬	◊	□	□	◊
X-Phi$_N$	◊	¬	◊	◊	◊	□

The second aspect is interesting to us because critics have tended to lump different views together under the heading "x-phi," as though there was only one variant of it. But as we have learnt in this chapter, there are multiple versions of empirically informed and experimental philosophy. As the above matrix shows, only two of these are logically tied to one another by implication, namely, E-Phi and X-Phi$_P$. All the other variants are logically independent of one another.

- E-Phi, for example, merely advocates for the use of empirical methods when it comes to certain philosophical questions. This commitment does not, however, imply – or, for that matter, rule out – that there are non-classical experimental questions (X-Phi$_C$), that we should use experimental methods in philosophy (X-Phi$_P$), or that we should shun MAP (X-Phi$_N$).
- X-Phi$_C$ merely favours a wider understanding of philosophy that includes non-classical questions. It is silent on the use of empirical and experimental methods in the pursuit of answers to classical questions (E-Phi and X-Phi$_P$, respectively). Furthermore, it neither endorses nor rejects MAP (X-Phi$_N$).
- X-Phi$_P$ is the endorsement of experimental methods in regard to certain classical questions. As such, X-Phi$_P$ merely implies E-Phi. However, it does not assert or dispute that there are non-classical philosophical questions (X-Phi$_C$), and it is not committed to dismissing MAP (X-Phi$_N$).
- X-Phi$_N$ merely rejects MAP and, with it, A-Phi, but is agnostic about the claim that there are non-classical philosophical questions (X-Phi$_C$). It, furthermore, does not take a stance when it comes to the use of empirical and experimental methods in the debate about classical philosophical questions (E-Phi and X-Phi$_P$, respectively). In principle, one may even combine X-Phi$_N$ with AC-Phi. It may be surprising, but this would indeed yield a consistent outlook. X-Phi$_N$, as we construed it, is merely the dismissal of A-Phi and its central method MAP. It is not the more sweeping suggestion that there are absolutely no tenable methods of a priori armchair reflection.[20]

In this section, we categorised AC-Phi, A-Phi, E-Phi, as well as X-Phi$_C$, X-Phi$_P$, and X-Phi$_N$ as metaphilosophical theses. Some of them advocate for the use of empirical and/or experimental methods, while others reject them. But how are any of these views to be justified in the first place? In asking this question, we go beyond the level of metaphilosophy. We ask a question that relates to a metaphilosophical question: How should we go about answering the question about the correct method for doing philosophy?

In principle, we can answer this question – let us call it a *metametaphilosophical* question – in two ways. The first is entirely a priori, and the second is (at least partly) a posteriori. Now we can combine both of these with the various views of philosophy that we have so far discussed. Table 1.2

Table 1.2. Metaphilosophical and Metametaphilosophical Views

	a priori metametaphilosophy	a posteri metametaphilosophy
AC-Phi	◊	◊
A-Phi	◊	◊
X-Phi$_C$	◊	◊
E-Phi	◊	◊
X-Phi$_P$	◊	◊
X-Phi$_N$	¬	□

shows the possible combinations. It tells us whether these views (row) are compatible with an a priori and a posteriori metametaphilosophy (column), respectively. As above, there can be a relationship of compatibility (◊), of incompatibility (¬), and of implication (□).

The above matrix shows a result that may be a bit surprising to some: Except for X-Phi$_N$, all views of philosophy are, from a strictly logical point of view, compatible with both an a priori view and a posteriori view of metametaphilosophy. That means, firstly, that the metaphilosophical views of AC-Phi and A-Phi that demand an aprioristic purism may, in principle, be justified using a posteriori – and even experimental – methods. To establish the reliability of a priori methods in philosophy one might try to show, using empirical studies of human cognitive processes, that these methods are, in fact, reliable.[21] Hence, we should distinguish between two forms of armchair philosophy, AC-Phi.

- The first form, AC-Phi$_{AC}$, is itself justified from the armchair, that is, using only a priori methods.
- The second form, AC-Phi$_E$, is not justified from the armchair, but through a posteriori methods.

Obviously, we may also draw an analogous distinction between A-Phi$_{AC}$ and A-Phi$_E$.

In addition, our result implies that there may be variants of empirically informed and experimental philosophy that may themselves be based on an a priori metametaphilosophical view. In fact, we have already come across an instance of this combination, namely, in the views of Joshua Knobe and Shaun Nichols. They defend themselves against the claim that the questions they propose to pursue are not, in fact, philosophical questions at all. They respond to this objection with, as they put it, a "quizzical stare." This retort may, of course, be interpreted as an a priori argument. In fact, it is reminiscent of the Cartesian appeal to the "light of reason" (fr.: "lumière naturelle"). Knobe and Nichols seem to want to say that it is simply *obvious* that their questions are also philosophical questions. In like manner, it may be possible to justify E-Phi and X-Phi$_P$ a priori. To this end, one could argue, perhaps, that an a priori investigation into the essence of philosophical argumentation suggests certain a posteriori questions that need to be addressed empirically or even experimentally.

Our inquiry, hence, makes clear that the supposedly clear-cut distinction between empirically informed and experimental philosophers, on the one hand, and analytic armchair philosophers, on the other hand, has to be differentiated further. It has to be differentiated, that is, because AC-Phi and A-Phi may themselves be justified a posteriori and even experimentally, while proponents of E-Phi, X-Phi$_C$, and X-Phi$_P$ may support their metaphilosophical views from, as it were, the metametaphilosophical armchair.

1.8 SUMMARY

In this chapter, we discussed metaphilosophical views of philosophy that are foils of x-phi, and we distinguished some versions of empirically informed and experimental philosophy.

In the first two sections, we began with traditional armchair philosophy (AC-Phi) and its narrower analytic version (A-Phi). Both of them claim that the appropriate method for solving philosophical problems consists in pure, a priori reflection and is independent of empirical considerations. Proponents of A-Phi believe, in addition to that, in a special form of a priori method, namely, the MAP. This method allows intuitions about philosophical thought experiments to play an important role in philosophical inquiry.

After that, we considered the first variant of x-phi, namely, X-Phi$_C$. We construed it as the cognitive science of philosophy. Unlike adherents of AC-Phi and A-Phi, its proponents do not believe that all philosophical questions are of a kind that can be addressed using only a priori methods. They believe, rather, that there are certain non-classical questions that we should also regard as genuinely philosophical. These questions, they believe, pertain not to first-order philosophical problems but to philosophical judgements about these problems as well as to the cognitive processes that underlie these judgements. These non-classical questions are, of course, amenable to a posteriori methods and experiments, in particular.

Like AC-Phi and A-Phi, empirically informed philosophy (E-Phi) focuses on classical philosophical questions (e.g. the free will problem). Unlike them, however, it advocates a posteriori methods to investigate them. Positive experimental philosophy (X-Phi$_P$) is a variant of E-Phi that proposes the use of particular a posteriori methods, namely, experiments.

In contrast, negative experimental philosophy (X-Phi$_N$) is agnostic when it comes to the appropriate methodology for doing philosophy. It only contains a negative methodological claim, namely, that A-Phi is flawed insofar as its method, MAP, is unsuited to answer philosophical questions.

Towards the end of the chapter, we examined the logical relations between the various views of philosophy. Firstly, we recorded that all of them are metaphilosophical views. Secondly, we analysed the relations between them from a logical point of view and found, thereby, that A-Phi is incompatible with all types of empirically informed and experimental philosophy. The latter, however, are to a large extent logically independent. Thirdly, we distinguished the level of metaphilosophy from the level of metametaphilosophy. On that basis, we observed that all metaphilosophical views of philosophy that we had hitherto discussed are, in principle, compatible both with an a priori and with an a posteriori metametaphilosophy – with the notable exception of X-Phi$_N$, which rejects A-Phi on an a posteriori basis. That means that the use of a priori and a posteriori methods in philosophy can itself be justified using either a priori or a posteriori arguments.

NOTES

1. Though armchair philosophers do believe that the only suitable instruments in the philosophical toolbox are a priori methods, this does not mean that they are not interested in making claims about the objects of our experience. The German philosopher Immanuel Kant famously held the view that a priori methods allow us rather significant insights into the objects of our experience. Williamson, too, points out that armchair philosophers are, of course, interested in the nature of reality (e.g. the nature of time).

2. The idea that philosophy differs from other fields of inquiry in virtue of the nature of its questions is not uncommon. See, for example, Griffiths & Stotz (2008).

3. We will address all of them in chapter 3.

4. Note that many philosophers use the term "method of cases" (e.g. Mallon et al. 2009) to refer, roughly, to what I call the "method of analytic philosophy." Recently, however, some of these philosophers have, surprisingly, distanced themselves from a central aspect of the method's characterisation, namely, the role of intuitions (in steps 4 and 5). See, for example, Colaço & Machery (2017) and Machery (2017). This was a response to claims by Cappelen (2012, 2014) and Deutsch (2015), who have argued that intuitions do not play any role in analytic philosophy. We will consider this point in section 4.3.5.

5. It should be mentioned that Glock does not address MAP explicitly. From the context, it is quite clear, however, that he has something very much akin to MAP in mind.

6. We may also ascribe this kind of view to Fiery Cushman and Al Mele. They say that experimental philosophy, which they practice, "uses empirical techniques to understand folk concepts" (Cushman & Mele 2008, 171). Cappelen (2014) puts forward a critique of this type of x-phi.

7. We will discuss this study in more detail in section 3.3.

8. See Chalmers (2011) for an insightful recent discussion of verbal disputes.

9. At this point, I should, perhaps, mention that experimental philosophers often view themselves as the *real* traditionalists (Knobe & Nichols 2008; Knobe 2010). Kwame Anthony Appiah puts forward a similar view when he says that "'experimental philosophy,' rather than being something new, is as old as the term 'philosophy'" (Appiah 2008, 2).

10. In regard to the a priori and a posteriori questions that pertain to the free will debate, see Björnsson & Pereboom (2016). We will come back to the issue of free will in section 3.4.

11. In fact, there are numerous empirical methods that researchers who practice empirically informed philosophy can use. For systematic reasons, we will ignore a large share of them. See, however, appendix C for an overview.

12. Graham & Horgan (1994, 223) explain what it means for a philosophical datum to have "squatter's rights" as follows: "It does not mean that such data get to squat forever or that they are indefeasible. But it does mean that our intuitive judgments should enjoy a high degree of prior epistemic reliability or warrant, namely that under an adequate theory of the ideology of philosophically significant concepts, those judgments will turn out generally correct" (Graham & Horgan 1994, 223).

13. There is at least one argument for the assessment that philosophy should base its premises on folk judgements rather than exclusively on the judgements of professional philosophers. We will encounter it in more detail in section 2.5. Those who endorse it insist that the significance of philosophical theories – for example, theories about free will – lies in the way in which they affect our self-image as human beings. Accordingly, they argue, it seems reasonable to require that these theories take seriously the concepts and notions that figure in the lifeworld of the folk and are mindful of the judgements that are central to the perspective of ordinary humans.

14. Note that this is my take on negative x-phi. As some authors have pointed out (e.g. Colaço & Machery 2017), there is no consensus on how to distinguish negative and positive x-phi.

15. Note that some proponents of X-Phi$_N$ have recently toned down their views. Rather than calling for the demise of analytic philosophy, Machery (2017, 208ff.) has recently argued that its method should be reformed or "rebooted." In my opinion, this makes his view look much more like X-Phi$_P$. For this reason, going forward, I shall interpret X-Phi$_N$ as it was originally intended.

16. Prinz (2008, 189–90) discusses a number of proposals as to how we may define philosophy. He also explains why, in each case, they fail. For similar remarks, see Nado (2017).

17. Further metaphilosophical questions relate to the premises of philosophising, its aims, and the differences between philosophy and other forms of inquiry (e.g. the natural sciences, logic, mathematics, and humanities). In addition, there are various branches within metaphilosophy that devote themselves to specific areas of philosophy (e.g. metaethics or metaepistemology). There are further, characteristic questions that are distinctive of these metaphilosophical areas (Moser 1999).

18. The concept of a "category error" is associated, in modern philosophy, with the work of Gilbert Ryle. See, for example, Ryle (1949/2002, 6 ff).

19. Those logical relations that are based on the principle of self-implication are, however, necessarily symmetric (grey cells).

20. Nevertheless, it would be highly unorthodox to combine X-Phi$_N$ and AC-Phi into one metaphilosophical position. At any rate, I know of no philosopher who has proposed to accept both of them.

21. The views put forward by Mortensen & Nagel (2016) may, perhaps, be interpreted as an instantiation of the combination of A-Phi and an a posteriori metametaphilosophy.

Chapter 2

Experimentally Informed Arguments

In the previous chapter, we distinguished between different views of philosophy. First, we considered armchair philosophy (AC-Phi) and, in particular, its variant analytic philosophy (A-Phi). Both claim that philosophical questions are to be answered using a priori methods only. After that, we moved on to empirically informed philosophy (E-Phi) and experimental philosophy (X-Phi$_C$, X-Phi$_P$, and X-Phi$_N$), which take issue with the apriorism of armchair philosophy.

Our analysis showed that one variant of experimental philosophy, namely, X-Phi$_C$, does not make any assertions as to how classical philosophical questions should be addressed methodically. In particular, it does not say that we should use a posteriori methods to tackle classical philosophical questions. X-Phi$_C$ merely claims that there are further philosophical problems in addition to the classical ones that do call for empirical investigation via experiment. Empirically informed philosophy (E-Phi) and its version positive experimental philosophy (X-Phi$_P$) do, however, maintain that we should use a posteriori methods to inquire into classical philosophical problems. X-Phi$_N$, on the other hand, does not commit itself to any positive view of philosophical methodology. It merely rejects, based on experimental evidence, A-Phi and the method that is central to it, namely, the MAP. In other words, E-Phi, X-Phi$_P$, and X-Phi$_N$ suppose that it is possible to bridge the logical gap between an empirical statement of fact and a non-empirical philosophical proposition. In this chapter, we will try to show that this assumption is, initial suspicions to the contrary notwithstanding, not all that implausible. There are, as we will show, empirical questions of philosophical relevance, and these can also be investigated experimentally.

We will seek to support the thesis that experimental research is, in fact, motivated by a close consideration of the way MAP functions. To support this thesis, we will use the following strategy. We will try to show that the relevance of experimental data to philosophical propositions parallels the relevance of experimental data from perceptual and cognitive psychology to empirical propositions. This strategy seems attractive because supposing that the workings of our psychology are relevant to the way we construe the world appears to be a rather uncontroversial premise.[1]

To develop our argument, we will first analyse how empirical theses are tested (section 2.1). After that, we will show that the examination of a philosophical assertion along the lines of MAP resembles the testing of an empirical claim in three ways (section 2.2). In a next step, we will explain how experimental data from perceptual and cognitive psychology may support (or call into question) the correctness of an empirical claim. After that, we will show that the same holds in the case of experimental data about the workings of intuition in philosophical argumentation. This, then, seems to provide a reasonable motivation for experimental research in philosophy (section 2.3). To make the argument for x-phi more concrete, we will supplement our largely abstract discussion of the first three sections with three specific argumentation schemes that might be used to develop experimentally informed arguments in philosophy (section 2.4). Towards the end of the chapter, we will identify a further argument to establish that experimental research may inform philosophical inquiry. Interestingly, this argument may even be acceptable to armchair philosophers (section 2.5). Its goal is not to show that experimental data can play a part in answering classical philosophical questions but, rather, in interpreting these questions. Finally, we will conclude with a summary of the results that we established throughout the chapter (section 2.6).

2.1 EMPIRICAL PROPOSITIONS

The examination of philosophical claims along the lines of MAP parallels the way in which empirical claims are examined, for example, in the sciences. In scientific investigation, the aim is often to identify general laws of the form "For all X it is true that Y." To illustrate this, let us consider a common example of a general empirical assertion.

(E) All swans are white.

Obviously, we can test this proposition through *observation*. We can, for example, walk through a park in our neighbourhood and look at the swans in the pond. Let us suppose we do this. We walk along the pond and look at each individual swan. All of them are white. What are we warranted to conclude from this? May we conclude that all swans are white?

Of course, such a far-reaching inference would not be justified. It would, after all, concern *all* swans that exist. Even though all swans we inspected were white, it would not be inconceivable that the next one we come across is of a different colour. This problem, which is known in philosophy as the *problem of induction*, was already pointed out by the Scottish philosopher David Hume (Hume 1739–40/1960).

Does this mean that we can never assess the proposition that all swans are white in terms of its truth value? That does not seem to be so. For it could be the case that the next swan we observe is, in fact, of a different colour. In that case, the proposition that all swans are white would be disconfirmed by a counter-example. When it comes to the examination of general empirical theses, the following principle, therefore, suggests itself:

Principle of Falsification

Individual facts that confirm a general empirical thesis do not prove it conclusively. A single fact that contradicts a general empirical thesis does, however, disprove it.

The *fact* that a particular swan is not white disproves, conclusively, the general empirical claim that all swans are white. If there exists only a single specimen that is a swan but not white, then the proposition is, in fact, false. That, however, does not mean that we have to dismiss the thesis that all swans are white once a given swan appears to be of a different colour. Our observation may, after all, be erroneous. An individual recalcitrant observation does not, therefore, disprove a general empirical thesis conclusively for there may be a plausible explanation that can make this observation consistent with the thesis after all.

- Perhaps we observed a bird that appeared to be a swan but is not.
- Perhaps the light was too dim or the distance too far so that we might have erred in our colour perception.
- Perhaps some jokester played a trick on us by painting a white swan black.[2]

Nevertheless, we should, of course, reject the proposition that all swans are white if we repeatedly make observations that are not in line with it. Individual observations may all be subject to error, but even a small number of them may drastically increase the likelihood of a general empirical claim being false. Then, it would be unreasonable to keep believing it. Let us suppose, for example, that we make four observations. If correct, each observation would topple the claim that all swans are white. Let us suppose, however, that all of them are highly error-prone. The likelihood of them being false, let us assume, is 75 percent in each case. On that supposition, the probability of a mistake in all four observations is only $(75 \text{ percent})^4 = 31.64 \text{ percent}$.[3] It would, hence, be reasonable to reject the hypothesis that all swans are white. It is, after all, more likely to be false than it is to be true. Crucially, it does not even play a role how many white swans we have observed so far. Even if that number were in the millions, a small number of recalcitrant observations would suffice to discredit the claim that all swans are white. In the case of observation, the following general principle, hence, appears to suggest itself:

Principle of Asymmetry

Observations that conflict with a general thesis carry much more weight than observations that confirm it.

2.2 PHILOSOPHICAL PROPOSITIONS

The examination of a philosophical proposition along the lines of MAP resembles the examination of an empirical statement of fact in three ways.

Feature 1

Many philosophical propositions are general theses of the form "For all X it is true that Y."

Feature 2

In philosophy, we can distinguish between statements of fact and observations.

Feature 3

A general philosophical proposition is disproven by a single fact that contradicts it (Principle of Falsification). However, one philosophical observation that speaks against a general philosophical proposition is usually not enough to discredit it entirely. Nevertheless, observed counter-examples do carry a very high weight in philosophical inquiry (Principle of Asymmetry).

For the sake of clarity, it seems well advised to illustrate these three commonalities between empirical and philosophical propositions using a simple example. To this end, let us consider the question "What is knowledge?" that we have encountered in section 1.2. We already know that there is a standard answer to this question. It is called the *standard analysis of knowledge*.

This analysis construes knowledge as justified true belief. The philosophical proposition that is being proposed is, hence, the following:

Standard Analysis of Knowledge

Knowledge is justified true belief.

This philosophical thesis is a general proposition of the form "For all X it is true that Y." After all, the standard analysis of knowledge says that *in all situations*, it is true that if a person believes p, if she is justified in believing p, and if p is true, then she knows that p. To that extent, it is of the same kind as the general, empirical thesis that all swans are white (Feature 1).[4]

Furthermore, we can distinguish between facts and observations (Feature 2).

- Anna knows that p.
- Anna believes that p.
- Anna has a justification for believing that p.
- p is true.

All of these are *facts* that may or may not obtain.

Now, how can we *observe* them? It is clear that the kind of observation that plays a role in the case of philosophical propositions is of a different kind than the kind of observation that we use in the empirical case that we discussed in the previous section. When we want to find out whether all swans are white, we resort to *sense data* or, more particularly, to *visual data*. When it comes to philosophical propositions, this can be ruled out because it would not work. After all, we cannot *see* that a person knows that p. We cannot *hear* it either. How, then, can we observe it?

In fact, we have already answered this question in the previous chapter. In modern analytic philosophy, a particular method has become the standard: it is the methodical use of *intuitions*. Intuitions are, as it were, philosophical observations.[5]

But what is an intuition? Different philosophers have answered this question in rather different ways (Cohnitz & Haukioja 2015; Pust 2014).[6] Some seem to believe that intuitions are simply opinions (e.g. Lewis 1983). On that view, when we say that we have the intuition that p, we merely want to express that we *believe* that p. This interpretation of the concept of intuition is problematic, however. It is, after all, commonly acknowledged that a person who is having an intuition can arrive at the conclusion that this intuition is mistaken (Bealer 1996, 1999). I can consistently say that I have the intuition that p though, on reflection, I have arrived at the view that p is false. For example, it may seem to me as though the set of points in n-dimensional space must be larger than the set of points on a straight line. Due to Georg Cantor's proof, I may, however, arrive at the conclusion that this intuition is false.[7] Accordingly, we should have the conceptual resources to distinguish between an opinion and an intuition. That is possible only if we do not identify the one with the other.

Philosophical paradoxes are a case in point. A paradox is a set of propositions that all appear to be correct, but jointly yield a contradiction and, hence, cannot all be true at once. One way of solving a paradox consists in dissolving the contradiction. To this end, one shows that the apparent contradiction is not, in point of fact, a genuine contradiction. A second way of solving a paradox consists in rejecting one of the propositions. In that case, one would say that the proposition in question merely seemed to be true (philosophical observation) but, actually, is not (fact).

An intuition should, hence, not be construed as an opinion but as an immediate *impression* (Mukerji 2014). When we want to ascertain whether a person knows that p, we ask whether it *seems* to us as though she knows that p. By asking this, we *observe*, as it were, the *fact* that the person knows that p. Hence, we can distinguish between facts and observations in philosophy, too. Also, the relation between the two is analogous to the empirical case. Philosophical observations – that is, intuitions – support our judgements about philosophical matters of fact. The observation that a person appears to know that p supports the proposition that she actually knows that p.

The fact that a person believes, truthfully and justifiedly, that p and does not know that p disproves the thesis that knowledge is justified true belief (Principle of Falsification). Our intuition that a person believes truthfully and justifiedly that p and does not know that p casts doubt on the thesis that knowledge is justified true belief. But it does not, strictly speaking, disprove it. There is, after all, the possibility that our intuition may deceive us. Nevertheless, the Principle of Asymmetry reigns in philosophy, too. That is, counter-examples that we observe through intuition carry great weight (Feature 3).[8]

2.3 THE RELEVANCE OF EXPERIMENTAL DATA

When we want to test a general empirical claim, we make observations. As I have already mentioned, these observations are error-prone. There are, however, different degrees of error-proneness, and these degrees play a role in assessing the reliability of the convictions that we form based on our observations. It is important to note that the likelihood of an observation being correct does not only depend on the source from which it comes. The circumstances in which the observations are made also play a great role.

Consider our sense of vision. It is usually very reliable. When we visually observe a state of affairs, we may conclude, with a high degree of probability, that our observation does, in fact, adequately represent reality. When we see a bird that looks like a swan and is white, we may conclude that we are, in all likelihood, looking at a white swan. But we cannot trust our visual sense in all circumstances. When the lighting conditions are suboptimal, or when we observe objects at a distance, we should obviously trust our eyes less.

Also, there are *optical illusions*. If, for example, we try to judge the relative lengths of the two horizontal lines in figure 2.1, we are likely to commit an error. It may seem as though the one on top is longer but, in fact, they are of the same length. This so-called Müller-Lyer illusion illustrates that we are not always able to gauge the length of lines relative to one another. The fins that are attached to them play a part in deceiving us. If they point away from the line (as in figure 2.1, top), this makes them look longer. In contrast, if the fins point inwards (as in figure 2.1, bottom), this makes them appear shorter. In this case, we call our perception an optical illusion because the perceived lengths of the lines do not adequately represent their actual lengths.[9]

The possibility of optical illusions of this kind suggests that our sense of vision is sometimes unreliable. But this is not the only reason why it may be reasonable for us to doubt its deliverances. Not only do we sometimes perceive aspects of a state of affairs inaccurately. In addition, we sometimes *fail to perceive* certain things. The American psychologists Daniel J. Simons and Christopher F. Chabris made this clear in a well-known experiment (Simons & Chabris 1999). They had their subjects watch a short video that showed a number of persons passing around a basketball. Half of the persons in the video wore white shirts. The other half of them wore black shirts. Subjects were asked to count the number of passes that members of the white team threw. Simons and Chabris specifically asked them to ignore the passes thrown by those who wore a black shirt. About three-quarters of a minute in, something unexpected happened: A woman wearing a black gorilla costume

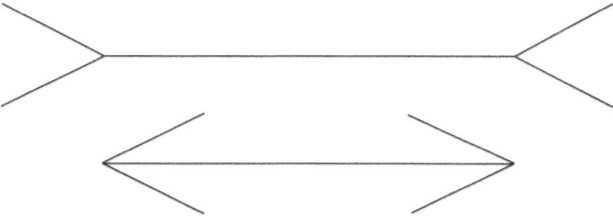

Figure 2.1. The Müller-Lyer Illusion

walked through the shot and was visible for a couple of seconds. After having watched the entire clip and having counted the number of passes thrown, subjects were asked whether they had noticed anything out of the ordinary. From their answers, Simons and Chabris were able to conclude that half of their participants did not even notice the woman in the gorilla costume. They were so busy counting the passes that their cognitive faculties were fully engaged and did not process that additional piece of information.

We should, hence, conclude that it would be unreasonable to trust our visual observation unconditionally. Rather, we should allow for the possibility of optical illusions, and we should consider that there might be gaps in our perceptions. In that connection, we might find it helpful to consult experimental research from *perceptual* and *cognitive psychology*. That research makes us aware of the possibility of errors and blind spots which, in turn, can help us to form a more accurate understanding of the reliability of our observations. When we look at two lines with shafts pointing in opposite directions, we should consider the possibility that the one is not actually longer than the other.[10] And when we are carrying out a cognitively strenuous task, we should be open to the possibility that we are not able to process all details of a situation. In other words, our empirical knowledge about the limitations of our perceptual apparatus and of our cognitive abilities can help us to assess the probability that our observations are correct.

In the previous section, we drew an analogy between empirical observations and philosophical intuitions. The latter, we said, were, in a sense, *philosophical observations*. Through our intuitions, we can observe certain facts that are of interest to philosophers, for example, the fact that a person knows (or does not know) a given proposition. We also stated that intuitions play a role in philosophical inquiry that is analogous to the role that sensual observations play in the examination of empirical facts. When we sensually observe a putative fact, that is a reason to believe that it does, in fact, obtain. Now, we saw that the error-proneness of empirical observation creates a relevance for experimental studies into the workings of our perceptual and cognitive faculties. Because of the apparent analogy between the role of empirical observations and the role of philosophical intuitions, it is not too far to seek that experimental research about the empirical properties of intuitions may be relevant to philosophical inquiry, too. After all, if we can gauge the reliability of empirical observations through experimental research, why should we not be able to use it to assess, also, the reliability of intuitions in philosophical inquiry?

At first glance, one consideration seems to suggest that there is, in fact, a relevant disanalogy between the empirical and the philosophical case. Usually, we can determine quite easily whether our observations are mistaken. In the case of our intuitions, this seems to be much more difficult, however.

Before we tackle this argument, it is important to spell out what it says. So let us do this first.

We can easily ascertain whether a given visual perception is, in fact, based on a visual illusion. For example, having looked at figure 2.1, we can take out a ruler and measure whether the two lines are, indeed, of the same of length. We can also check whether our observations contain gaps. In the case of Simons and Chabris's experiment, we can go back to the clip and ascertain whether the gorilla was, in fact, there. Also, many observations can be checked through independent sensual perceptions. For example, at this moment, it seems to me as though there is a notebook in front of me. I am quite sure that my visual sense does not deceive me. After all, I can reach for the notebook and touch it. My sense of touch confirms my visual impressions. When I strike the keys, I can also hear certain sounds. (Some of them are disconcerting. Maybe I should get a new notebook.) In the case of an intuition about a philosophical thought experiment, this seems to be different, though. Here, my immediate impression that, say, a person knows that p is all I have. There is no method of observation that allows me to confirm or disconfirm my impression. That seems to suggest that we cannot check intuitions using empirical means. There is no ruler that I can use to "measure" an intuition and no other sense impression that we may use to put our intuitions to the test (Cummins 1998). Does this exclude, then, the possibility that we may assess the reliability of our intuitions empirically as we can do in the case of our sensual perceptions?

That is not necessarily so. There is a counter-argument that may, in broad strokes, be stated thus: Though there is no external standard that we can use to check our intuitions, we are, nevertheless, able to ascertain whether they possess certain empirical properties. And these empirical properties may be relevant to the assessment of their reliability. This thought allows us to formulate the following argument:[11]

The Argument from Reliability

(P1) Our intuition that p possesses the empirical property E. (Empirical premise)
(P2) If an intuition possesses the empirical property E, then it is *pro tanto* (un)reliable. (Bridging premise)
(C) Our intuition that p is *pro tanto* (un)reliable.

From this general scheme, we can derive two kinds of experimentally informed arguments, namely, arguments that *increase the credibility* of a given intuition and arguments that *decrease the credibility* of a given intuition. Proponents of E-Phi and X-Phi$_P$ employ both kinds of arguments, while adherents of X-Phi$_N$ only use the latter.

It is important to note that individual arguments which follow the above scheme have only limited force. Any given experimentally informed argument merely increases or decreases the credibility of a given intuition, and it does so only *pro tanto*. That is, it speaks to the credibility of the intuition only insofar as it possesses the empirical property in question. In other words, an experimentally informed argument usually does not allow us to make any definite pronouncements on the credibility of a particular intuition.

Nevertheless, experimentally informed arguments can have a great influence on the debate about a philosophical issue. Many such debates are at a stalemate. Philosophers of opposing camps insist on premises that, they say, are intuitive though members of the other side reject them. This "intuition mongering" may make it hard to figure out whose views are more persuasive because it makes every appeal to intuition weak (Mizrahi 2012). In that situation, an experimentally informed argument may tip the scales in favour of the one or the other view. They can have a significant payoff if they succeed in showing that the intuitions that are used on one side of the debate are more credible than those on the other side.

One of the areas of philosophy in which we can observe the impact that experimentally informed arguments can have is *normative ethics*. The modern debate in this field has been coined, in large part, by the controversy between consequentialists and deontologists. Consequentialists believe that it is always morally permissible to do what has the best consequences. On its face, this idea is quite attractive. It does seem to line up with what we intuitively believe. Deontologists, however, reject the consequentialist viewpoint. To criticise it, they draw attention to intuitions about individual scenarios in which consequentialism leads to rather counter-intuitive results. Hence, in the debate between consequentialists and deontologists, we face the problem that consequentialism is intuitively appealing in the abstract, while it leads to intuitively unpalatable results in concrete cases (Nida-Rümelin 1997b). This coexistence of supporting and opposing intuitions creates an unproductive argumentative stalemate in which philosophers on opposite sides keep on touting the intuitive appeal of the premises that inform their view.[12] Some consequentialist moral philosophers (especially Greene 2008 and Singer 2005) tried to get out of it using experimentally informed arguments. To this end, they argued that the intuitions about cases, which tend to undermine consequentialism, should not be trusted. Citing neuroscientific data, they argued that intuitions underlying the deontological perspective typically derive from emotionally induced reactions, while the principled explanations deontologist philosophers come up with should be properly regarded as rationalisations of these emotional responses. In contrast, Greene and Singer maintain, consequentialist theories are not based on emotional responses but are, rather, the product of cognitive processes that seem more reliable. Hence, these authors conclude, the weight of deontological arguments should, plausibly, be discounted, and the balance of reasons supports the consequentialist side.[13]

2.4 BRIDGING THE GAP

In the previous section, we introduced a general scheme for experimentally informed arguments: the argument from reliability. We distinguished two variants of it and discussed their potential reach. In this section, we shall examine the philosophical plausibility of these arguments further. As Jonah Schupbach notes, "The concept of Reliability is relative and normative." That means that "some thing cannot be reliable full stop; it can only be reliable relative to some specified norm" (Schupbach 2017, 696). Accordingly, a concrete version of the general scheme has to specify a concrete property of intuitions and a norm for ascribing (un)reliability to them based on this property. The properties we will discuss in this section are the following.

Property 1

There is agreement (or disagreement) about the intuition that p.

Property 2

The intuition that p is caused by a factor that is irrelevant to the issue at hand.

Property 3

The intuition that p is susceptible to framing effects.

2.4.1 Agreement and Disagreement

Philosophers often begin their discussion of a philosophical question by remarking that a particular answer to it seems to concur with ideas that most people find intuitively plausible. We already came across an example of this in section 1.5, where we considered some aspects of the debate about the free will problem. In this debate, contributors often claim that most people intuitively accept the view of incompatibilism. It is the notion that the complete causal determination of the course of the world rules out the possibility of free will. Robert Kane, for example, who is a prominent author in the debate, writes the following: "In my experience," he says, "most persons resist the idea that free will and determinism might be compatible when they first encounter it" (Kane 2005, 12). This alleged agreement about the intuitiveness of incompatibilism increases its philosophical credentials – at least so long as we are unaware of substantive reasons to doubt it. In other words, incompatibilism has "squatter's rights."

This line of reasoning follows the scheme of the argument from agreement, which is a variant of the argument from reliability.

The Argument from Agreement

(P1) There is agreement on the intuition that p.
(P2) If there is agreement on the intuition that p, then this intuition is *pro tanto* reliable.
(C) The intuition that p is *pro tanto* reliable.

This argument follows, then, in the footsteps of modern analytic philosophers. It seems as though experimental philosophers who pick it up simply carry on the discussion that analytic philosophers have had for a long time. To that extent, their reasoning along the lines of the argument from agreement seems sound. If any, it seems to be sounder than the arguments that analytic philosophers have produced in the past. After all, to support the empirical premise P1, experimental philosophers do not settle for mere anecdotes ("In my experience . . ."). They try to ascertain whether P1 can, in fact, be supported by empirical evidence. They are prepared, for example, to test, through experiments, whether incompatibilism is aptly called the intuitive view.[14]

In the past, experimental researchers have often discovered that philosophers misjudge what laypeople do and do not find intuitive. As we saw in section 1.5, Nahmias et al. (2005, 2006) found evidence suggesting that most people found the compatibilist (not the incompatibilist!) judgements intuitively plausible when they had to judge certain scenarios. In other cases, experimental philosophers have confronted us with the result that there is disagreement on a particular intuition. As we discussed in section 1.6, Weinberg et al. (2001) found that members of different ethnic groups report significantly different intuitions about the concept of knowledge. The phenomenon of intuitive disagreement generally plays a great role in the debates of experimental philosophers (see textbox 2.1). Such findings, they argue, warrant us to regard these intuitions as *pro tanto* unreliable.

TEXTBOX 2.1.   DIMENSIONS OF DISAGREEMENT

Experimental philosophers have found interpersonal disagreements among various dimensions. Early on, Weinberg et al. (2001) reported disagreements between ethnic and socioeconomic groups. After that,

> investigations about further kinds of differences followed, for example, differences between the sexes (Buckwalter & Stich 2014; Seyedsayamdost 2014), age groups (Colaço et al. 2014), and personality types (Feltz & Cokely 2009). For a recent overview of the literature, see Machery (2017, chapter 2).

Experimental philosophers who are interested in findings about disagreement often extract philosophical conclusions from them using a form of the general argument from reliability: the argument from disagreement.[15]

The Argument from Disagreement

(P1)   There is disagreement on the intuition that p.
(P2)   If there is disagreement on the intuition that p, then this intuition is *pro tanto* unreliable.
(C)   The intuition that p is *pro tanto* unreliable.

This argument, too, has its roots in traditional philosophical practice. In his influential book *The Methods of Ethics* (1907), Henry Sidgwick employs it. He writes that

> the denial by another of a proposition that I have affirmed has a tendency to impair my confidence in its validity. . . . For if I find any of my judgments, intuitive or inferential, in direct conflict with a judgment of some other mind, there must be error somewhere: and if I have no more reason to suspect error in the other mind than in my own, reflective comparison between the two judgments necessarily reduces me temporarily to a state of neutrality. (Sidgwick 1907, 341–42)

Sidgwick thus believes that our judgements – and our intuitive judgements, in particular – lose their credibility once we find out that other people, who seem reasonable to us, do not share them. He even goes a step further. If we have "no more reason to suspect error in the other mind," then we should suspend judgement – at least temporarily. Hence, we should not treat the fact that proposition p seems intuitive *to us* as evidence that p is likely correct. Experimental philosophers who exploit the argument from disagreement to draw conclusions from their experimental research can properly claim that they are using a way of arguing that Henry Sidgwick has employed long before them.

At this point, I should, however, add a qualification that Sidgwick also makes in his discussion.[16] He says that we should suspend judgement "if we have no more reason to suspect error in the other mind" than in our own. But it is well known, from research in cognitive psychology, that human beings often err when they trust their intuitions. Let us consider an example that illustrates this.

Bat-and-Ball Problem

A bat and a ball cost $1.10 in total. The bat costs $1.00 more than the ball. How much does the ball cost?

The psychologist Shane Frederick asked students of Princeton University and the University of Michigan to answer this question. As Kahneman (2003) reports, over 50 percent said that the answer was 10ct. This result should not have us doubt that the correct answer is, in fact, 5ct. After all, the problem has exactly one correct solution, and it follows from the laws of arithmetic. It is neither here nor there whether this solution is intuitive, and it is equally immaterial whether there is disagreement on its intuitiveness.

The example of the Bat-and-Ball problem allows us to draw two conclusions regarding the argument from agreement and the argument from disagreement:

- The argument from disagreement only casts doubt on the intuition that p if there is no independent way of ascertaining whether p is correct (e.g. the laws of arithmetic).[17]
- Similarly, the argument from agreement only increases the credibility of the intuition that p if there is no independent way of checking whether p is correct.

2.4.2 Irrelevant Factors

Let us take stock, then. Usually, the empirical fact that most people have the intuition that p supports the idea that this intuition is correct. Likewise, the fact of intuitive disagreement renders the respective intuition less credible. These two findings, at any rate, were the quintessence of the argument from agreement and the argument from disagreement that we have considered in the previous section. The two arguments, however, do not allow us to draw any definite conclusions. The fact that there is agreement about a given intuition does not imply that we should trust it, all things considered. Similarly, the fact that there is disagreement about a particular intuition does not allow us to draw the sweeping conclusion that it is unreliable, period. There are three reasons for this.

The first reason is, as we already said in the previous section, that there might be an independent way of checking whether a given intuition is correct. In the Bat-and-Ball problem, the laws of arithmetic provide such a way. In that case, people's intuitive judgements are, hence, neither here nor there.

The second reason is trivial. It might be that there merely seems to be an intuitive disagreement when, in fact, there is not. This can happen when the parties that are disagreeing interpret certain phrases differently. In that case, we face a mere *verbal dispute*.[18] (Analogously, in the case of a mere seeming agreement, we may speak of a verbal agreement.)

The third reason – and this is the one that shall concern us here – consists in the fact that intuitions may sometimes be explained (or explained away) by an *error theory*. Such a theory explains causally why a person has a given intuition, where – crucially! – the factor that provides the explanation is irrelevant to the question whether the intuition is correct or not. An analogy between the philosophical and the empirical case may make clear what this means.

When we try to ascertain whether an empirical thesis is correct, it is normally reasonable to trust our eyes. If we visually perceive a given state of affairs, we may reasonably conclude that our perception accurately represents reality. For example, if we perceive an object as blue, it is normally reasonable to conclude that it is, in fact, blue. After all, the purported fact that the object is blue can causally explain why we perceive it so. However, if we have, say, ingested a pill that causes us to perceive everything as blue, we can no longer trust our colour perceptions. In that case, if an object seems blue to us, this might be causally explained by one of two factors. Either this object is, in fact, blue, or the pill creates this illusion. The second explanation draws on a factor that does not have anything to do with the purported fact that the object is, indeed, blue. It is blue, or it is not, and this does not depend on whether we have taken the pill.

In the philosophical case, this is quite similar. When we examine a philosophical thesis, it is normally reasonable to trust our intuitions – at least to a certain degree. For example, if a normative-ethical theory says that a given act is morally permissible though it seems clearly wrong to us, it is reasonable to treat the theory with suspicion. However, even in that instance, it may be possible to explain our intuition in a way that debunks it. Perhaps it is possible to show, through experiments, that our intuitions are likely caused by a factor that should be irrelevant to the answer to the respective ethical question. In that case, our intuition may be called into question along the lines of the following argumentation scheme.

The Argument from Irrelevant Factors

(P1) Our intuition that *p* is caused by an irrelevant factor.
(P2) If an intuition is caused by an irrelevant factor, it is *pro tanto* unreliable.
(C) Our intuition that *p* is *pro tanto* unreliable.

There is evidence that our moral judgements are affected by a large number of factors, and at least some of them seem to be irrelevant to the respective moral questions. Let us consider an example that illustrates this.

Haidt et al. (1993) found that moral judgements are influenced, among other things, by emotional states (e.g. disgust). They gave participants scenarios like the following:

> A brother and sister like to kiss each other on the mouth. When nobody is around, they find a secret hiding place and kiss each other on the mouth, passionately. (Haidt et al. 1993, 617)

In this scenario, the two siblings do something that may cause disgust at least in some people: they kiss each other, and they enjoy it! However, that enjoyment does not seem to come at anyone else's expense. Haidt et al. (1993) asked their subjects to evaluate the siblings' behaviour and analysed the data. By doing this, they unearthed an interesting result. Apparently, it was possible to predict how subjects would judge the siblings' behaviour by asking them a simple question. That question was: "Would it bother you to see this?" (Haidt et al. 1993, 625). Those who said that it would were significantly more likely to judge what the siblings are doing as wrong. We may, hence, debunk this moral intuition using the above argumentation scheme.

(P1) The intuition that it is wrong for a brother and a sister to kiss each other passionately is caused by an irrelevant factor, namely, the feeling of disgust.
(P2) If an intuition is caused by an irrelevant factor, it is *pro tanto* unreliable.
(C) The intuition that it is wrong for a brother and a sister to kiss each other passionately is *pro tanto* unreliable.

This argument is, as we already noted, deductively valid, and the second premise, P2, may be taken as uncontroversial. The soundness of the argument hinges, thus, on the persuasiveness of the first premise, P1. Its plausibility depends, in turn, not only on the question whether the feeling of disgust does, in fact, cause the respective intuition. It also depends on whether we may justifiably regard this cause as irrelevant. Now, what should we say about this?

It seems we can argue as follows: Whether the siblings' behaviour is morally wrong or not depends, plausibly, on whether they harm others with it.[19] The fact that other people would be made to feel uneasy if they had to witness their kissing does not, by itself, fulfil this condition. After all, there is nobody forcing anyone to watch them do it. They have their secret hiding place! Hence, the fact that it *would* make certain people uncomfortable to see the siblings kissing each other may properly be regarded as irrelevant to the assessment of their behaviour.

The plausibility of this reasoning does, however, depend on the *background theory* that we assume. In a paper entitled "The Wisdom of Repugnance"

(1997), the American philosopher Leon Kass has, for example, put forward the view that we should, indeed, trust our gut feelings when it comes to moral issues. When we find a given human practice repulsive, for example, Kass takes this to be an indication that we should reject it as immoral.[20] In other words, Kass would not be impressed by the experimental result that a given moral intuition is driven by the emotion of disgust because, to him, disgust is not an irrelevant factor.

I believe we can draw an important lesson from our discussion that pertains to the dialectic force of the argument from irrelevant factors. Its persuasiveness depends, crucially, on whether or not all parties to the debate do, indeed, accept the factor in question as irrelevant. Those who do not take this into consideration may commit a fallacy that argumentation theorists call "begging the question." That is, they may base their arguments on a supposition that those who do not share their conclusion would not accept.

2.4.3 Framing Effects

There are, however, certain factors that causally affect our intuitions, and they should, undoubtedly, count as irrelevant. So-called *framing effects* are one such factor. Before we discuss them, we should draw a distinction between three types, namely, verbal framing effects, context effects, and order effects.[21] We shall discuss them in turn.

A *verbal framing effect* obtains when two conditions are fulfilled:

- We may describe a given state of affairs in at least two logically equivalent ways.
- The choice of the formulation has a psychological influence on the way we assess it.

It is important to distinguish verbal framing effects from similar, language-related phenomena. Learned rhetoricians have, for example, known since antiquity that language is a powerful tool. They are aware that the verbal framing of circumstances greatly affects our thinking. Using loaded terms, we can, for example, communicate tacit assumptions that our interlocutors are unlikely to question.[22] We may, for example, describe a military intervention as an "unprovoked attack" rather than a "preemptive strike." In that case, our verbal frame communicates an entirely different judgement to the listener than if we had used the second formulation. "Unprovoked attack" and "preemptive strike" say different things. Verbal framing effects are different in that regard. Here, the same message is being communicated, albeit in different words.

Let us illustrate this using a well-known example from a famous paper by the Israeli psychologists Amos Tversky and Daniel Kahneman. They were interested in how our intuitions about decision problems change as their formulation changes. To investigate it, Tversky and Kahneman gave their subjects the following scenario:

> Imagine that the U.S. is preparing for an outbreak of an unusual Asian disease which is expected to kill 600 people. Two alternative programs to fight the disease, A and B, have been proposed. Assume that the exact scientific estimates of the consequences of the programs are as follows: (Tversky & Kahneman 1981, 453)

In addition, the first group of participants received the following information about options A and B:

> If program A is adopted, 200 people will be saved. If program B is adopted, there is a 1/3 probability that 600 people will be saved, and a 2/3 probability that no people will be saved. (Tversky & Kahneman 1981, 453)

The second group was given a choice between options C and D. Tversky and Kahneman described their effects as follows:

> If program C is adopted, 400 people will die. If program D is adopted, there is a 1/3 probability that nobody will die and a 2/3 probability that 600 people will die. (Tversky & Kahneman 1981, 453)

All participants were subsequently asked to choose either between A and B (in the first group) or between C and D (in the second group). In the first group, 72 percent of participants favoured option A, and 28 percent preferred option B. In contrast, 22 percent of subjects in the first group said that they would choose option C, while 78 percent selected option D.

This result is remarkable because the choice between A and B is logically equivalent to the choice between C and D. The two choices merely came in different verbal frames.

- Participants in the first group were told that option A would save 200 out of 600 lives. In other words, 400 people would die as a result of adopting A. The latter information is, hence, the same information that Tversky and Kahneman used to describe the consequences of option C to subjects in the second group.
- Participants in the first group furthermore received the information that choosing B would, with a probability of 1/3, result in all 600 people being saved and would, with a probability of 2/3, lead to nobody being saved. In other words, B would lead to no deaths with a probability of 1/3 and would leave all 600 persons dead with a probability of 2/3. The latter information about B is, hence, identical to the information about D that Tversky and Kahneman gave to participants in the second group.

Context effects are framing effects that are independent of the verbal framing of the choice options. We speak of a context effect if the following two conditions are fulfilled:

- We may describe a given state of affairs against the background of at least two different contexts. These contexts do not, however, alter the respective state.
- The context in which the state of affairs is presented has a psychological influence on the way we assess it.

The context that is being varied may, for example, consist in other circumstances that are being provided along with the state of affairs to be judged. We may, for example, conduct an experiment to find out whether a given case is assessed differently if it is accompanied by another case B as opposed to C. To investigate this, we could, for example, divide participants into two groups. We would then have subjects in the first group judge A alongside B and subjects in the second group judge A alongside C. After that, we would analyse the responses in both groups statistically to find out whether the varied context did, in fact, make a significant difference.

Order effects are a specific class of context effects. They require that the following two conditions are fulfilled:

- There are at least two cases.
- The order in which we assess them has a psychological influence on the content of our assessment.

To find out whether there is an order effect in the evaluation of a case A in regard to B, we could conduct the following experiment. Once more, we would divide our research participants into two groups. Those in the first group would then get to judge A and B in the order AB, while those in the second group would be asked to evaluate the two cases in the order BA. Once more, we would analyse whether there are significant differences in the responses of the two groups.[23]

When we find out that a given intuition is, in all likelihood, subject to a framing effect, this reduces its reliability according to the following argumentation scheme:

The Argument from Framing Effects

(P1) The intuition that *p* is subject to a framing effect.
(P2) If an intuition is subject to a framing effect, it is *pro tanto* unreliable.
(C)   The intuition that *p* is *pro tanto* unreliable.

It should be noted, once again, that the argument is deductively valid. Hence, to assess it critically, we should consider its premises.

Regarding the first premise, we might ask, for example, whether the experimental study that purports to provide evidence for the existence of a framing effect in a given intuition does, in fact, establish this. If we talk about a verbal framing effect, we should ask whether the different formulations that researchers used to frame the case were, indeed, logically equivalent. In the case of an alleged context effect, we should ask how we can exclude the possibility that variations in context led subjects to different interpretations of the relevant case. And as regards order effects, we should ask, similarly, whether it is possible that research participants understood the cases differently when they had to judge them in a different order.

Concerning the second premise, we should ask whether the empirical fact that a given intuition is subject to a framing effect does, plausibly, discredit it, as claimed. In that connection, it is necessary to consider the *effect size*. After all, framing effects only cast doubt on the epistemic credentials of a given intuition if they are of a sufficient size.

What does this mean? Suppose we ask our subjects in an experiment to state, on a scale from 1 to 5, how they would judge a given act. They can choose between the following options: 1 (= wrong), 2 (= somewhat wrong), 3 (= neither wrong nor laudable), 4 (= somewhat laudable), and 5 (= laudable). Now, if we found that, under the first frame, the average judgement subjects reported were 1.2 and under the second 4.6, then the effect size would be very large. In contrast, if we found that the variation was between 2.1 under the first frame and 2.4 under the second, the effect size would be smaller, and we should, perhaps, not dismiss the intuition as unreliable because of this. After all, many of our sources of knowledge are subject to the random influence of irrelevant factors (Boyd & Nagel 2014). Take, for example, our sense of temperature, which is, demonstrably, subject to a similar effect. To test it, you can conduct the following experiment: Put your left hand into cold water and your right one into hot water. After a while, take both of them out, and quickly put them into lukewarm water. On your left hand, you will perceive the lukewarm water as warmer than on your right hand. This does not mean that your thermoception is generally unreliable.

2.5 RELEVANT QUESTIONS

In the previous sections, we showed how we could use experimental findings to advance the discussion of philosophical issues. The key lesson we learnt can be summarised thus: when philosophers engage in philosophical inquiry, they ask certain questions. To answer them, they give reasons why particular answers to them might be correct, and some of these reasons rely on intuitions about thought experiments. This, at any rate, is the paradigmatic method of modern analytic philosophy (MAP). Experimental research can help us to ascertain whether the intuitions that form the premises of the philosophers' arguments are indeed reliable. To this end, we may examine whether there is agreement on them. We may also look for irrelevant factors that drive them and for various types of framing effects, in particular. This way, we obtain information that can help us to weigh the arguments on the table by the reliability of the intuitions that are cited in support of them.

At this point, we may make an observation, namely, that the way in which experimental research connects with philosophical inquiry lies in the way philosophical questions are *answered*. This, however, is not the only way. Experimental research may contribute to philosophy by investigating how philosophical questions should be *asked* in the first place. Let me explain.

Philosophy is a very diverse field that accommodates questions of very different kinds. Many of those are very abstract and largely of purely theoretical interest. As such, they do not speak to the way we live our lives. We may, perhaps, regard the questions that philosophers of mathematics pursue in that way. There are, however, different questions that do, undoubtedly, relate to our lifeworld, and the answers to these questions do, arguably, have an impact on our lives. They coin the way we see ourselves and affect the image that we form of our fellow humans. One classical philosophical question that makes this especially clear is the issue of free will that we have already encountered above. The answers we give to that problem affect how we think of our own agency and the agency of others. That, in turn, coins the way we understand the concept of responsibility and that of morality more broadly. However, it is not entirely clear how we should interpret the complex of questions that attach to this particular issue. There are, after all, different interpretations, as we have already discussed in section 1.5.[24] Frank Jackson, hence, asks:

> What then are the interesting philosophical questions that we are seeking to address when we debate the existence of free action and its compatibility with determinism? (Jackson 1998, 31)

Evidently, Jackson does not think it arbitrary which interpretation of the free will problem we adopt. To him, it is important that these questions are *interesting*. But what does that mean? Jackson gives us a criterion for it.

> What we are seeking to address is whether free action *according to our ordinary conception*, or something suitably close to our ordinary conception, exists and is compatible with determinism. (Jackson 1998, 31; emphasis in the original)

So Jackson says that the concept of free will that we presuppose in our philosophical discussions should not be a technical notion. He thinks that we should ask, rather, whether free will, as it is ordinarily understood, can be reconciled with what empirical research findings from, say, cognitive science and neuroscience reveal.[25] Jackson, hence, encourages us to use the concept of free will in its everyday interpretation or, at least, in a sufficiently similar way.

The question arises, however, how we determine what the everyday interpretation of a philosophical concept is. Experimental philosophers do, of course, have an answer to this question. It matches, quite closely, what the late Wittgenstein suggested in his *Philosophical Investigations* (1958/1986):

> One cannot guess how a word functions. One has to *look at* its use and learn from that. (Wittgenstein 1958/1986, §340; emphasis in the original)

Experimental philosophers suggest that we follow this insight (though they hardly ever attribute it to Wittgenstein). They propose that we investigate how philosophical laypersons use key philosophical concepts. To this end, we can ask them to describe, say, the concept of free will, or we have them judge whether a given person acted of their own free will in a given case.[26] After that, we draw conclusions from their replies that help us to characterise the folk concept of free will. This new concept may then help us to reframe classical philosophical questions that revolve around it.[27]

Let us record the following, then: There is a further way in which experimental research may contribute to philosophy. Its findings may not only help us to judge the reliability of the intuitions on which philosophers base their arguments. They may also help us to understand certain classical philosophical questions better. They do that by informing us about the folk usage of key philosophical terms. In so doing, they allow us to reinterpret classical philosophical questions in a way that is most relevant to our lives. Interestingly, this experimental contribution to philosophy is not at odds with AC-Phi, that is, the view that philosophers should answer philosophical questions from the armchair. Once we have found, through experiments, the most natural interpretation of certain philosophical questions, armchair philosophers may pick up the thread and pursue these questions in the traditional way.[28]

Before concluding this section, we should try to pre-empt a possible misunderstanding. Nobody suggests that philosophers should slavishly cling to the way in which laypersons use certain concepts. Nobody suggests, that is, that philosophers should adopt the folk concepts that we investigate using experimental studies in their crude form. To be sure, it is sometimes advisable to modify certain concepts to make for easier use or to introduce technical notions that are unprecedented in our everyday thinking. Folk concepts may, after all, be incoherent. This may be the case, for example, if certain components of the concept do not fit with its other parts or some concepts contradict others. Whenever this happens, philosophers should try to improve the inventory of philosophical concepts that is at their disposal.[29]

In fact, the metaphor of the *conceptual inventory* suggests one reasonable way of doing the readjusting. Philosophers should, it seems, behave like good interior designers. Now, what is the point behind this analogy?[30] To answer this question, let us assume your flat is overstuffed and non-functional. Moving is out of the question. At the same time, you are not willing to part with much of your stuff. Hence, you are calling up an interior designer and assign her the job of remodelling your place. You do realise that, for better or worse, some of the old things in your home need to go. But you would be more than surprised if the designer proposed to throw everything out and replace it all with new items. If that plan were implemented, you likely would not recognise the place as *your* place. Instead, you would probably expect the designer to suggest reorganising some elements of your living space and replacing others to make better use of the available room. You are prepared to get rid of some things if that is necessary to implement a good plan. You would be willing, for example, to replace the old wardrobe with a newer, more practical model. In other words, you would accept a remodelling proposal that promises to increase the comfort of living. But you are only willing to go so far. After the process has been completed, you should still be able to recognise the place as *your* place. A good interior designer should bear that in mind.

Philosophers behave like good interior designers if they take seriously our self-image and the concepts that attach to it, if they are willing to work with them, and if they make conceptual adjustments in a parsimonious way and only when they are necessary. Philosophical conceptions of free will, personal identity, rationality, morality, and so on are inextricably linked to the way we live our lives and to our self-perception. As such, they have to be recognisably informed by how we ordinarily conceive of these concepts.

The American philosopher John Searle makes this point rather elegantly when he says: "There is exactly one overriding question in contemporary philosophy . . .: How do we fit in?" (Searle 2007, 4). In other words, how does our self-image fit in with the "basic facts" that characterise our world? It is obvious that a philosophy that tries to address this question has to be empirically informed. After all, the basic facts are fundamental empirical facts about the nature of our world (e.g. the theory of evolution by natural selection). As such, they cannot be uncovered through armchair investigation. However, it seems equally clear that our self-image, which philosophy should reconcile with the basic facts, also has to be empirically informed. Experimental philosophy, it seems, is well equipped to assist us by empirically investigating our human self-image and the concepts that form it.

2.6 SUMMARY

Proponents of E-Phi and X-Phi$_p$ believe that we should deploy experimental methods directly in the pursuit of answers to classical philosophical questions. Adherents of X-Phi$_N$ argue that experimental findings suggest we should not trust A-Phi and its central method (MAP). E-Phi, X-Phi$_p$, and X-Phi$_N$ are, hence, based on the idea that a posteriori methods allow us to attain information from which we can draw philosophical or, at least, philosophically relevant conclusions. In this chapter, we analysed how this claim can be made plausible.

To this end, we first examined the role that findings from perceptual and cognitive psychology play when it comes to testing the reliability of empirical claims. After that, we showed that there is an analogous point of connection between empirical research findings and philosophical inquiry. We formulated a general argumentation scheme that clarifies the role of experimental results in philosophy, and we discussed three concrete manifestations of this scheme in the practice of x-phi.

The quintessence was that empirical and experimental findings could be relevant to the extent that they allow us to draw inferences about the reliability of intuitions that are customarily used as premises in philosophical discussions. They may conceivably permit us to adjudicate debates that have reached a stalemate. Armed with new empirical results about the trustworthiness of particular intuitions, we may readjust the weights that we assign to the arguments in a given controversy. We can increase the weight of those arguments whose intuitive premises have tended to be confirmed through empirical investigation and reduce the weight of those arguments whose premises seem worthy of doubt. Adherents of X-Phi$_N$ even go a step further. To undermine MAP, they have gathered data that they take to demonstrate the general unreliability of philosophical intuitions.

We also discussed why experimentally informed arguments might be problematic. Each of the three argumentation schemes is open to certain critical questions that experimental philosophers are well advised to answer carefully before they draw philosophical inferences from the empirical evidence.

Towards the end of the chapter, we discussed a further way in which experimental research findings may contribute to philosophy. We recognised that x-phi could join the philosophical debate at an even earlier stage, namely, at the point where the interpretation of classical philosophical questions is negotiated. As we noted, the task of a good part of modern philosophy is to reconcile our human self-image with what we know, from an empirical-scientific viewpoint, about the way the world functions. To do this, we need a host of empirical information about our world. However, we also need a good amount of empirical research into the way we view ourselves and into the concepts that figure in the making of our self-image. Experimentally informed arguments in philosophy may help us to provide the latter.

NOTES

1. Arguments that rest on analogies, I should point out, are oftentimes quite weak (see Mukerji 2017, chapter 9). I should add, therefore, that the analogy we will draw on merely serves the purpose to illustrate. It does not bear any argumentative weight.

2. This possible explanation, which is reminiscent of a thought experiment by Dretske (1970), is unlikely, but it is not impossible. A while ago, an Italian zoo dyed chow chow puppies black and white in order to pass them off as pandas.

3. The calculation of the overall probability that all observations are false is, of course, only valid if it may be assumed that the individual probabilities of erroneous observations are independent of one another.

4. Of course, there are also philosophical propositions that only relate to individual cases, for example, the judgement that "Anna knows that Bert loves her" or "It is immoral that Christina is lying to Daniel."

5. Some philosophers seem to prefer to think of intuitions, not as philosophical observations, but as *philosophical sensations*. Nagel et al. (2013, 653), for example, seem to express this attitude when they talk about the "perception of knowledge."

6. As Nado (2016) remarks, there is no property that philosophers would unanimously agree to view as the essential characteristic of the entire class of intuitions.

7. Like me, Cantor also found this result highly counter-intuitive. In a letter to Richard Dedekind, he wrote, "I see it, but I don't believe it!" ("Je le vois, mais je'n le crois pas!") (quoted in Wallace 2003, 259).

8. The thought experiments proposed by Edmund Gettier are a case in point. In Gettier (1963), he used them as counter-examples against the standard analysis of knowledge. His critique was so damaging that most philosophers immediately accepted Gettier's arguments and rejected the standard analysis of knowledge.

9. Interestingly, this illusion does not appear to work with all people, as intercultural studies have shown. The San foragers of the Kalahari seem to be immune to it (Segall et al. 1966).

10. If you are from the Kalahari, you might be fine, however (see footnote 9, this chapter).

11. The following scheme is a generalised form of an argumentation scheme that I proposed in Mukerji (2014).

12. Michael Ridge diagnoses this type of stalemate in normative ethics. He says that "much contemporary first-order moral theory revolves around the debate between consequentialists and deontologists," which "often seems to come down to irresolvable first-order intuition mongering about runaway trolleys, drowning children in shallow ponds, lying to murderers at doors, and the like" (Ridge 2015, 17). Shortly after that, he says: "What seems to be needed is an argument for either consequentialism or deontology which does not depend so heavily on first-order moral intuitions"

(Ridge 2015, 17). Though Ridge himself certainly does not have an experimentally informed argument in mind, it is clear that such an argument may fulfil his criteria.

13. I have criticised certain aspects of this argument elsewhere (Mukerji 2014, 2016). See also Heinzelmann (2018) and Paulo (forthcoming). For a general critique of consequentialism from a deontological perspective, see Nida-Rümelin (1997a, 1997b, 2018).

14. For this reason, Pust (2014) has called this type of experimental research the "verification project" within x-phi.

15. I use the term "argument from disagreement" in the sense in which I used it in Mukerji (2014, 230ff). Other philosophers, for example, Kauppinen (2007, 107ff.), employ the term differently, however.

16. Also, it is necessary to calibrate the concept of disagreement precisely, as I argue in Mukerji (2014). However, I shall not address this problem here.

17. See Ludwig (2007, 147–48) for an example which illustrates this.

18. On verbal disputes, see section 1.4 as well as footnote 8 (chapter 1).

19. To give a principled justification for this judgement, we may point towards John Stuart Mill's famous "harm principle" that he proposes in his influential treatise *On Liberty* (1859). This principle is usually employed to formulate conditions for the legitimacy of state interference with individual freedoms. In the present case, it plausibly caries over from the political context to an issue in private morality.

20. In fact, Kass (1997) is concerned to formulate an argument against human cloning. However, the reasoning he offers is general. For a critical rejoinder, see Pinker (2008).

21. We borrow this distinction from Sinnott-Armstrong (2008).

22. Two classic papers by C. L. Stevenson (1937, 1938) contain an influential analysis of such loaded terms.

23. Swain et al. (2008) conducted an influential study of this kind in epistemology. We will discuss it in section 3.1.3.

24. The subtitle of Daniel Dennett's influential book *Elbow Room* (1984) makes this clear. It is: *The Varieties of Free Will worth Wanting*.

25. In a series of publications, the German philosopher Julian Nida-Rümelin has argued, rather extensively, for a similar position (Nida-Rümelin 2009, 2016). According to him, philosophy should pay attention to our "Lebensform" (life form), which comprises our everyday practices and customs as well as the way we interact and communicate with one another. This position, too, seems to be open to empirical considerations in a way similar to Jackson's view.

26. The first strategy would involve qualitative research methods, which will not be the focus of our discussion (see, however, appendix C). The second strategy is pursued, for example, by Nahmias et al. (2005, 2006), whose study we have encountered in section 1.5 and which we will discuss in more detail in section 3.4.

27. In section 4.1, we will introduce an argumentation scheme that captures this reasoning more formally.

28. In saying this, I am, of course, only pointing out a logical possibility. I do not believe that staunch armchair philosophers would be excited about the proposal that experimental philosophers might assist them in determining the relevant interpretations of their questions.

29. A much-discussed method of doing this is Carnapian explication. See appendix C.2 on formal methods and Machery (2017, chapter 7) for further discussion.

30. To reiterate what I said in footnote 1 (this chapter), it is quite problematic to base arguments on analogies. However, the analogies we are employing here should not be regarded as bearing any argumentative load. The intention in using it is merely to illustrate.

Chapter 3

Experimental Studies

In the previous two chapters, we discussed different versions of empirically informed and experimental philosophy, and we examined how it is possible to bridge the gap between empirical research and philosophical inquiry. To illustrate, we resorted to examples of experimental findings that, as some philosophers have argued, are of philosophical relevance. In this chapter, we will focus on x-phi studies in more depth. We will discuss the most influential contributions that proponents of x-phi have made and how they have affected various philosophical debates up to the present day.

In doing that, we will try to categorise the arguments that experimental philosophers have put forward using the concepts that we have introduced earlier. We will attempt to identify, most importantly, which understanding of experimental philosophy – that is, X-Phi$_C$, X-Phi$_P$, and X-Phi$_N$ – the respective study expresses.

In the following sections, we will look at experimental studies that address *knowledge* (section 3.1), *reference* (section 3.2), *intentional action* (section 3.3), and *free will* (section 3.4) before we conclude the chapter with a *summary* (section 3.5).[1] The first four sections (sections 3.1–3.4) will have a uniform structure. First, we will introduce some background theory about the area that the respective studies address. After that, we will home in on pioneering experimental studies. Finally, we will conclude with a discussion in light of subsequent findings and a brief and selective review of recent developments.

3.1 KNOWLEDGE

Epistemology is the theory of *knowledge*. It addresses questions like the following:

- What is knowledge?
- What is the structure of knowledge?

- Is it possible to attain knowledge and, if so, how?
- What are possible objects of knowledge?

These questions are about various aspects of knowledge. All these aspects are connected in complicated ways. There is, hence, much to say about the various epistemological questions and their connections with one another. In the following, we will not do this, however. Rather, we will focus on the most basic one of these questions. It is the question: "What is knowledge?"

3.1.1 What Is Knowledge?

There is a classical answer to this question. We already addressed it in sections 1.2 and 2.2 to illustrate the application of the MAP. It is the following proposition.

> ***Standard Analysis of Knowledge***
>
> Knowledge is justified true belief.

On the standard analysis, a person knows if and only if the following conditions hold.

> ***Condition 1 (Belief Condition)***
>
> The person *believes* that p is true.

> ***Condition 2 (Truth Condition)***
>
> p is true.

> ***Condition 3 (Justification Condition)***
>
> The person has a justification for believing that p is true.

In many cases, the standard analysis gives us an intuitively sound answer to the question whether a person knows. Thought Experiment 1 is an example of this.

> ***Thought Experiment 1***
>
> Anna wants to know what time it is. So she consults her watch, which displays 2:51 pm at the time. On that basis, Anna forms the belief that it is 2:51 pm. It is, in fact, 2:51 pm. Does Anna *know* that it is 2:51 pm?

Intuitively, Anna has knowledge in this case. Checking whether Conditions 1, 2, and 3 are fulfilled yields the same result. So the standard analysis yields the intuitively correct answer in this case. It does not, however, do that in all cases. Thought Experiment 2 demonstrates this. It is a counter-example to the standard analysis.

Thought Experiment 2

> Anna wants to know what time it is. So she consults her watch, which displays 2:51 pm at the time. On that basis, Anna forms the belief that it is 2:51 pm. It is, in fact, 2:51 pm. *However, the reason why the watch displays the correct time is that it stopped yesterday precisely at 2:51 pm.* Does Anna know that it is 2:51 pm?

The intuitively correct answer seems to be that, no, she does not know. Nevertheless, the standard analysis implies, in this case too, that Anna knows it is 2:51 pm. The three conditions are, after all, still fulfilled. Anna believes that it is 2:51 pm (Condition 1), it is, in fact, 2:51 pm (Condition 2), and Anna has a justification for believing that it is 2:51 pm (Condition 3).

The standard analysis seems to get it right only in one regard: the three conditions do, in fact, seem to be necessary for the existence of knowledge. However, the standard analysis claims to be more than that. It claims to be an *analysis*, that is, a statement of *necessary and sufficient conditions*. This contention does not seem to be correct, as Thought Experiment 2 shows. Here, all three conditions that should, on the standard analysis, be sufficient for the existence of knowledge are fulfilled. But Anna does not seem to know that it is 2:51 pm. The reason for this seems to lie in the fact that there is an element of chance in her belief. That is, she would, most likely, believe that it is 2:51 pm even if it was, in fact, 2:45 pm or 3:03 pm (see, also, textbox 3.1).

TEXTBOX 3.1. IS KNOWLEDGE JUSTIFIED TRUE BELIEF?

The view that knowledge may be analysed as justified true belief is often traced back to Plato's dialogue *Theaetetus*. There, however, it is in fact concluded that we do not know what knowledge is. The view that it might be justified true belief is merely considered as a possibility. For an instructive discussion of the knowledge problem in Plato's *Theaetetus*, see Chappell (2013). Nevertheless, this idea later became the standard account. The discovery that there are counter-examples to it is usually attributed to Edmund Gettier. According to most philosophers, Gettier disproved the standard analysis of knowledge conclusively in a

> three-page paper (Gettier 1963) though some have remained sceptical about this (e.g. Sartwell 1991). In it, he used two counter-examples that function much like the case in Thought Experiment 2. As is less well known, however, other philosophers had invented similar cases in the past. In fact, the clock case, which we have used for illustration, was introduced by Bertrand Russell in his book *Human Knowledge – Its Scope and Limits* (1948), which was published before Gettier's paper. Even earlier than that, the Medieval philosopher Peter of Mantua produced a similar counter-example to the standard analysis (Boh 1985).

Since epistemologists have been aware that it is possible to construct cases like Thought Experiment 2 that disprove the standard analysis, they have tried to formulate an analysis of knowledge that would not be open to such counter-examples. One possibility that they pursued was *reliabilism*. Those who subscribe to the reliabilist view of knowledge think that Condition 3 (Justification Condition) needs to be refined. They suggest that we should only regard a conviction as justified if it was formed using a reliable method. This solution would, indeed, solve the problem that the standard analysis encountered in Thought Experiment 2. Anna forms her belief that it is 2:51 pm based on an unreliable method. She consults a broken watch, which is, of course, no reliable instrument. Accordingly, we may say, that Anna is not, in fact, justified in believing that it is 2:51 pm and, hence, does not know it.

So far, so good. Reliabilists do, however, run into other sorts of trouble. For we can, as Lehrer (1990) has argued, construct different sorts of counter-examples. These present a scenario in which a person forms a true belief based on a reliable process but is not aware that this process is, indeed, reliable. In such a case, it does not seem as though the person has knowledge. Thought Experiment 3 makes this clear.

Thought Experiment 3

Bert is kidnapped by a crazy, yet very able, brain surgeon, who implants into his brain a digital clock. It is wired up to his brain in a way which ensures that whenever Bert thinks about the time the correct time just pops into his mind. However, he does not know that the implanted timepiece guides his thoughts. Also, he does not bother to check whether he is always correct about the time. At some point, Bert forms the belief that it is 3:00 pm. It is, in fact, 3:00 pm. Does Bert know that it is 3:00 pm?

In Thought Experiment 3 it seems, as many philosophers believe, intuitively implausible to say that Bert knows that it is 3:00 pm. We have this intuition even though Bert has a correct belief that it is 3:00 pm, which is the result of a reliable process. Here, the reliability of the process does not seem to be enough to ensure a justified belief. In addition, it seems, it should be required that Bert be aware of it. The reliability of the process as such appears to be insufficient.

At this point, we might replace or refine the reliabilist proposal to attempt to arrive at a more solid analysis of knowledge. This project only seems reasonable, however, if we take it for granted that the intuitions we use to evaluate different proposals are themselves trustworthy. Perhaps, that is not the case. In fact, Jonathan Weinberg, Shaun Nichols, and Stephen Stich claimed precisely this in their influential paper "Normativity and Epistemic Intuitions" (2001). Let us consider it in more detail.

3.1.2 Weinberg et al. (2001)

Weinberg et al. (2001) argue that the intuitions analytic epistemologists use to test analyses of knowledge are not trustworthy. Their study was the first contribution to the experimental study of epistemology and may be seen as an instance of negative experimental philosophy (X-Phi$_N$). The authors criticise the application of MAP, which is the standard methodology of epistemologists. The latter, Weinberg et al. (2001) insist, are taken in by an "intuition-driven romanticism."

Stephen Stich's book *The Fragmentation of Reason* (1990) may be seen as the origin of the argument that the authors advance. In it, Stich points out that there may be cultures unlike ours, and the people in these cultures may have developed cognitive processes that differ from our own. The mere possibility of such cultures, reasons Stich, suggests that our culturally evolved cognitive processes and, in particular, our intuitions do not possess any justificatory force. This, he thinks, holds at least if it is not possible to explain why our processes are better than those of other people. The mere fact that we have the processes we have is simply a historical accident, not evidence of their reliability.

Weinberg et al. (2001) concede that there may be a counter-argument to this line of reasoning. Perhaps, a critic may say, Stich's possible cultures are merely "philosophical fictions?" Perhaps they are not psychologically possible, after all? Perhaps all people in all cultures have the same cognitive processes? In their own words:

> While it may be logically possible that there are groups of people whose reasoning patterns and epistemic intuitions differ systematically from our own, there

is no reason to suppose that it is nomologically or psychologically possible. (Weinberg et al. 2001, 435)

This reply, the authors say, does not convince them. But they do acknowledge that "a plausible case might be made for privileging normative claims based on actual intuitions over normative claims based on intuitions that are merely logically possible" (Weinberg et al. 2001, 435). To counter it, they set out to show that some people do have these logically possible intuitions. Following Stich's reasoning, it would be possible to exploit this result to discredit the methodical use of intuitions in epistemology, that is, MAP.

Now, where could we find such people? To answer that question, Weinberg et al. (2001) have something to go on, namely, two interesting results from the psychological literature.

- The *first result* goes back to the work of a psychological research team led by Richard Nisbett, who has been a long-time co-operator of Stich. In a much-discussed study entitled "Culture and systems of thought: Holistic versus analytic cognition," Nisbett et al. (2001) found that East Asian subjects differed in their cognitive processes from subjects of Western descent. The latter, the authors argue, have a more analytic style of thinking than the former.
- The *second result* is based on work done by a team around the psychologist Jonathan Haidt.[2] Haidt et al. (1993) examined moral judgements and paid particular attention to a certain subclass of actions. These were actions that harm nobody but may lead to negative emotional responses (e.g. disgust) in some people. The authors found that subjects with high socioeconomic status judged actions in that category significantly more favourably than subjects with low socioeconomic status.

Though the studies by the two research teams led by Nisbett and Haidt, respectively, do not allow us to draw any conclusions about the interpersonal variability of epistemic intuitions that Weinberg et al. (2001) are interested in, they do, arguably, suggest two research hypotheses.

Hypothesis 1

Epistemic intuitions vary from culture to culture.

Hypothesis 2

Epistemic intuitions vary from one socioeconomic group to another.

Weinberg et al. (2001) tested these two hypotheses using various questionnaires. We will confine ourselves to two of their results.

To test Hypothesis 1, Weinberg et al. (2001) recruited members of different ethnic groups. Among them were Westerners, that is, Americans of European descent (W), East Asians (EA), and people from the Indian subcontinent (SC). They each received the following case that resembles our Thought Experiment 2 from the previous section:

Car

Bob has a friend, Jill, who has driven a Buick for many years. Bob therefore thinks that Jill drives an American car. He is not aware, however, that her Buick has recently been stolen, and he is also not aware that Jill has replaced it with a Pontiac, which is a different kind of American car. Does Bob really know that Jill drives an American car, or does he only believe it? (Weinberg et al. 2001, 443)

The options participants could choose from were "Really Knows" and "Only Believes."

Among the 66 subjects in the W-group, a clear majority of 49 persons (=74 percent) picked the option "Only Believes." To them, Bob did not seem to know that Jill drives an American car. Interestingly, 13 out of 23 subjects (=57 percent) in the EA-group ascribed knowledge to Bob. To them, it seemed as though Bob knew that Jill drives an American car. Even more dramatic was the difference between the W-group and the SC-group. In the latter, only 9 out of 23 persons (=39 percent) picked the reply "Only Believes" that the majority of Westerners had favoured. In the SC-group, most subjects judged Bob knows that Jill drives an American car.

To test Hypothesis 2, Weinberg et al. (2001) worked with two groups. One had high socioeconomic status (High SES). The other had low socioeconomic status (Low SES). Whether an individual had High SES was determined by the amount of education he or she had received. For the purpose of the study, anyone with at least one year of college education counted as High SES. Everybody else was assigned to the other group. Weinberg et al. (2001) used, among other things, the following scenario. They gave it to 14 Low SES individuals and 35 High SES individuals.

Cancer Conspiracy

It's clear that smoking cigarettes increases the likelihood of getting cancer. However, there is now a great deal of evidence that just using nicotine by itself without smoking (i.e. by taking a nicotine pill) does not increase the likelihood of getting cancer. Jim knows about the evidence and as a result, he believes that using nicotine does not increase the likelihood of getting cancer. It is possible that the tobacco companies dishonestly made up and publicised this evidence that using nicotine does not increase the likelihood of cancer, and that the evidence is really false and misleading. Now, the tobacco companies did not actually make up this evidence, but Jim is not aware of this fact. Does Jim really know that using nicotine doesn't increase the likelihood of getting cancer, or does he only believe it? (Weinberg et al. 2001, 444)

Participants were again able to choose between "Really Knows" and "Only Believes." In the Low SES group, 12 chose "Really Knows" (=86 percent), and two chose "Only Believes" (=14 percent). In the High SES group, a different picture arose. Here, only 6 participants picked the option "Really Knows" (=17 percent), and 29 opted for "Only Believes" (=83 percent).

In summary, we can, therefore, record the following: Weinberg et al. (2001) were able to find evidence both for Hypothesis 1 and Hypothesis 2. Their study suggests that epistemic intuitions vary between cultural groups and between groups of different socioeconomic statuses.

These two results can be exploited with the aid of two argumentation schemes that we discussed in section 2.4.1. The first is the argument from disagreement. After all, Weinberg et al. (2001) report data which show that different ethnic and socioeconomic groups disagree in their epistemic intuitions.

The Argument from Disagreement

(P1) There is disagreement on epistemic intuitions.
(P2) If there is disagreement on an intuition, then it is *pro tanto* unreliable.
(C) Our epistemic intuitions are *pro tanto* unreliable.

There is a second scheme that one could employ to put the results of Weinberg et al. (2001) to philosophical use. They suggest, after all, that subjects' intuitions are affected by irrelevant factors, namely, their cultural background or socioeconomic status. Accordingly, the Argument from Irrelevant Factors suggests itself. It may come in two forms.

Argument from Intercultural Variation

(P1) Our epistemic intuitions are caused, in part, by our cultural background, which is an irrelevant factor.
(P2) If our epistemic intuitions are caused by an irrelevant factor, then they are *pro tanto* unreliable.
(C) Our epistemic intuitions are *pro tanto* unreliable.

Argument from Socioeconomic Variation

(P1) Our epistemic intuitions are caused, in part, by our socioeconomic background, which is an irrelevant factor.

(P2) If our epistemic intuitions are caused by an irrelevant factor, then they are *pro tanto* unreliable.
(C) Our epistemic intuitions are *pro tanto* unreliable.

3.1.3 Swain et al. (2008)

Weinberg et al. (2001) formulate not only Hypotheses 1 and 2 that we discussed in the previous section. They also propose the following hypotheses:

Hypothesis 3

Epistemic intuitions vary as a function of how many philosophy courses a person has had.

Hypothesis 4

Epistemic intuitions depend, in part, on the order in which cases are presented.

However, Weinberg et al. (2001) do not provide evidence for these conjectures. This is where Stacey Swain, Joshua Alexander, and Jonathan Weinberg pick up with their study.

Swain et al. (2008) report on an experiment they conducted. It was designed to test Hypothesis 4. Like Weinberg et al. (2001), they sought to use the results to construct an argument against the methodical use of intuitions in epistemology. As such, their study may also be categorised as an expression of X-Phi$_N$. The argument they put forward is the Argument from Framing Effects, which we considered in section 2.4.3.

The Argument from Framing Effects

(P1) The intuition that p is subject to a framing effect.
(P2) If an intuition is subject to a framing effect, it is *pro tanto* unreliable.
(C) The intuition that p is *pro tanto* unreliable.

To support the first premise, Swain et al. (2008) focus on a case that resembles our Thought Experiment 3 from section 3.1.1, which was a stylised version of Keith Lehrer's *Truetemp* scenario. As we discussed, Lehrer uses this case to argue against the view of reliabilism in the philosophy of knowledge. To recapitulate, reliabilism claims that a person knows p if and only if she believes that p is true, p is, in fact, true, and she formed her conviction that p based on a reliable process. According to Lehrer's view, the conditions reliabilism proposes are not sufficient. If the person does not have reason to presume that the process through which she forms her belief is reliable, then we should not attribute knowledge to her. The Truetemp case, thinks Lehrer, makes this clear.

Now, Swain et al. (2008) ask whether the intuitions that Lehrer's argument is based on are reliable. To this end, they report on an experiment they conducted with the aid of 220 students of Indiana University Bloomington. Students were given a version of a questionnaire that contained a variant of the Truetemp case (C).

Charles (C)

One day Charles was knocked out by a falling rock; as a result his brain was "rewired" so that he is always right whenever he estimates the temperature where he is. Charles is unaware that his brain has been altered in this way. A few weeks later, this brain rewiring leads him to believe that it is 71 degrees in his room. Apart from his estimation, he has no other reasons to think that it is 71 degrees. In fact, it is 71 degrees (Swain et al. 2008, 154).

Subjects also received three further cases, which can be summarised as follows:

- In case D, Dave plays a game in which he flips a coin. Sometimes, he gets a "special feeling" and anticipates that the next time he flips the coin it will come up heads. He is right about this roughly 50 percent of the time. Before his next flip, he gets that same special feeling and thinks that the coin will come up heads. It does.
- In case S, Suzy is driving her car. She looks out of the window and sees a barn. So she forms the belief that there is a barn beside the road. What she does not know is that the countryside is used as a film set. The film-makers have put up many fake barns which look like real ones. Suzy, however, is looking at the only barn that is not fake.
- In case K, Karen, who is a professor of chemistry, reads a scientific article in a well-reputed journal. In this article, it is explained that, when mixed, two floor disinfectants, Cleano Plus and Washaway, create a dangerous gas that is lethal to humans. The janitor is about to mix the two disinfectants. Karen sees this and tries to warn him. She yells: "Get away! Mixing those two products creates a poisonous gas!"

After reading these scenarios, participants were asked to which extent they would agree that the four protagonists – Dave, Charles, Suzy, and Karen – *knew*, respectively, that it is 71 degrees, that the coin will come up heads, and so on. In each case, they could select one of the following options:

Strongly agree/Agree/Neutral/Disagree/Strongly disagree

Each version of the questionnaire contained the four cases C, D, S, and K. They differed, however, in the *order* in which subjects received them. Overall, there were eight different variants of the questionnaire that state the four cases in eight different orders. These were randomly assigned to the students. The particular order in which cases were presented was not random, however. Swain et al. (2008) tried to find out how their subjects would evaluate C depending on whether or not they had considered K or D, respectively, before that. That is, they wanted to find out whether the inclination to attribute knowledge to Charles depended on which cases they had thought about before.

Now, why did Swain et al. (2008) think K and D to be particularly relevant? The answer is simple: K and D seemed to be well suited as contrast cases for C:

- K is a clear case of knowledge. The chemistry professor Karen knows, based on her expertise in chemistry, that a mixture of Cleano Plus and Washaway produces a poisonous gas.
- D, on the other hand, is a clear case of non-knowledge. To be sure, Dave believes that the coin will come up heads, and it does. However, his belief is based on a mere feeling that leads him astray half the time.

We may suspect, then, that subjects should have had a stronger inclination to ascribe knowledge to Charles in C if they had previously considered D and a comparatively lesser proclivity to do this if they had just considered K. Indeed, the results that Swain et al. (2008) report support precisely this. To analyse them, they encoded the answers using numerical values: 5 (= "Strongly agree"), 4 (= "Agree"), 3 (= "Neutral"), 2 (= "Disagree"), and 1 (= "Strongly disagree"). Table 3.1 shows the average values for C in the different versions of the questionnaire.

As table 3.1 demonstrates, there appeared to be an order effect, which according to Swain et al. (2008), was statistically significant. Subjects' inclination to ascribe knowledge to Charles in C was

- comparatively small when participants had previously been confronted with K (2.4 in the case of order KCDS and 2.9 in the case of order DSKC),

Table 3.1. Results of Swain et al. (2008)

Version of questionnaire	Average value of C
KCDS	2.4
CSDK	2.6
SCDK	2.9
DSKC	2.9
CDSK	3.0
CKDS	3.0
DCSK	3.2
DSCK	3.6

- in the mid-range (i.e. between 2.6 and 3.0) when C was the first case that participants read, and
- comparatively high when subjects had previously considered D (3.2 in the case of order DCSK and 3.6 in the case of order DSCK).

These data seem to suggest a remarkable conclusion, which suggests itself once we consider that a value of 3.0 represents a neutral stance (i.e. neither agreement nor disagreement). Swain et al. (2008) were apparently able to show that the strength of agreement and disagreement, respectively, to the assertion "Charles knows that it is 71 degrees in his room." varied according to the order of cases. In addition, they were able to show, it seems, that this order effect was strong enough to turn a moderate average disagreement into a moderate average agreement. As Swain et al. (2008) put it, "Intuitions about the Truetemp Case reverse direction depending on whether the case is presented after a case of clear non-knowledge" (Swain et al. 2008, 144).

3.1.4 Discussion

Both Weinberg et al. (2001) and Swain et al. (2008) arrive at sceptical conclusions about the reliability of epistemic intuitions. But is this the final word on the matter? Of course, the discussion continued after these two contributions. So let us examine some aspects of the debate that ensued.

To start, we should observe the following: The sceptical conclusions that the two teams of authors suggest are quite far-reaching. With their findings, they attempt to support X-Phi$_N$. That is, they try to cast doubt on the method of using intuitions about cases (MAP), at least in epistemology. Though they do concede that further studies are called for, they propose, nevertheless, to view their results as a serious blow to the method of inquiry central to A-Phi. This conclusion seems premature for three reasons:

(1) The number of subjects that were included in the studies was small – especially in the case of Weinberg et al. (2001).
(2) Neither Weinberg et al. (2001) nor Swain et al. (2008) were able to find statistically significant results in all cases. Weinberg et al. (2001), for example, found significant differences between the EA-group and the W-group only in two cases. In two further cases, they did not find any. Similarly, Swain et al. (2008) did not find a framing effect in case S.
(3) Also, Weinberg et al. (2001) and Swain et al. (2008) only tested some of the many thought experiments that play a role in epistemology, and they did so only with one experimental design. So it is unclear whether their findings are robust throughout designs.

To establish the rather sweeping conclusions Weinberg et al. (2001) and Swain et al. (2008) have in mind, it would have to be shown that similar experimental results can also be found in larger groups, in other thought experiments, and using other research designs that seem equally legitimate. After all, one of the cornerstones of the scientific method is the *replication of results*. The principle is that research findings are only to be taken seriously if different researchers have been able to confirm them independently (see textbox 3.2)!

TEXTBOX 3.2. THE REPLICABILITY OF X-PHI FINDINGS

In recent years, experimental psychology has undergone a crisis which has come to be known as #repligate. Many central findings in the field did not replicate when researchers reran the requisite experiments. Various reasons for this have been identified (for a concise discussion, see Doris 2015, 44–49). One is that experimental psychologists have, generally speaking, not prioritised replication efforts. According to a study by Makel et al. (2012), in the top-100 most influential psychology journals (measured by impact factor), only 1.07 percent of the papers that these journals had published were attempts to replicate prior results. This raises the worry that x-phi, which largely relies on methods associated with experimental psychology, might also be in trouble. In fact, it could be even worse since x-phi practitioners are mostly philosophers who, as some have argued (e.g. Cullen 2010; Deutsch 2009), lack the proper training to conduct experimental studies. In addition, Seyedsayamdost (2015) has critically noted that there has not been a single attempt to replicate the findings reported by Weinberg et al. (2001) in almost ten years since the publication of their study. Recently, however, Colombo et al. (2018) have reported encouraging results about at least one aspect of the methodological soundness of x-phi studies. Focusing specifically on statistical inconsistencies, they found that "rates of inconsistencies are lower than for other disciplines in the behavioral and social sciences." Furthermore, a number of prominent x-phi researchers have teamed up for the X-Phi Replicability Project (XRP), which seeks to estimate the replicability of x-phi studies. The first published report estimated that roughly three out of four x-phi studies replicate (Cova & Strickland et al. forthcoming).

Furthermore, some of the arguments that figure prominently in the two papers we discussed seem doubt-worthy. The Argument from Socioeconomic

Variation that Weinberg et al. (2001) employ may be criticised because the socioeconomic background of participants may not be an irrelevant factor, after all (Cullen 2010). It could be that persons who have spent less time in the educational system seem to judge cases like Cancer Conspiracy differently, not because they form fundamentally different judgements about it, but because they did not pay close enough attention to the details of the case. This leads us to a methodological point: To exclude these competing explanations, we would have to make sure that we get the same (or at least similar) results if we present the cases in a way that makes it easier to understand and compute their most crucial aspects. Turri (2013) tested this experimentally and arrived at the conclusion that intuitions are almost uniform if the cases are presented in a structured form that makes their content more easily accessible.[3]

But not only the presentation of the scenarios may have influenced the subjects' judgements. The same may hold for both the number of options from which subjects could choose and their exact formulations. Nagel et al. (2013) attempted to replicate the results that Weinberg et al. (2001) had found in their Car Case.[4] They gave their subjects the same formulation of the case but included further options as possible replies. In their study, subjects could choose "Unclear." In other words, they could remain agnostic. In this experimental design, Nagel et al. (2013) were unable to find statistically significant differences between the intuitions of different ethnic groups.

The formulation of the reply options may also have played a role. In the Car Case, Weinberg et al. (2001) had their subjects choose from the options "Really Knows" and "Only Believes." This formulation may have been taken to suggest that the subjects were expected to attribute knowledge rather restrictively, namely, in the sense of "real knowledge." Cullen (2010) investigated this possibility in a simple comparative study. He assigned his subjects to one of two groups. One group received the Car Case and were asked, like in the original study, to answer the question: "Does Bob really know that Jill drives an American car, or does he only believe it?" Subjects could choose from the same possible replies, namely, "Really Knows" and "Only Believes." The second group also got the Car Case and received the same question. Cullen, however, asked them to choose either "Knows" or "Does Not Know," dropping the adverbs "really." In the first group, 29 percent chose "Really Knows," while significantly more subjects – that is, 42 percent – chose "Knows."

Moreover, Cullen mentions an important point of criticism regarding Swain et al. (2008). They concluded that epistemic intuitions are liable to order effects because their data suggest that their subjects were more inclined to attribute knowledge to Charles if they had previously considered D (clear case of non-knowledge) and less inclined if they had thought about K (clear case of knowledge). But the differences in the subjects' willingness to attribute knowledge to Charles may, as Cullen points out, be explained rather differently. We can understand this if we consider the task of participants in an x-phi study from their point of view. Participants get a questionnaire that contains, as far as they are concerned, rather strange cases and thought experiments. These may make sense to professional philosophers. Laypersons, however, cannot know the intention behind them. They presumably ask themselves why the experimenters confront them with these scenarios and which replies they might expect.[5] To answer that question for themselves, they likely try to draw inferences from the context in which the thought experiments appear. If we first present K to them (clear case of knowledge) and then C (less clear case), they may be tempted to infer from this that the experimenters are expecting them not to attribute knowledge in this case. If, on the other hand, we first have them examine D (clear case of nonknowledge) and then C, they may deduce from the contrast between the two cases that the experimenters are expecting them to categorise the latter as a case of knowledge. It is unclear whether the order effect Swain et al. (2008) believe to have found may, at least partly, be explained by the expectations participants perceived.

In general, we may record that there is, at this point, quite a bit of evidence that disconfirms the original results that Weinberg et al. (2001) and Swain et al. (2008) reported (Knobe 2015b). An extensive intercultural study confirms this (Machery & Stich et al. 2015). The authors worked with 521 subjects from the United States, Brazil, India, and Japan and presented cases to them in their respective mother tongues (English, Portuguese, Bengali, and Japanese). They were interested whether persons from different cultures would share the "Gettier Intuition." That is, they sought to establish whether they would deny knowledge in cases like Thought Experiment 2 (see sections 1.2 and 3.1.1), where a person's justified true belief is only accidentally correct. The study showed no significant differences between groups: "Indians, Americans, Brazilians, and Japanese tend to share the Gettier intuition" (Machery & Stich et al. 2015, 7).

At this point, a critic of x-phi may polemically remark that the debate Weinberg et al. (2001) initiated about the reliability of epistemic intuitions was a complete waste of time.[6] After all, over ten years of discussion has led us to the conclusion that empirically informed doubts about the tenability of the methodical use of intuitions in epistemology are unfounded, and this was what analytic philosophers had assumed all along. I do not think, however, that the debate was in vain. There are two reasons for this.

Firstly, it did yield an interesting foundational result for the metaphilosophical discussion about philosophical methodology. Though it does not lead to a new paradigm, it is nevertheless important. For it counters one potential counter-argument against the conventional analytic methodology in epistemology.[7] As such, it puts epistemological inquiry on a more solid foundation.

Secondly, proponents of X-Phi$_C$ may argue that the results the debate has yielded are philosophically interesting in and of themselves. The fact that knowledge ascriptions of people from different cultural backgrounds are rather uniform may generate interesting hypotheses about the underlying cognitive processes, and this may stimulate further research in the cognitive science of philosophy (Knobe 2015a).

3.1.5 Recent Developments

In recent years, many interesting studies followed Weinberg et al.'s (2001) and Swain et al.'s (2008) contributions to the experimental study of epistemology. Unsurprisingly, these papers have considerably broadened the scope of research and have addressed many further questions. In the following, I briefly want to discuss three of them.

Turri et al. (2017), for example, have studied the issue of *doxastic voluntarism* experimentally. Championed, among others, by Augustine of Canterbury, Thomas Aquinas, René Descartes, Blaise Pascal, and William James, doxastic voluntarism maintains that we can bring ourselves, at will, to believe a proposition. This, of course, is a controversial thesis, which many authors in the history of philosophy have denied. Especially in contemporary philosophy, the view that one could willingly induce a belief seems to have fallen out of favour, as Turri et al. (2017) note. As they explain, doxastic involuntarists, who reject voluntarism, commonly use two types of arguments. The first is conceptual and holds that the notion of voluntary belief does not even make sense. The second is psychological. It cites psychological reasons for the falsehood of doxastic voluntarism. Though the notion of a voluntary belief may be possible conceptually, say proponents of this second argument, it is impossible as a matter of psychological fact. To support their reasoning, they frequently use examples of occasions where they tried to bring themselves to believe a given proposition – and did so, of course, unsuccessfully. As Turri et al. (2017) note, however, the psychological argument would lose much of its credibility if it would turn out, as a matter of folk psychology, that ordinary people judge voluntary belief to be possible. In addition, this would discredit the idea that doxastic voluntarism is conceptually impossible. To investigate whether ordinary folk actually do think that voluntary belief is possible, Turri and colleagues ran a series of experiments and found that subjects did, indeed, tend to view belief as voluntary. In fact, their first two experiments seemed to demonstrate that belief was judged more voluntary than other kinds of mental state, for example, knowledge, opinion, and faith.[8] These results are obviously interesting from the perspective of X-Phi$_C$ since they shed light on the folk concept of belief. Furthermore, proponents of X-Phi$_p$ will find them interesting because they bear directly on the classical philosophical question what belief is. If Turri et al. (2017) are correct, the common arguments of doxastic involuntarists are likely flawed. To the extent that doxastic involuntarists can be shown to rely on conceptual intuitions about the impossibility of voluntary belief, a proponent of X-Phi$_N$ may point to these results to provide further evidence that philosophical intuitions are unreliable.

Andow (2017) has recently investigated folk judgements about epistemic consequentialism. His study dovetails rather nicely with the inquiry by Turri et al. (2017) that we have just discussed. If it is conceptually and psychologically possible to bring oneself to believe a given proposition voluntarily, as Turri's et al. (2017) subjects believe, then the question arises whether this is in line with the demands of epistemic rationality. The question arises, that is, whether it is epistemically permissible. Epistemic consequentialism speaks to this issue. It is similar to consequentialism in ethics, which holds that whether an act is morally permissible depends on whether it maximises moral value.[9] In like manner, epistemic consequentialism claims that whether holding a particular belief is epistemically permissible for an epistemic agent depends on whether that belief maximises epistemic value. We can illustrate what epistemic consequentialism implies by considering a case like the Truth Fairy scenario proposed by Elstein & Jenkins (forthcoming). The truth fairy, suppose, is a very powerful being and offers you the following deal. You accept a given proposition *p* as true. In return, the truth fairy will maximise your epistemic value. She will guarantee, that is, that your beliefs are justified, true, and knowledgeable to the highest possible extent. Is it, then, epistemically permissible for you to take her up on the offer? Epistemic consequentialism answers this question in the affirmative. Andow's (2017) question is whether the folk agree. To be sure, many philosophers have stated that accepting the truth fairy's offer is unacceptable. However, as Andow notes, "it is tempting to think that the unacceptability of believing, in the Truth Fairy case, is," given what we already know about the reliability of philosopher's judgements, "something of a 'philosopher's reaction' and thus the relevant resistance to epistemic consequentialism is something of a 'philosopher's worry'" (Andow 2017, 2635). In other words, what philosophers think may not be a reliable guide to what ordinary folk believe. However, as Andow reports, based on the results of two experiments, the philosophers' judgements do seem to mirror the folk's intuitions in this case. His findings suggest that the folk are generally inclined to judge that it is permissible for an epistemic agent to make changes that maximise epistemic value. They reject it, however, if this means that the agent takes on board a belief that is false or not backed up by evidence.

Again, these results may be viewed, firstly, through the lens of X-Phi$_C$ as, primarily, interesting findings about the nature of the folk view of epistemic permissibility. As Andow notes, however, his findings may also be regarded as contributing to a first-order philosophical question, namely, the controversy about the correct view of epistemic permissibility in the epistemological debate. This should interest champions of X-Phi$_P$. To the extent that the arguments of epistemic anti-consequentialists rely on claims about the intuitiveness of their view, Andow's results empirically strengthen these philosophers' position. Finally, critics of X-Phi$_N$ may use the result to point out that there is at least some evidence that philosophers' intuitions are shared by the folk.

There is a third recent development in the area of experimental epistemology that seems worth mentioning to me. In the earlier discussion section, recall, we have already touched on the contribution by Machery & Stich et al. (2015). These authors report that, by and large, people in different cultures and language communities tend to share the Gettier intuition. That is, they tend to share the view that justified true belief is not necessarily knowledge in cases like the ones raised by Gettier (1963). This finding, however, does not imply that people in all parts of the world share the same intuitions about all aspects of the concept of knowledge. There might, for all we know, be differences, and these differences might be interesting to investigate. What is more, contemporary epistemologists have likely missed these differences because they have, as Stich & Mizumoto (2018b) emphasise, focused almost entirely on the way in which epistemic terms like "know" are used in "our language," where "our language" is almost exclusively taken to mean "contemporary English." Since, according to Stich and Mizumoto, there is, at this point, no reason to believe that the characteristics of epistemic terms in English are universally shared by epistemic terms in other languages, there is a clear motivation to investigate the latter. The contributions to the volume *Epistemology for the Rest of the World* (2018) edited by Stich & Mizumoto (2018a) take initial steps towards doing this. Should it turn out, based on empirical findings, that the characteristics of epistemic terms like "know" are not, in fact, universally shared across language communities, this raises the question how philosophers should respond to this. One response could be to plead for a fragmentation of the epistemological project into English epistemology, Japanese epistemology, and so on. Another could be to integrate the multiple findings into "a multi-linguistic and multi-cultural epistemology" (Stich & Mizumoto 2018b, xiv). In any case, there is reason to suspect that future cross-cultural studies of epistemic terms and their characteristics will provide much fodder for thought in the epistemological debate.

3.2 REFERENCE

In the previous section, we discussed experimental contributions to the philosophical debate about epistemology. To René Descartes, that part of philosophy was central to the entire discipline. So he called it the *prima philosophia* or "first philosophy." However, through the influence of Gottlob Frege, Bertrand Russell, Ludwig Wittgenstein, and the Vienna Circle, philosophy underwent what has come to be known as the "linguistic turn" in the first half of the twentieth century. Its role was increasingly understood as the analysis of concepts and the clarification of notions that scientists used. Language itself increasingly became a topic that philosophers discussed. One of the central questions that played a great role from the beginning was that of the nature of reference. Experimental philosophers have also made contributions to this area. In the following, we will consider some aspects of the debates that they started. Before that, however, we will consider some facets of the theory of reference that have played a role in the debate.

3.2.1 What Is Reference?

We use language to make statements about the world. According to a naïve view, we can do this because every linguistic term refers to an object that is, as it were, "out there." This idea is, of course, mistaken.[10] In fact, we can show this very easily. Consider, for example, the sentence "Snow is white." The word "snow" is probably the most unproblematic of the three. "Snow," we may say, refers to all the snow in the world. The word "white" is more tricky than "snow." Apparently, it does not refer to a concrete object out there but, rather, to a property of physical objects. Perhaps we should say, then, that the expression "white" refers to an *abstract* thing. Be that as it may. In any case, there is a third word, namely, the copula verb "is," which does not seem to refer to anything at all. Linguistically speaking, its function is to link the subject of the sentence "snow" with the predicate "white." By doing that, it does not refer to an object like the word "snow" refers to snow. In addition, there are many words like "very" or "fortunately" that cannot be assigned to any object in the world.

Nevertheless, the naïve view of language may contain a kernel of truth. It is not obviously false so long as we confine it to *singular terms*. These are terms we use to talk about individual objects in the world. It seems as though we can assign each and every such term an object to which it refers.

Among the singular terms, two categories are distinguished in particular: *descriptions* and *proper names*. "The 44th president of the United States of America" is an example of a description. "Barack Hussein Obama" is an example of a proper name. Both refer to the same object, namely, the person Barack Obama.

There is, however, a problem with this theory of reference. It becomes apparent once we consider the following three statements.

(1) "Barack Hussein Obama is the 44th president of the United States of America."

(2) "Barack Hussein Obama is Barack Hussein Obama."
(3) "The 44th president of the United States of America is the 44th president of the United States of America."

All three are statements of identity. They have the form (1) a = b, (2) a = a, and (3) b = b. A statement of identity is true if the expressions to the left and right of the identity sign "=" refer to the same thing. Because the expressions "Barack Hussein Obama" and "the 44th president of the United States of America" refer to the same object, all three statements are true. But only (1) contains a cognitively valuable piece of information. (2) and (3), on the other hand, are uninformative. How can that be?

Gottlob Frege proposed to distinguish between the *Bedeutung* or reference of a term, that is, the object it points to, and the *Sinn* or meaning (Frege 1892).[11] Though the terms "Barack Hussein Obama" and "the 44th president of the United States of America" have the same reference, they do not have the same meaning. The two refer to Barack Obama in different ways. One calls him by his name; the other describes his person in terms of the office he once held. Accordingly, a person who fell into a coma in 2007 and wakes up today does not know that Barack Obama was the 44th president of the United States of America. (1) would help her to acquire that knowledge. (2) and (3) would do nothing of the sort. (2) refers to Barack Obama only as "Barack Hussein Obama," and (3) only refers to the 44th president of the United States of America as "the 44th president of the United States of America." However, both ways of referring are necessary, as Frege points out, to arrive at an informative statement.

Frege's theory does, however, lead to a problem: How do we interpret singular terms that have a meaning but do not refer to any object? How do we interpret statements like the following?

(4) "The present King of France is bald."

This sentence is evidently meaningful. Hence, it seems reasonable to expect that it has a truth value (either *true* or *false*). But we cannot determine its truth value, it appears, since the term "the present King of France" has no referent. Frege seems to be committed, then, to the idea that there are meaningful expressions without truth value.

Bertrand Russell tried to remedy this nuisance through his famous *theory of definite descriptions* (Russell 1905). On this theory, (4) can be split up into three components as follows:

(5) There is at least one thing that is presently King of France.
(6) There is at most one thing that it is presently King of France.
(7) If something is King of France, then it is bald.

(4) is true, according to Russell's view, if and only if (5), (6), and (7) are jointly true. But (5) is false because there is nothing that is presently King of France. Through the analysis of (4) into its logical conjuncts (5), (6), and (7), it is, hence, possible to assign a truth value to the statement "The present King of France is bald." That statement is false.

Russell's theory of definite descriptions appears to be incomplete as a theory of singular terms. It seems, after all, that we cannot apply it to proper names. Russell fills this void, however, with his theory of descriptions for proper names. According to this theory, proper names *stand for descriptions*.

Russell's Descriptivist Theory of Proper Names

The reference of a proper name is fixed by a description that is associated with it.

If you hear the name "Arnold Schwarzenegger," you perhaps associate the description "the actor who played the main role in James Cameron's science-fiction thriller *The Terminator*" with it. In that case, the reference of the name "Arnold Schwarzenegger" is fixed by that description, according to Russell's theory.

Saul Kripke famously criticised Russell's ideas (Kripke 1972/1980).[12] A series of experimental studies followed up on his contribution. We shall discuss it in the next section.

3.2.2 Machery et al. (2004)

To counter Russell's descriptivist theory of proper names, Saul Kripke introduced a scenario that he intended as a counter-example to it. In it, a person comes to associate a false description with a proper name. Kripke's case features an icon of the history of philosophy, namely, the famous logician Kurt Gödel. He proved two theorems that are nowadays known as his *incompleteness theorems* of arithmetic. However, the scenario that Kripke envisions supposes, blasphemously, that Gödel did not, in fact, prove these theorems. Instead, a man named "Schmidt" did. Gödel merely got a hold of the manuscript and then published it under his name. Hence, we associate his name with the description "the person who proved the incompleteness theorems of arithmetic." But in Kripke's scenario, Schmidt satisfies this description. According to Russell's theory, everybody who uses the name "Gödel" actually refers to Schmidt.

To Kripke, this reasoning represents a counter-example to Russell's theory because he thinks it is obvious that we refer to Gödel when we use the name "Gödel." He draws from this the conclusion that Russell's theory is false and presents, as an alternative, his *causal-historical theory* of proper names.

On this view, the intuition that "Gödel" refers to Gödel can be explained by the fact that "Gödel" originally referred to Gödel and was handed down to us through a chain of uses in which that name was employed to refer to that person.[13]

Kripke's Causal-Historical Theory of Proper Names

A proper name refers to that thing or person that speakers originally referred to when they first used it if there is an unbroken chain of uses to the present day.

Machery et al. (2004) observe that Kripke's argument for his theory and against Russell's presupposes that Kripke's intuitions about referential relations are reliable. As they insist, however, this premise is an unverified empirical claim. Machery et al. (2004) believe it is possible that a variant of Hypothesis 1 of Weinberg et al. (2001) may turn out to be true regarding intuitions about proper names. If that were true, it would suggest that Kripke's entire argument is doubt-worthy. Furthermore, such a result would justify doubts about the central method of the analytic philosophy of language (MAP). Accordingly, we may regard the study by Machery et al. (2004) as yet another expression of X-Phi$_N$.

To test their hypothesis, Machery et al. (2004) conducted an experiment with 42 students of Rutgers University at New Jersey and 31 students of the University of Hong Kong. In it, they gave their subjects the following thought experiment that they had modelled after Kripke's scenario.

Gödel 1

Suppose that John has learned in college that Gödel is the man who proved an important mathematical theorem, called the incompleteness of arithmetic. John is quite good at mathematics and he can give an accurate statement of the incompleteness theorem, which he attributes to Gödel as the discoverer. But this is the only thing that he has heard about Gödel. Now suppose that Gödel was not the author of this theorem. A man called "Schmidt," whose body was found in Vienna under mysterious circumstances many years ago, actually did the work in question. His friend Gödel somehow got hold of the manuscript and claimed credit for the work, which was thereafter attributed to Gödel. Thus, he has been known as the man who proved the incompleteness of arithmetic. Most people who have heard the name "Gödel" are like John; the claim that Gödel discovered the incompleteness theorem is the only thing they have ever heard about Gödel.

Having read the case, participants were asked what John is talking about when he uses the name "Gödel." The options were:

(A) the person who really discovered the incompleteness of arithmetic? or
(B) the person who got hold of the manuscript and claimed credit for the work? (Machery et al. 2004, B6).

In addition, subjects received another scenario, Gödel 2, which was very similar to Gödel 1. This case is about Ivy, who is assumed to be a student in Hong Kong. She learns in her astronomy class that Tsu Ch'ung Chih first discovered the exact time of the summer and winter solstices. This, it is assumed, is the only piece of information she receives about Tsu Ch'ung Chih. However, as the story goes, Tsu Ch'ung Chih did not, in fact, make the discovery that is attributed to him. In fact, he stole it from another astronomer who died right after making it. This theft, however, has remained undetected such that, nowadays, many people associate the discovery of the precise times of the solstices with Tsu Ch'ung Chih. In fact, this is the only thing they think they know about him. Upon considering this case, participants were asked who Ivy is talking about when she uses the name "Tsu Ch'ung Chih:"

(A) the person who actually determined the exact time of the summer and winter solstices or
(B) the person who stole the discovery of the exact times of the summer and winter solstices.

In both cases, option A matches with the answer that Russell's theory would suggest, while B fits Kripke's view. Machery et al. (2004) were interested whether the subjects' replies would support the former or the latter and whether there would be significant differences between the two groups. To this end, they coded the answers numerically. Those who selected A twice and, hence, judged both cases fully in line with Russell's theory were assigned the number 0. Students who chose A and B once got a 1. And those who judged that B was correct in both cases, which was fully in line with Kripke's theory, received the number 2.

The analysis of the data yielded two interesting results:

- Firstly, there was a significant difference between the two groups. Westerners and Chinese students showed significant differences in the way they assessed the two cases. The average value of the former was 1.13. In contrast, the latter received a value of 0.63. That is, the Western students from Rutgers University appeared to show a slight inclination to judge according to Kripke's theory, while the Chinese students of Hong Kong University seemed to concur, mostly, with Russell's theory.
- Secondly, the data that Machery et al. (2004) uncovered contained a comparatively high standard deviation, namely, 0.88 in the Rutgers group and

0.84 in the Hong Kong group. That suggests that there was a comparatively large degree of intuitive disagreement within each group.

From these findings, we can derive arguments, according to the schemes we discussed in sections 2.4.1 and 3.1.2. The first is a version of the Argument from Disagreement and the second a variant of the Argument from Irrelevant Factors.

Argument from Disagreement

(P1)   There is disagreement on intuitions about referential relations.
(P2)   If there is disagreement on an intuition, then it is *pro tanto* unreliable.
(C)   Intuitions about referential relations are *pro tanto* unreliable.

Argument from Intercultural Variation

(P1)   Our intuitions about referential relations are caused, in part, by our cultural background, which is an irrelevant factor.
(P2)   If an intuition is caused by an irrelevant factor, then it is *pro tanto* unreliable.
(C)   Our intuitions about referential relations are *pro tanto* unreliable.

These two arguments do not, of course, appear explicitly in Machery et al. (2004). But the authors' remarks make it clear that they would subscribe to the Argument from Disagreement (or an argument sufficiently similar to it). They say, for example, that they find it "wildly implausible" that the intuitions of philosophers who are under the influence of Western culture are a more reliable indicator of the correct theory of reference than the intuitions people have in other cultures and language communities. They also call into question the methodical use of intuitions in the theory of reference. "In the absence of a principled argument about why philosophers' intuitions are superior," they say, "this project smacks of narcissism in the extreme" (Machery et al. 2004, B9). What Machery et al. (2004) argue fits, in principle, with Sidgwick's remarks about the problem of disagreement, which we discussed in section 2.4.1.

3.2.3 Discussion

Now, what should we make of these results? In our discussion of the studies by Weinberg et al. (2001) and Swain et al. (2008) in section 3.1, we observed that it is important to ask whether the findings have been replicated. In experimental epistemology, the surprising data on epistemic intuitions that Weinberg et al. (2001) and Swain et al. (2008) reported could largely not be backed up by subsequent studies. What about the results that Machery et al. (2004) report?

Firstly, we should note that the authors are rather circumspect in the way they deal with their findings, as the following statement illustrates.

> We found the predicted systematic cultural differences on one of the best known thought experiments in recent philosophy of language, Kripke's Gödel case. However, we have no illusions that our experiment is the final empirical word on the issue. Rather, our findings raise a number of salient questions for future research. (Machery et al. 2004, B8)

In a follow-up paper that was published five years later, they say:

> We have no illusions that our experiments are the final empirical word on the issue. This is a newly emerging type of research, and obviously it is too early to draw any definite conclusion about the variation of intuitions about reference. (Mallon et al. 2009, 342)

Moreover, the results from their original study turned out to replicate in subsequent inquiries.[14] In fact, the data Machery et al. (2004) report on were themselves drawn from the replication of a previous pilot study. And what they found was then supported by further experiments that were conducted by other researchers (see textbox 3.3).

TEXTBOX 3.3. EMPIRICAL FINDINGS FOLLOWING MACHERY ET AL. (2004)

Though the findings Machery et al. (2004) reported have subsequently been challenged by other researchers, they have mostly held up. Beebe & Undercoffer (2015), for example, conducted one such study. They note that the Gödel case contains wrongdoing on the part of the imagined Gödel character. This, they argue, may have an effect on participants' judgements. Through experimental studies on the Knobe effect (see section 3.3), we know that the moral valence of an action can influence the intuitions that subjects report. Beebe & Undercoffer (2015) report testing this possibility but finding no evidence for it. Similarly, Sytsma et al. (2015) found no evidence that intuitions about reference were significantly distorted by ambiguities in the original vignettes. Machery (2014) provides an instructive overview of earlier experimental studies on reference as do Beebe & Undercoffer (2016). The latter

> also investigate hitherto unanswered empirical hypotheses which claim that the results by Machery et al. (2004) may have been distorted. Their data suggest that all of these explanations should be rejected. Maybe the most interesting result in recent x-phi of reference is the finding by Li et al. (2018) that differences between Westerners and Easterners seem to be in place already by the age of seven.

Also, when researchers tried to replicate the findings of Machery et al. (2004), they tried to accommodate points of criticism that objectors had put forward. Sometimes they did this in collaboration with their critics. Deutsch (2009), for example, has pointed out that the question that Machery et al. (2004) asked their subjects was ambiguous.[15] At the end of Gödel 1, they formulated their question as follows:

> When John uses the name "Gödel," is he talking about:
>
> (A) the person who really discovered the incompleteness of arithmetic? or
> (B) the person who got hold of the manuscript and claimed credit for the work? (Machery et al. 2004, B6).

As Deutsch remarks, this formulation of the question may, plausibly, be interpreted in two ways:[16]

> *Interpretation 1 (Speaker Meaning)*
>
> When John uses the name "Gödel," to whom does he *intend* to refer?
>
> *Interpretation 2 (Semantic Meaning)*
>
> When John uses the name "Gödel," to whom does this name refer?

Theories of reference make assertions about semantic meaning. As such, they give us an answer to Interpretation 2 of the question but are agnostic regarding Interpretation 1. Referential intuitions can, hence, only conflict with a theory of reference if they are about Interpretation 2. The research design that Machery et al. (2004) used was not suited, however, to draw conclusions as to whether participants did, in fact, answer the question in this interpretation.

Édouard Machery and Justin Sytsma tried to settle this issue in a collaborative study that they conducted along with Max Deutsch (Machery & Sytsma et al. 2015). To this end, they repeated the experiment from Machery et al.

(2004) with 82 American students and 47 Chinese students. In the American group, 62.2 percent chose B, and in the Chinese group, 63.8 percent favoured A. After that, Machery & Stysma et al. (2015) conducted another experiment with 79 American subjects and 49 Chinese subjects. This time, they slightly altered the formulation of the question:

> When John uses the name "Gödel," *regardless of whom he might intend to be talking about*, is he *actually* talking about:
>
> (A) the person who really discovered the incompleteness of arithmetic? or
> (B) the person who got hold of the manuscript and claimed credit for the work?
> (Machery & Sytsma et al. 2015, 69; emphasis in the original).

In this formulation of the question, it cannot be read along the lines of Interpretation 1 because subjects are explicitly instructed to ignore the speaker meaning and only pay attention to the semantic meaning, that is, to Interpretation 2. The results of this second experiment did not differ significantly from the results of the first. In the American group, 59.5 percent chose option B, and in the Chinese group, 61.2 percent opted for A.[17]

Machery & Sytsma et al. (2015) were, hence, able to confirm the earlier position of Machery et al. (2004). They showed that intuitions about the reference of proper names, which loom large in the analytic philosophy of language, seem to vary between cultures as well as within cultures, and they do that even if there is no room for pragmatic misinterpretation.[18]

3.2.4 Recent Developments

Following the study by Machery et al. (2004), experimental research in the x-phi of language and, more specifically, the theory of reference branched off into different directions and subsequently addressed further interesting questions. One area where these studies produced ripple effects is the metaphilosophical debate. Machery et al. (2004) and Mallon et al. (2009) can be read as supporting X-Phi$_N$. After all, these authors have shown, it seems, that there is reason to doubt the reliability of philosophers' intuitions, at least in the philosophy of language. This is exactly what proponents of X-Phi$_N$ would hypothesise.

In addition, though, the studies we have considered in sections 3.2.2 and 3.2.3 have provided evidence that a particular class of arguments, so-called arguments from references, are defective. As Mallon et al. (2009) explain, these arguments "derive philosophically significant conclusions from the assumption of one or another theory of reference" (Mallon et al. 2009, 332). Now, if the empirical studies on reference that we have discussed are any indication, then we should doubt that any philosopher working today may justifiedly claim to be in possession of the *correct* theory of reference. Accordingly, arguments from reference lose their credibility, and this, it may be argued, is very problematic for many areas of philosophy where these arguments are in frequent use.

One example that illustrates this problem is the philosophy of race.[19] In this area, *race eliminativists*, who think that races are not biologically real, oppose race realists, who believe that they are. Anthony Appiah, for example, who is an eliminativist, writes: "The truth is that there are no races: there is nothing in the world that can do all we ask 'race' to do for us." As Robin Andreasen (2000) points out, however, arguments like this tacitly rely on a particular description that ordinary folk associate with the term "race." Then, they go on to show that there is, as Appiah says, "nothing in the world" that conforms to that description. In other words, the argument is that the term "race," as it is commonly understood, does not refer. Against this, Andreasen argues that

> descriptions associated with a kind term [in this case "race;" NM] do not form part of its meaning, thus even if scientists were to later discover that some of these descriptions are false of the objects originally referred to, the term is still taken to refer. (Andreasen 2000, S662)

The upshot is that we get different conclusions about the ontological status of race if we use different theories of reference. Since there is, following the arguments by Machery et al. (2004) and Mallon et al. (2009), no reason to suspect that, using our intuitions, we can determine what the correct theory of reference is, these arguments all seem to be defective. This conclusion extends, of course, to Andreasen's own race-realist position that she argues for based on a different theory of reference.

There might, however, be a way to repair arguments from reference. One can try to show that there is a way to determine the correct theory of reference that does not depend on anybody's intuitions. Pinder (2017) has recently proposed such an approach. It relies on Carnap's (1950/1962) method of *explication*, which can be understood as a form of conceptual engineering.[20] The idea behind this method is to start with a vague common-sense concept, which Carnap calls the "explicandum," and to replace it with an engineered concept, which Carnap calls the "explicatum." The replacement, it is important to note, is not arbitrary but follows stringent quality criteria that Carnap discusses and motivates.[21] Pinder thinks, therefore, that it is possible to provide an intuition-independent, non-arbitrary basis for specific theories of reference that fix the meaning of terms like "race" and are immune to criticisms based on experimental findings. To illustrate how such an "explication defence" of a theory of reference might work, he shows how Robin Andreasen's reasoning for her race realist position may be recast in terms of a Carnapian explication.[22] If successful, his approach may show traditionally minded philosophers a way out of the predicament that experimental critiques have gotten them into.[23]

Another way for traditionalists to answer experimental critiques of theories of references was suggested by Max Deutsch. He argues against the "received view" that "that we should proceed by consulting our intuitive judgments about language" (Devitt 2012, 554). According to Deutsch, contributors like Kripke do not, in fact, appeal to intuitions to support their theories of reference, and even if they were, this would be the wrong way to go about it. Accordingly, he concludes, "it is safe to say, right now, that experimental work on intuitions about the Gödel Case is irrelevant" (Deutsch 2015a, 25). His argument has, in fact, a wider scope than that. Like Cappelen (2012, 2014), he doubts more generally, that philosophers appeal to intuitions as evidence in any area of philosophy. For that reason, his worries are best addressed along with a number of fundamental criticisms of x-phi in chapter 4.

Finally, it is worth pointing towards further interesting developments in the experimental philosophy of language. While initial experimental research focused on theories of reference for proper names, subsequent studies also investigated theories of reference for natural kind concepts (Genone & Lombrozo 2012).[24] In addition, experimental philosophers increasingly turned to the investigation of philosophically significant concepts along the lines of X-Phi$_C$.[25] Bear & Knobe (2017), for example, investigated what ordinary folk understand by "normal." Plausibly, this term should either be interpreted as descriptive such that it refers to, for example, the statistical average, or what is normal should be judged relative to a normative standard, for example, the ideal. Interestingly, Bear and Knobe found that their participants seemed to factor in both descriptive and normative considerations when trying to assess whether something is normal. This result chimes rather nicely with Joshua Knobe's view that descriptive and normative considerations mix and mingle in ordinary people's assessment of factual matters (Knobe 2014a). This conclusion partially depends on the most prominent result in x-phi, which has come to be known as the "Knobe effect." We shall turn to it in the next section.

3.3 INTENTIONAL ACTION

Experimental philosophers have not only contributed to epistemology and the philosophy of language. They have tried to advance philosophical action theory as well. At the core of the x-phi debate, which has mainly revolved around a very influential paper by Joshua Knobe (Knobe 2003), is the question whether an unintended side effect may properly be regarded as intentional.[26] In this section, we will consider this problem. We will begin with the question: "What is intentional action?"

3.3.1 What Is Intentional Action?

The philosophical theory of action revolves around questions that arise when persons act. At its core is the issue what, essentially, makes a given action an action. In the discussion of philosophical questions like this one, it has proven useful to distinguish the object of interest – in this case, *action* – from another object in what may be called a "comparative study." In epistemology, we ask, for example, what distinguishes knowledge from mere belief. An answer to that question would, we hope, bring us closer to an answer to the question about the nature of knowledge. Regarding the question "What is an action?" we may ask: "What distinguishes an action from other occurrences that merely *happen*?"

Wittgenstein asked more concretely: "What is left over if I subtract the fact that my arm goes up from the fact that I raise my arm?" (Wittgenstein 1953/1999, §621). The point that Wittgenstein is driving at is that my arm can rise even if I do not raise it. The rising of my arm may be the causal upshot of a muscle contraction, or it may be the result of another person raising it. A physiotherapist who is treating my shoulder muscles may, for example, say: "I will now move your arm up and down. While I do this, I would like you to relax it completely." In this case, my arm would go up without *me* raising it.

Evidently, we can, hence, answer Wittgenstein's question as follows: If I subtract the fact that my arm goes up from the fact that I raise my arm, then my *intention* to raise it is left over. I raise my arm if I have the intention to raise it and it does, indeed, go up.

With this answer, we are on the right track. However, it is not sufficiently precise yet. As it turns out, it is not enough to connect the concept of action with the concept of intention. Furthermore, we have to differentiate the latter concept. That gets clear once we encounter certain cases. In them, a person forms a prior intention to make something happen, which then happens, though we would not, intuitively, take this to be an instance of an action.

Suppose I decide to raise my arm. After I have formed this intention, my muscles contract spontaneously such that my arm goes up. In this case, it seems as though I did not raise my arm even though I formed the intention to raise it, and it did, in fact, go up. This problem disappears once we differentiate between two kinds of intentions, namely, *prior intentions* (intention$_P$) and *intentions in the action* (intention$_A$) (Searle 1983). In the case just described, I decided to raise my arm. By doing that, I formed an intention$_P$. This intention$_P$ may be fulfilled or remain unfulfilled. If it is, in fact, fulfilled, this happens through an action in which the person who is acting acts on an intention$_A$. If I form the intention$_P$ to raise my arm, this intention$_P$ is fulfilled by the fact that it goes up while I intend$_A$ to raise it.

An action without an intention$_A$ is, hence, impossible. But how can it be possible that we say something like this: "Sorry, I did not intend to do this." This statement does not seem nonsensical. But it concedes that there was an action which was not intended.

The first possible interpretation is to take "intend" as referring to an intention$_P$. It is, after all, possible to do something without forming such an intention that precedes the action. John Searle makes this clear by pointing out that it is possible to reply to the question "When you suddenly hit that man, did you first form the intention to hit him?" by saying "No, I just hit him" (Searle 1983, 84). The point is that an intention$_P$ is neither necessary nor sufficient for there to be an action. We can act without forming a prior intention to act. Nevertheless, this possibility does not do much to help us make sense of the expression "Sorry, I did not intend to do this." It is obviously meant to excuse the person saying it. If it would mean "I did not intend to do this, I just did it," this would be a bad apology.

There is a second, more suitable interpretation, which distinguishes a further sense in which the word "intention" can be used. On this interpretation, a given behaviour can be attributed to a person as intentional in this third sense only if there exists at least one description of it on which it was not accompanied by an intention$_A$. That does not mean, however, that the person's behaviour was intentional$_A$ under all descriptions. When somebody says "Sorry, I did not intend to do this," the phrase "to do this" refers to a description of the behaviour that they did not intend$_A$.

To bring this out more clearly, let us elaborate a bit further on the previous example. I may intentionally$_A$ raise my arm without thereby intending$_A$ to do anything else. Suppose I attend a talk by a fellow academic. The speaker has asked the audience not to ask questions during the presentation. Because the topic is quite boring (yes, that sometimes happens!), I get quite sleepy and feel the urge to yawn while stretching out my arms. I do that, and, in so doing, I raise my right arm above my head. I do this intentionally$_A$. Now, suppose that the speaker sees this and misinterprets it as an attempt on my part to ask a question. He replies by saying: "I specifically requested that there would not be any questions during the talk. Please ask your question after I have finished." I might apologise then by replying: "Excuse me. I did not intend$_A$ to signal that I had a question." That is true. When I raised my arm, this action was accompanied by an intention$_A$. But it was not the intention to indicate that I wished to ask a question. (Well, perhaps it would not help in this situation if I explained myself any further…)

We can infer which intention$_A$ is guiding a behaviour by asking a further question: What is the *motivating intention* (intention$_M$) behind it?

That question, in turn, is answered by asking what the reason for it was. The speaker in the previous example might follow up by saying: "But you raised your arm. To me, this indicates that you wanted to ask a question." In reply, I might say: "I did raise my arm, but not to indicate that I had a question." Perhaps I might make this plausible by also saying: "I was not even aware that you could see me in the back row." Saying this would clarify that I did not have the intention$_M$ that the speaker was attributing to me and that I, hence, did not intend$_A$ to signal that I wanted to ask a question when I raised my arm. I do this by emphasising that I did not even know that the raising of my arm could be understood in that way (Anscombe 1957/2000, §6). As it turns out, then, a given action may be intentional$_A$ under one description ("I raise my arm.") and not intentional$_A$ under another ("I indicate that I want to ask a question."). Hence, there can be things we do unintentionally$_A$.

In the previous case, we saw that the question what a person intends$_M$ is plausibly relevant to the question what she intends$_A$ while she acts. It is not far to seek that there might be a close connection between the two types of intention, such that I intend$_A$ an act if and only if I have an accompanying intention$_M$ to do it. Bratman (1984) calls this view of the connection between intention$_A$ and intention$_M$ the *simple view*. Though it seems reasonable on the face of it, it is not uncontested. Some philosophers believe that it is possible to act intentionally$_A$ without forming an intention$_M$ to do it.[27] Many x-phi researchers have investigated the controversy between proponents of these two views. Knobe (2003) broke the first ground.

3.3.2 Knobe (2003)

Is the simple view justified, or is it not? Gilbert Harman gives the following example to show that it is not:

> A sniper shoots at a soldier from a distance, trying to kill him. . . . In firing his gun, the sniper knowingly alerts the enemy to his presence. He does this intentionally, thinking that the gain is worth the possible cost. But he certainly does not intend to alert the enemy to his presence. (Harman 1976, 433)

The example stands to reason. The soldier fires his shot with the intention$_M$ to hit an enemy combatant. While doing it, he knows that he his thereby alerting the enemy to his presence. He does that intentionally$_A$. But it would be implausible to suggest that he intends$_M$ it.

Michael Bratman, who also criticises the simple view, points out, however, that "it is a view towards which commonsense initially leans" (Bratman 1984, 378). But is this true? Do most people think of the simple view as intuitive?

This is the question that Joshua Knobe tackled in the hitherto most quoted x-phi paper (Knobe 2003).[28] He investigates when people judge in line with the simple view and when they do not. To this end, he reports about an experiment in which he asked subjects to assess the following case:

Experiment 1 ("help condition")

The vice-president of a company went to the chairman of the board and said, "We are thinking of starting a new program. It will help us increase profits, and it will also help the environment."

The chairman of the board answered, "I don't care at all about helping the environment. I just want to make as much profit as I can. Let's start the new program."

They started the new programme. Sure enough, the environment was helped (Knobe 2003, 191).

In Experiment 1, Knobe asked participants "whether they thought the chairman *intentionally* helped the environment" (Knobe 2003, 191; emphasis in the original), and 77 percent said "no" to this.

This result suggests that philosophical laypersons have a concept of intentional action that matches the simple view. The chairman says, beyond any doubt, that he does not have the intention$_M$ to help the environment. He only cares about his bottom line. On the simple view, we should not attribute to him the intention$_A$ to help the environment. This is how the majority of Knobe's subjects saw it.

Knobe reports, however, that the subjects' answers changed when he changed one aspect of the case description. In a second experiment with different participants, he replaced the word "help" with "harm."

Experiment 2 ("harm condition")

The vice-president of a company went to the chairman of the board and said, "We are thinking of starting a new program. It will help us increase profits, but it will also harm the environment."

The chairman of the board answered, "I don't care at all about harming the environment. I just want to make as much profit as I can. Let's start the new program."

They started the new programme. Sure enough, the environment was harmed (Knobe 2003, 191).

Once more, Knobe asked his subjects "whether they thought the chairman *intentionally* harmed the environment" (Knobe 2003, 192; emphasis in the original). In this case, 82 percent said "yes."

This result from Experiment 2 does not fit the simple view anymore. After all, the chairman makes it clear, once again, that he does not care about the environment but only about his profits. He did thus not have the intention$_M$ to harm the environment. Nevertheless, the majority of participants in Knobe's study thought that he had the intention$_A$ to do this.

In the course of the x-phi debate, it turned out that the judgement asymmetry which Knobe found in his experiments is a robust result. A number of studies have been able to replicate this so-called Knobe effect or side-effect effect.[29] Some researchers even found it in subjects from different cultures and language communities,[30] with children (Leslie et al. 2006, Pellizzoni et al. 2009), as well as with persons who have autism spectrum disorder and Asperger syndrome (Zalla & Leboyer 2011). More recently, Kneer & Bourgeois-Gironde (2018) found that even professional judges appear to show the Knobe effect when they are asked to assess whether a defendant has caused a merely foreseen side effect intentionally. It does seem worthwhile, therefore, to spend some time thinking about its possible interpretations and its philosophical status.

3.3.3 Discussion

The Knobe effect is very interesting. There are at least three reasons for this. Firstly, it is an empirical psychological result about the way humans judge philosophically relevant scenarios. From the perspective of X-Phi$_C$, it is thus interesting in its own right. It tells us that judgements people make about actions and their intentions follow a more complex structure than philosophers had previously thought.

Secondly, those experimental philosophers who adhere to X-Phi$_P$ may propose to exploit the Knobe effect as a result that is potentially interesting for the debate in philosophical action theory. In section 2.5, we discussed that many philosophical discussions aim to pursue questions that are of relevance to our lifeworld, and we saw that experimental findings could assist philosophers in finding out which interpretations are, in fact, relevant. The Knobe effect may play a part here. It indicates that philosophical laypersons have a particular concept of intentional action that differs from the simple view. Proponents of the simple view, it may be argued, merely engage in a metaphysics of action that the folk find utterly irrelevant to their lifeworld. Such a departure from the layperson's understanding of intentional action may, on occasion, turn out to be justified, as we discussed in section 2.5. But those who propose it owe us good reasons.

Thirdly, Knobe's finding plausibly transcends action theory insofar as it has implications for our understanding of philosophy as a whole. Whether we regard the bringing about of a given side effect as intentional$_A$ depends, it seems, on whether or not it is good or bad. This way of judging violates a well-entrenched view in philosophy that may be called the *two-worlds paradigm*. According to that idea, answers to factual questions are independent of answers to normative questions and vice versa. Knobe's result seems to indicate, however, that philosophical laypeople are inclined to judge the factual question about the intention$_A$ behind an act based on their normative assessment of its effects. Hence, their normative judgements seem to mix and mingle with their factual judgements. To be sure, this does not prove conclusively that the two-worlds paradigm is flawed because philosophers do not have to cling slavishly to the judgements of laypersons. However, it does give them a considerable burden of proof. They have to justify their stance if they disagree with the folk.

It is evident that these three reasons why the Knobe effect is interesting are subject to certain suppositions. Whether one accepts the first reason depends on whether one accepts X-Phi$_C$ as a metaphilosophical view. Those who do not may regard the Knobe effect as a philosophically uninteresting psychological finding. Whether one accepts the second and third reason depends, it seems to me, on two factors. Firstly, one has to accept X-Phi$_P$, that is, the idea that experimental findings are relevant to classical philosophical questions. Secondly, one has to adopt a particular interpretation of the Knobe effect. One has to adopt the view that the result tells us something about how philosophical laypersons understand the concept of intentional$_A$ action. If it were possible to explain the effect away, then it should not affect the debate in philosophical action theory at all. In that case, it should not be seen as a blow to the two-worlds paradigm either. If it were possible to show that the judgement asymmetry that philosophical laypersons exhibit is based on a mistake, then we might only be able to exploit this finding, drawing on X-Phi$_N$, to argue that philosophical intuitions and their methodical use in analytic philosophy (MAP) are unreliable. Hence, the interpretation of the Knobe effect is tremendously important to gauge its philosophical consequences. For this reason, a large part of the x-phi debate since 2003 has pursued the question how it might be explained.

In the literature, different explanations have been proposed.[31] Broadly speaking, they are of two types.

- Proponents of the first type of explanation suspect that the judgement asymmetry observed by Knobe is based on a performance error in the application of the concept of intentional$_A$ action.
- Others, including Knobe himself, suppose that the Knobe effect tells us something about the folk concept of intentional$_A$ action.

Early on, Adams & Steadman (2004a, b) put forward an *error theory*, that is, an explanation of the first type, arguing that the subjects Knobe worked with likely drew pragmatic inferences from his scenarios.[32] Strictly speaking, such pragmatic inferences are not logically valid. They may, however, appear appealing to laypersons based on everyday reasoning practices.[33] The crucial issue is, according to Adams and Steadman, the connection between the attribution of intentional$_A$ action, on the one hand, and the attribution of praise and blame, on the other. If a person intentionally$_A$ does something good, praise seems to be the proper response, and if she intentionally$_A$ does something bad, it appears appropriate to blame her. In Knobe's Experiment 1, subjects did not seem to be inclined to praise the chairman. To be sure, what he does helps the environment. But he does not care about that and, hence, he does not appear to be praiseworthy. His indifferent attitude explains, according to Adams and Steadman, why Knobe's subjects judge that the chairman did not help the environment intentionally$_A$. In Experiment 2, however, they seemed to be inclined to blame him because what he does harms the environment, which he callously ignores. But here, Knobe did not offer a reply option that subjects could choose to express this judgement. Therefore, they chose the only available option that would, from a pragmatic perspective, reflect what they wanted to say. Subjects, ascribed, that is, the intention$_A$ to harm the environment to the chairman.

On its face, the error theory Adams and Steadman propose is, admittedly, quite plausible. After all, we do sometimes use phrases like "You did that intentionally!" when we want to blame another person. This, however, does not necessitate that the explanation is correct. And even if there were something to it, this would not mean that it explains the whole Knobe effect. The only possibility to settle the question whether the pragmatic explanation that Adams and Steadman offer is appropriate is to run further experiments.

Nichols & Ulatowski (2007) tried their luck doing this.[34] To this end, they gave their participants Experiment 2 and asked them to pick one of the two options as an answer:

i. The chairman *intentionally* harmed the environment.
ii. The chairman didn't *intentionally* harm the environment (Nichols & Ulatowski 2007, 352).

Sixty-eight per cent chose (i).

After that, Nichols and Ulatowski did another experiment with different participants. Again, they gave them Experiment 2. This time, however, they offered the following options:

i. The chairman *intentionally* harmed the environment, and he is responsible for it.
ii. The chairman didn't *intentionally* harm the environment, but he is responsible for it (Nichols & Ulatowski 2007, 352–53).

This formulation of the options clarifies that the chairman can be blamed even if he did not act intentionally$_A$ when he harmed the environment. Now, the error theory that Adams' and Steadman's offer allows us to make a prediction in this case: Here, the Knobe effect should disappear. That is, subjects should pick option (ii). As Nichols and Ulatowski report, however, that was not the case. In fact, 67 percent chose option (i). The re-description of the options had no discernable effect! Hence, though initially plausible, Adams' and Steadman's explanation for the Knobe effect does not seem to be adequate.

Malle & Nelson (2003) propose an alternative error theory which also allows praise and blame to play a decisive role. However, these authors do not focus on pragmatic inferences. Instead, they suppose that the emotional responses which underlie pragmatic inferences could be the key to understanding the Knobe effect. The authors point out that negative emotions which accompany blameworthy actions can distort our verdicts such that we misapply the concept of intentional$_A$ action. They give an everyday example to illustrate this:

> When a couple fights, for example, the intense negative affect that emerges will bias each person into believing that everything the other does is intentional and motivated by malevolence. (Malle & Nelson 2003, 575)

From this, Malle & Nelson (2003) draw a conclusion that seems relevant for the explanation of the Knobe effect.

> Similarly, the vengefulness toward a person who is accused of having committed a crime will all but rule out considerations that the person may have committed the act in question unintentionally. (Malle & Nelson 2003, 575)

So it is possible that the folk concept of intentional$_A$ action does comport with the simple view, after all. Knobe's data from Experiment 2 that appear to contradict this may, then, be the result of a misapplication of that concept. Many of Knobe's participants, it may be argued, had an emotionally induced inclination to blame the chairman so that they attributed to him, despite better judgement, the intention$_A$ to harm the environment.

This explanation is not implausible either. However, there is empirical evidence that raises doubts. Wright & Bengson (2009) and Nadelhoffer (2004b), for example, report that, in some experiments, subjects judged that a person intentionally$_A$ brought about a side effect but did not blame her for it. Young et al. (2006) present evidence of subjects with damage to the ventromedial prefrontal cortex, which is a region of the brain that plays a large role in the processing of information. These persons' assessments of Experiments 1 and 2 did not differ significantly from the judgements of participants who did not have damage in that brain region. Diaz et al. (2017) have recently found, more specifically, that the Knobe effect does not seem to be caused by anger. These results call Malle's and Nelson's error theory into question.

Knobe himself has proposed an explanation of the second type. He suspects that the Knobe effect does not result from the misapplication of the folk concept of intentional$_A$ action. The folk, hypothesises Knobe, do apply that concept correctly. The concept itself, however, has normative components. He thinks that two kinds of evaluations are logically related in the context of intentional$_A$ action, namely, the moral quality of the intended$_M$ and unintended$_M$ side effects as praise- or blameworthy. Figure 3.1 illustrates this.[35]

Figure 3.1 shows three connections that are to be interpreted as follows:

1. If an anticipated, but unintended$_M$, side effect is regarded as bad, this is a factor that prompts us to blame the agent.
2. If, in addition, we judge that the person brought about the side effect intentionally$_A$, this increases our inclination to blame her.

These two connections largely reflect the orthodox view. Knobe, however, sees a further connection.

3. If we judge that an anticipated, but unintended$_M$, side effect is bad, this increases our inclination to judge that the agent brought it about intentionally$_A$.

Mele & Cushman (2007), however, report that some of their experimental findings cast doubt on Knobe's explanation. They used the following thought experiment to test it.

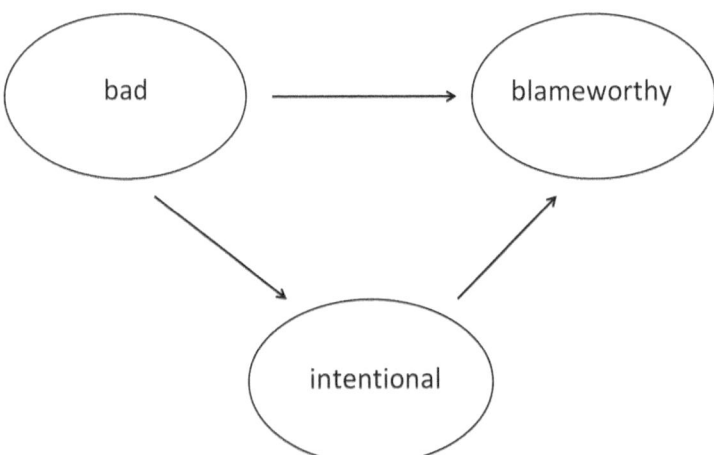

Figure 3.1. Knobe's Cognitive Reconstruction of the Concept of Intentional Action

Pond

Al said to Ann: "You know, if you fill in that pond in the empty lot next to your house, you're going to make the kids who look for frogs there sad." Ann replied: "I know that I'll make those kids sad. I like those kids, and I'll definitely regret making them sad. But the pond is a breeding ground for mosquitoes; and because I own the lot, I am responsible for it. It must be filled in." Ann filled in the pond, and, sure enough, the kids were sad. Did Ann intentionally make the kids sad? (Mele & Cushman 2007, 193)

On Knobe's explanation, we should be inclined to say that Ann intentionally$_A$ made the kids sad. After all, this case fulfils all the criteria he states. Though Ann does not intend$_M$ to make the kids sad, she anticipates that she will do this if she fills in the pond. She does, and the bad side effect actually occurs. Accordingly, we should judge that Ann made the kids sad intentionally$_A$. Intuitively, however, this does not seem to be correct. Mele's and Cushman's participants confirmed this. They were asked to rate, on a 7-point scale, whether Ann had intentionally$_A$ made the kids sad. Values above 4 counted as indicating agreement. Only 28 percent did agree by choosing a value of 5 or higher, while the average value of responses was 3.19. Participants, that is, tended not to agree that Ann intentionally$_A$ made the kids sad.

If we compare Knobe's Experiment 2 with Pond, we find that the attitudes of the main characters differ regarding the side effects in question. The chairman avowedly does not care whether he helps or harms the environment. Ann, on the other hand, regrets that she makes the kids sad. This difference seems to be relevant. Accordingly, Joshua Knobe and his co-author Dean Pettit proposed a new explanation.

Pettit & Knobe (2009) hypothesise that we ascribe intentional$_A$ action based on the attitude that the person who is acting exhibits towards the side effect. They think that there are certain criteria that make an attitude appropriate to have.[36]

- The person acting should have a pro-attitude towards a good side effect. If she knowingly produces a good side effect but feels neutral or negative about it, we do not ascribe it to her as intentional$_A$.
- The person acting should have a con-attitude towards a bad side effect. If she knowingly produces a bad side effect but feels neutral or positive about it, we do ascribe it to her as intentional$_A$.

This hypothesis explains Knobe's Experiment 1 and Experiment 2.

- In Experiment 1, most people say that the chairman did not help the environment intentionally$_A$. He knew that what he did would help the environment. This result is a positive side effect. A pro-attitude would be appropriate.

The chairman, however, has a neutral attitude. Hence, we judge that he did not help the environment intentionally$_A$.

- In Experiment 2, most people say that the chairman intentionally$_A$ harmed the environment. He knew that what he did would harm the environment. This result is a negative side effect. A con-attitude would be appropriate. The chairman, however, has a neutral attitude. Hence, we judge that he did harm the environment intentionally$_A$.

Pettit's and Knobe's proposal also plausibly explains Pond:

- In Pond, most people say that Ann did not make the kids sad intentionally$_A$. She knew that what she did would have this bad side effect. A con-attitude towards it would be appropriate. Ann does have a con-attitude (i.e. regret). Hence, we judge that Ann did not make the kids sad intentionally$_A$.

Even though the hypothesis Pettit and Knobe propose can explain all these cases, it, too, does not seem to be fully adequate. This is because there is experimental evidence that conflicts with it. Interestingly, it comes from a paper that Knobe himself has published earlier (Knobe 2007b). In it, he reports on an experiment in which he tested how subjects would respond to a thought experiment about a situation in Nazi Germany. The CEO of a company has to decide whether to implement an organisational measure. The vice-president informs him about the anticipated consequences of that measure. In the first version of the thought experiment, they were described as follows:

> *Nazi Law 1 ("violate condition")*
>
> The vice-president of the corporation said: "By making those changes, you'll definitely be increasing our profits. But you'll also be *violating* the requirements of the racial identification law."
>
> The CEO said: "Look, I know that I'll be *violating the requirements of the law*, but I don't care one bit about that. All I care about is making as much profit as I can. Let's make those organizational changes!" (Knobe 2007b, 105; emphasis in the original).

In the second version of the thought experiment, consequences were described this way:

> *Nazi Law 2 ("fulfil condition")*
>
> The vice-president of the corporation said: "By making those changes, you'll definitely be increasing our profits. But you'll also be *fulfilling* the requirements of the racial identification law."
>
> The CEO said: "Look, I know that I'll be *fulfilling the requirements of the law*, but I don't care one bit about that. All I care about is making as much profit as

I can. Let's make those organizational changes!" (Knobe 2007b, 106; emphasis in the original).

Both in Nazi Law 1 and in Nazi Law 2, the CEO is only interested in making profits. He would increase profits if he were to implement the respective measure. In Nazi Law 1, doing this would, however, violate the racial identification law. In Nazi Law 2, on the other hand, the CEO would thereby fulfil it. Knobe wanted to make sure his subjects would understand that complying with the racial identification law would be a bad consequence, and not complying with it would be good. So he added the following comment:

> The purpose of the law was to help identify people of certain races so that they could be rounded up and sent to concentration camps. (Knobe 2007b, 105)

On the explanation that Pettit & Knobe (2009) put forward, participants should judge the two cases as follows.

- In Nazi Law 1, they should judge that the CEO did not violate the racial identification law intentionally$_A$. After all, violating that law was to be regarded as a *good* consequence. The CEO should, therefore, have a pro-attitude, but he did not.
- In Nazi Law 2, participants should respond that the CEO did have the intention$_A$ to comply with the racial identification law. Compliance, after all, is a bad consequence. The CEO should thus have a con-attitude. In fact, however, he does not care about it. He has a neutral attitude.

As Knobe (2007b) reports, his subjects judged these cases differently, however.

- Some 81 percent said that the CEO violated the law intentionally$_A$ in Nazi Law 1.
- In contrast, only 30 percent said that he fulfilled the law intentionally$_A$ in Nazi Law 2.

These results from Knobe (2007b) suggest that social norms may play a role in the ascription of intentional$_A$ action. And, interestingly, this effect seems to be largely independent of the moral quality of these norms.

At the beginning of this section, we started out with the observation that the philosophical consequences of the Knobe effect depend, to a great extent, on its explanation. We have considered two entirely different explanatory approaches. On the first, the Knobe effect does not tell us anything about the way philosophical laypersons understand the concept of intentional$_A$ action. Instead, it merely tells us that they tend, on occasion, to fall prey to cognitive errors. On the second approach, which Knobe himself favours, the Knobe effect reveals how the folk understand the concept of intentional$_A$ action. A lot of research has been done in the past ten years or so. Nevertheless, "what the correct account should look like," is, to use the words of Cova et al. (2016, 1306) "still a riddle." Since no interpretation has hitherto been able to explain all the data that is available, we cannot say, with sufficient assurance, which approach is preferable. Accordingly, it is hard, at this point, to gauge the philosophical consequences of the Knobe effect.

3.3.4 Recent Developments

As in the case of experimental epistemology and the experimental philosophy of language, a number of interesting developments followed the initial studies in the experimental theory of action by Knobe and his colleagues. One such development occurred, for example, in legal philosophy. Here, Cohen-Eliya & Porat (2015) have recently argued that the Knobe effect has implications for the way we view constitutional law. As they explain, it is common for courts to investigate whether a governmental organisation intended to harm rights with a given action. For example, in *Schneider v. State*, which is a famous American legal case of the 1930s, the American Supreme Court decided that it was unconstitutional for a municipality to prohibit Jehovah's witnesses from distributing handbills. The municipality argued that the distributors of handbills would litter public streets and insisted that this problem outweighed the distributors' right to free speech. In its ruling, the Supreme Court determined, however, that the littering issue was a trivial problem in comparison to the free speech issue. The judges concluded, therefore, that the municipality had used the former problem as a subterfuge and gathered that it, in fact, intended to harm the free speech rights of Jehovah's witnesses. Accordingly, they ruled it unconstitutional. Now, as Cohen-Eliya and Porat observe, though it has been a common practice in constitutional law to consider the intention to harm rights as an important factor, the indifference to harming rights has so far been neglected. On their view, however, government actions that betray an indifference to harming rights are similarly problematic. Central to their argument is a particular view of the Knobe effect. As the authors propose, it can be explained "as an assessment of respect or disrespect":

> Intentionally harming a person or an interest conveys lack of respect for that person or interest. Accordingly, the same disrespect is also present when we do not care about that person or interest. The identity in attitudes is translated in people's minds into an identity in terms of intentionality. (Cohen-Eliya & Porat 2015, 240)

This being so, Cohen-Eliya and Porat argue, if it is impermissible for governments to *intend* to harm rights, it should also be impermissible for them to be *indifferent* to harming rights. After all, both the intention to harm and the indifference to harming betray a morally problematic attitude, namely, a disrespect for persons and their rights.[37]

This argument is somewhat problematic since it relies on an explanation of the Knobe effect that Cohen-Eliya and Porat do not support with empirical evidence. Nevertheless, their contribution is valuable because it illustrates how practitioners of X-Phi$_p$ could use the Knobe effect to infer substantive philosophical conclusions from it. There is, in principle, no reason why these conclusions should only concern the area of constitutional law. As a matter of fact, Cohen-Eliya and Porat also discuss how the Knobe effect might be relevant to normative ethics more generally. According to a well-known ethical doctrine, the *doctrine of double effect*, an act that has a bad side effect may, nevertheless, be morally permissible if the agent does not bring it about intentionally. If we combine this doctrine with the previously mentioned simple view, the moral status of the act would depend on whether or not the agent positively intended the bad side effect. As we know through the research by Knobe and colleagues, most people tend to judge that an agent has intentionally brought about a bad side effect even in cases where she, like the chairman in Knobe's Experiment 2, does not care about it. Now, if we assume, following Knobe, that this judgement is not simply a performance error, this implies that the doctrine of double effect is considerably less permissive than many ethicists have previously thought. Not only does it forbid acts with bad intended side effects. It also forbids acts with bad side effects that the agent merely foresees and is indifferent to. It remains to be seen which conclusions proponents and opponents of the doctrine of double effect draw from the Knobe effect.[38]

A further interesting development was the study by Utikal & Fischbacher (2014). They tested the Knobe effect using a different methodology, namely, that of *experimental economics*.[39] Previously, all studies about the Knobe effect had relied on written vignettes that participants had to read and assess. In contrast, Utikal and Fischbacher converted the story that these vignettes contained into an incentivised game that players they had recruited for their experiment had to play. Player 1 played the role of the chairman who had to decide whether to take a given action that would foreseeably produce a given side effect for player 2. The incentive structure of the game was such that player 1 would benefit from taking the action. Player 2 represented the environment. This person would be helped/harmed by the side effect of player 1's action. Player 3 was a third-party spectator. After the chairman's decision, this player had to decide whether to punish or reward player 1 by deducting or adding a monetary reward. In this experimental setup, the Knobe effect would be confirmed if "player 3 punishes player 1 for negative side effects but does not reward him for positive ones" (Utikal & Fischbacher

2014, 223). Interestingly, Utikal and Fischbacher confirmed the Knobe effect in some of their experimental settings but not in others. Whether the Knobe effect showed up in their data seemed to depend on the relative economic status of player 1 vis-à-vis player 2 and on the magnitude of the side effect. It arose only when player 1 was of higher economic status (i.e. received a higher monetary reward) than player 2, and the side effect was small. In other settings, it did not arise or was even reversed.

The study by Utikal & Fischbacher (2014) is interesting for several reasons, not least because it uses a different methodology to investigate the Knobe effect. This allows the authors to find evidence that the Knobe effect is not mediated through the language of vignettes but is a direct consequence of the economic determinants of the setting. This said, the study is also somewhat problematic. Most importantly, we should observe that Utikal and Fischbacher do not test people's judgements about intentionality directly. Rather, they work with proxies. Judgements about intentionality are identified with willingness to praise and blame, and this willingness is then measured by the participants willingness to punish and reward, respectively. As the authors concede, there is, of course, no guarantee "that the perception of intention is identical to the assignment of blame and praise" (Utikal & Fischbacher 2014, 232). Nevertheless, their study is certainly innovative, and their findings should stimulate further interesting research on the Knobe effect.

Another recent development to do with the Knobe effect is a series of studies reported by Michael & Szigetic (2018). They examined whether the Knobe effect, which had previously only been tested with cases that involved the actions of an individual (e.g. the chairman), would generalise to the group level. In other words, they wanted to find out whether participants would still show the judgement asymmetry that Knobe uncovered when asked to judge the collective action of a group of individuals. To test this, they reformulated Knobe's original vignette by replacing the chairman with a group of representatives from the research and development (R&D) department of a company. When asked to consider a programme that would maximise profits and harm/help the environment, they say: "*We* don't care at all about harming [or helping] the environment. *We* just want to make as much profit as we can. Let's start the new program" (Michael & Szigetic 2018, 4; emphasis added, NM). The authors confirmed the Knobe effect in this scenario. There is, however, a simple deflationary explanation for this, namely, that participants ascribed (or withheld) intentionality distributively, that is, to each member of the group individually and not to the group per se. To test this possibility, Michael and Szigetic gave their participants further vignettes clarifying the situation as follows:

> For various reasons, each individual member of the board personally opposed the program and tried to prevent it from being implemented. Nevertheless, the

interests of the company and the shareholders prevailed and the board decided to implement the new program. (Michael & Szigetic 2018, 6)

Even with this clarification, Michael and Szigetic found a Knobe effect in their subjects' judgements. They also found it when they highlighted the role of a particular individual who appears to be especially responsible for the forming of the group's decision.

The contribution of Michael & Szigetic (2018) is interesting not only because it shows that the Knobe effect generalises in yet another way but also because their specific finding contradicts philosophers' previously held beliefs about the folk psychology of morality. Some authors have thought, for example, that "a lack of personified elements in organizations makes them more difficult targets for moral judgments" (Tyler & Mentovich 2010, 212). If Michael and Szigetic are correct, this assessment is false or, at least, too sweeping. Ordinary folk, it seems, do not generally find it problematic to blame and praise groups.[40]

Furthermore, proponents of X-Phi$_p$ might find Michael's and Szigetic's results interesting because they could have direct implications for the first-order philosophical debate about collectivism and individualism in social ontology. Collectivists claim that collectives are appropriate bearers of intentions and legitimate objects of moral judgement. Individualists deny this. Following Tyler & Mentovich (2010), one might think that collectivists bear the burden of proof for their view. After all, if most people find it counter-intuitive to ascribe attitudes to collectives, individualism should be considered the default position. Michael and Szigetic's experiments, however, provide at least some evidence that ordinary people might not find collectivism so counter-intuitive. There is, hence, reason to think that philosophers' armchair speculations about folk intuitions regarding collectivism were mistaken. This should not come as a surprise. By now, x-phi studies have amassed plenty of evidence that philosophers frequently misjudge the way ordinary people think. One debate which has shown this particularly clearly is the debate between compatibilists and incompatibilists about free will. We shall turn to it in the next section.

3.4 FREE WILL

Apart from questions about the nature of knowledge, reference, and intentional action, experimental philosophers have taken a keen interest in the problem of free will. In fact, this issue has been at the centre of the x-phi debate for a rather long time, considering x-phi's short overall lifespan. In this section, we will consider an influential study that has addressed it and discussed it against the background of more recent contributions. Before we do that, however, we should get clear on the fundamental questions and positions that play a role in the free will debate. Hence, we shall start with the question: What is free will?[41]

3.4.1 What Is Free Will?

The question whether we do or do not have free will is the central substantive question on which the free will debate focuses.

> *Central Substantive Question*
>
> Do we have free will?

There are two possible answers. We can affirm it, thus adopting the view that we do have free will, or we can negate it, thus rejecting the idea that we have free will. What, however, do we even say when we give one of these answers? That depends on our take on the central conceptual question in the free will debate.

> *Central Conceptual Question*
>
> What is free will?

This question is discussed, first and foremost, against the background of the problem of determinism. Determinism is the thesis that the entire course of the world follows natural laws that dictate, precisely, what happens at each point in time.

> *Determinism*
>
> The whole course of the world is predetermined, with necessity, by the initial conditions of the universe and the natural laws.

If determinism is true, can we have free will?[42] There are two possible answers to this conceptual question: the compatibilist position and the incompatibilist position.

> *Compatibilism*
>
> Free will is possible even if determinism is true.

> *Incompatibilism*
>
> Free will is impossible if determinism is true.

Both compatibilists and incompatibilists can give an affirmative or a negative answer to the central substantive question about free will. That is, both can adopt or reject the view that we do have free will. Incompatibilists, however, have a harder time doing this. They need to argue for a position that many philosophers find metaphysically suspect, namely, libertarianism. It is the conjunction of three views.

Libertarianism

(T1) We do possess free will.
(T2) Free will and determinism are incompatible.
(T3) Determinism is false.

Given the first two theses, the third is logically inevitable. Of course, those who think free will is impossible, given the truth of determinism, and who do believe in the existence of free will have to reject determinism. Hence, T3 is redundant.[43]

To be sure, libertarians about free will do not hold that there are no deterministic processes at all. This idea would be incompatible with our scientific world view. They claim, rather, that there are certain processes that are not completely deterministic. These processes, they think, occur in human agents who act freely. On the libertarian view, these agents can make genuine decisions that are not necessitated by the laws of nature. Instead, they are caused by the agents themselves, who libertarians take to be "unmoved prime movers," as it were. In the debate about free will, this type of causality is, hence, called *agent causality* (as opposed to the deterministic *event causality*).

The opaque metaphor of the unmoved prime mover already suggests that the concept of agent causality and, with it, the doctrine of libertarianism might be metaphysically problematic. From a scientific point of view, it certainly has a plausibility problem because libertarians, it seems, see the agent as being outside of the natural order. We may, hence, regard their view as the expression of an "obscure and panicky metaphysics" (Strawson 1974/2008, 27), to use Peter Strawson's words. It seems, however, that those who would like to defend free will have to endorse libertarianism because, at first glance, the compatibilist view is counter-intuitive. At any rate, many philosophers assume this. If we consider the conditions that are intuitively necessary for the existence of free will, this idea seems prima facie reasonable.

Necessary Conditions for the Existence of Free Will

A person who acts can only have free will if

(1) she has a *choice* between different options for acting,
(2) this choice is *genuinely hers*, and
(3) she has *control* over which decision she chooses.

Condition (1) is the *condition of alternate possibilities*. It cannot be fulfilled, it seems, in a completely determinist universe. If the course of history is determined, with necessity, at each point in time, then there are apparently no options from which the agent can ever genuinely choose.

Condition (2) is the *condition of ownership*. It, too, appears to be unfulfillable if determinism is true. In that case, events that took place billions of years ago determined what a person would do today. Plausibly, then, nothing that happens now can be attributed to an agent as the owner of the action.

Condition (3) is the *condition of control*. For all it seems, it cannot be fulfilled under determinism either. If everything that happens in the life of a person is determined with necessity, she does not appear to be in control in any meaningful way.

These three ways of reasoning suggest that the compatibilist answer to the central conceptual question about free will should not strike people as intuitively plausible. Moreover, philosophers who take part in the free will debate often report that philosophical laypersons they talk to confirm this assessment. Robert Kane, for example, remarks: "In my experience, most persons resist the idea that free will and determinism might be compatible when they first encounter it" (Kane 2005, 12). Various other philosophers have gone on the record saying similar things.[44] Compatibilists do seem, then, to enter the debate about free will with a considerable burden of proof. If they cannot provide watertight arguments for their view, they should relinquish their position. They should, that is, either convert to libertarianism or deny free will.[45]

At this point, however, it is worthwhile to make a basic observation. The reasoning for the counter-intuitiveness of compatibilism is itself tied to conceptual premises. Its proponents have tried for centuries to show that we can and should interpret the necessary conditions for the existence of free will differently.[46] A prominent contemporary adherent of compatibilism, the American philosopher Daniel Dennett, has argued that his metaphysically less demanding view of free will does, in fact, exhibit all properties that we might wish for from the perspective of everyday life.[47] Even if determinism should be true – and Dennett clearly thinks it is – we can still attribute free will to other people in a way that would justify holding them responsible for what they do. Incompatibilists would, of course, deny this. For this reason, it is not too far to seek, as we remarked in section 2.5, to appeal to the judgements of philosophical laypersons, who are neutral about the issues on the table. We should, it seems, ask them to find out which concept of free will does, in fact, play a role from the perspective of our lifeworld.[48]

In section 1.4, we recorded that the debate about free will is remarkably open to empirical and experimental arguments. This is illustrated, for example, by the fact that neuroscientific research, especially that of Libet (2002), has given the debate an enormous stimulus. Interestingly, however, the folk concept of free will, in general, and the alleged counter-intuitiveness of the compatibilist concept, in particular, had never been tested experimentally before the advent of x-phi. To be sure, participants in the debate have reported that philosophy students and laypersons seem to reject compatibilism when they first considered it. These remarks, however, are merely based on anecdotes and do not constitute scientifically credible evidence. Nahmias et al. (2005, 2006) identified this research gap and tried to ascertain whether compatibilism is, in fact, counter-intuitive.

3.4.2 Nahmias et al. (2005, 2006)

Nahmias et al. (2005, 2006) appear to hold a view of philosophy that comports with X-Phi$_P$. They set out to test the hypothesis that philosophical laypersons will reject compatibilism as counter-intuitive to make a positive contribution to the debate about free will. To this end, they first formulate a prediction.

> *Incompatibilist Prediction*
>
> People will tend to judge that agents who act in a deterministic scenario do not act freely and are not morally responsible for what they do.

To test this prediction, Nahmias et al. (2005, 2006) chose students from Florida State University as subjects. These individuals were not familiar with the philosophical debate about free will and could, hence, be regarded as neutral on the main theoretical positions. Nahmias et al. (2005, 2006) presented them with suitable scenarios and asked them whether the persons acting in them did what they did of their own free will. In formulating the scenarios, the researchers took care to avoid terms like "determinism" or "determined." Instead, they aimed to describe their meaning in everyday language.[49] Nahmias et al. (2005, 2006) used the following case for their first experiment.

> *Bank Robbery*
>
> Imagine that in the next century we discover all the laws of nature, and we build a supercomputer which can deduce from these laws of nature and from the current state of everything in the world exactly what will be happening in the world at any future time. It can look at everything about the way the world is and predict everything about how it will be with 100 percent accuracy. Suppose that such a supercomputer existed, and it looks at the state of the universe at a certain time on 25 March, 2150 AD, 20 years before Jeremy Hall is born. The computer then deduces from this information and the laws of nature that Jeremy will definitely rob Fidelity Bank at 6:00 pm on 26 January, 2195. As always, the

supercomputer's prediction is correct; Jeremy robs Fidelity Bank at 6:00 pm on 26 January, 2195. (Nahmias et al. 2005, 566; 2006, 36)

After participants had read this scenario, Nahmias et al. (2005, 2006) asked them whether the protagonist, Jeremy, acted of his own free will. Sixteen out of 21 subjects (i.e. 76 percent) said that, yes, he did. This result evidently contradicts the above incompatibilist prediction. Since Jeremy's behaviour could be predicted using the supercomputer, it may count as fully determined. According to the incompatibilist prediction, participants should have judged that what Jeremy did was not an expression of his free will. But Nahmias et al. (2005, 2006) found the opposite result.

One way of dealing with this finding is to conclude that the incompatibilist prediction is likely false. Alternatively, we may consider the possibility that the subjects' judgements are based on an error in the application of the concept of free will. On one version of such an *error theory*, subjects' emotions interfered with their judgements.[50] The hypothesis is that they developed a negative emotion in response to Jeremy's action. This possibility is not implausible since Jeremy robs a bank, which most people would presumably react to with a negative emotion. That negative emotion, the theory goes, then gave rise to the wish to hold Jeremy responsible for what he did. But this is only justifiable, it seems, if he acted freely. Thus, subjects ascribed free will to Jeremy.

This error theory allows a prediction that can be tested: If the scenario is altered such that Jeremy does not rob a bank but saves a child (positive action) or goes for a jog (neutral action), then people should show no more inclination to ascribe free will to him. As Nahmias et al. (2005, 2006) report, however, when they ran the experiments, 15 out of 22 participants (i.e. 68 percent) said that Jeremy did save the child of his own free will, and 15 out of 19 (i.e. 79 percent) responded that he went jogging of his own free will. Hence, Nahmias et al. (2005, 2006) were unable to confirm the error theory on which emotional interference explains the compatibilist judgements that they had observed in the Bank Robbery case.

On a further alternative explanation, the deterministic aspect of the scenario that Nahmias et al. (2005, 2006) tested was not sufficiently visible. For this reason, they conducted another experiment using a case that emphasised the deterministic elements a bit more. This case is about two characters, Fred and Barney, who live in a world where what people believe and value is determined entirely by their genes and environment. Fred and Barney are assumed to be two identical twins who are given up for adoption by their mother. One, Fred, is adopted by the horrible Jerksons. This family values money above all other things. Accordingly, Fred, acquires this value, too. Barney, in contrast, is adopted by a much nicer family, the Kindersons. They value honesty above all else. Therefore, Barney acquires this value as well. One day, the following happens.

Fred and Barney

> One day Fred and Barney each happen to find a wallet containing $1,000 and the identification of the owner (neither man knows the owner). Each man is sure there is nobody else around. After deliberation, Fred Jerkson, because of his beliefs and values, keeps the money. After deliberation, Barney Kinderson, because of his beliefs and values, returns the wallet to its owner. (Nahmias et al. 2005, 570; 2006, 38)

In the rest of the vignette, it is reemphasised that Fred's and Barney's genes and environment fully determine their behaviour. Fred keeps the $1,000, while Barney returns it to the rightful owners. Had Fred grown up with the Kindersons, he, too, would have returned the money, and had Barney grown up with the Jerksons, he, too, would have kept it. Nevertheless, as Nahmias et al. (2005, 2006) report, 26 out of 34 participants (i.e. 76 percent) judged that Fred and Barney acted freely. Sixty per cent regarded Fred as morally responsible for his action, and 64 percent said this about Barney.

Nahmias et al. (2005, 2006) conclude from their data that the incompatibilist prediction is likely false and that incompatibilism does not appear to be supported by the intuitions of philosophical laypersons.

3.4.3 Discussion

The results of Nahmias et al. (2005, 2006) have received much attention in the x-phi debate and the debate about free will.[51] Other researchers proposed different interpretations of their data and tested different explanations, some of which Nahmias et al. (2005, 2006) had already tentatively ruled out. In an influential study, Nichols & Knobe (2007) remark, for example, that the case descriptions that Nahmias et al. (2005, 2006) used were all *concrete*. They hypothesise that though philosophical laypersons do, in fact, have an incompatibilist concept of free will, they are inclined to commit performance errors when they encounter a concrete scenario that triggers certain emotions. To (re)test this hypothesis, they did an experiment with 41 students of the University of Utah, who were separated into two groups. In the first step of the experiment, they gave their participants descriptions of two universes.

- The first, Universe A, was stipulated to be completely *deterministic*. Here, everything that happens, including human actions, was assumed to be entirely determined by prior causes.

- The second, Universe B, was supposed to be *indeterministic*. Here, prior causes were assumed not to determine human decisions and actions completely.

Having given the students a lengthier description of these two universes, Nichols and Knobe confronted the first group with the following *concrete* scenario:

Concrete Question

In Universe A, a man named Bill has become attracted to his secretary, and he decides that the only way to be with her is to kill his wife and 3 children. He knows that it is impossible to escape from his house in the event of a fire. Before he leaves on a business trip, he sets up a device in his basement that burns down the house and kills his family.

Is Bill fully morally responsible for killing his wife and children? (Nichols & Knobe 2007, 670)

Subjects were able to pick either "Yes" or "No" as answers. Nichols & Knobe (2007) report that a majority of 72 percent of participants who received this question chose "Yes." That means their judgements were in line with compatibilism. To them, the fact that Bill's behaviour was completely determined could be reconciled with the idea that he was responsible for murdering his family and that he ipso facto acted from his own free will. In other words, Nichols' and Knobe's finding in the first group lined up with what Nahmias et al. (2005, 2006) had established previously.

In the second group, however, this was not the case. Here, Nichols and Knobe asked participants the following *abstract* question:

Abstract Question

In Universe A [i.e. the deterministic universe, NM], is it possible for a person to be fully morally responsible for their actions? (Nichols & Knobe 2007, 670)

As the authors report, a clear majority of 86 percent chose the incompatibilist option, namely, "No." There was, hence, a discrepancy between the judgements of the subjects. In the first group, they gave an answer confirming compatibilism, while in the second group they gave an answer confirming incompatibilism. Nichols and Knobe consider various explanations for this difference. Two competing explanations are as follows:

Explanation 1

The observed discrepancy in the subjects' judgements is explained by the concreteness and abstractness, respectively, of the questions asked.

Explanation 2

The observed discrepancy in the subjects' judgements is explained by the difference in the emotions that the two questions elicited.

As noted earlier, Nichols and Knobe favour the second explanation, which they call the *affective performance error model*. However, the experiments we just discussed do not allow them to conclude that this model is, indeed, preferable. The second question differs, after all, from the first question both regarding its higher degree of abstractness and its lower degree of emotional charge. That means that both Explanation 1 and Explanation 2 (and even a combination of the two) might explain why participants reported compatibilist intuitions in one case and incompatibilist intuitions in the other case. For this reason, Nichols and Knobe conducted a further experiment that would exclude abstractness as a factor. To this end, they used two concrete scenarios that would induce different emotional reactions.

Rapist ("High Affect Condition")

As he has done many times in the past, Bill stalks and rapes a stranger. Is it possible that Bill is fully morally responsible for raping the stranger? (Nichols & Knobe 2007, 675)

Tax Cheat ("Low Affect Condition")

As he has done many times in the past, Mark arranges to cheat on his taxes. Is it possible that Mark is fully morally responsible for cheating on his taxes? (Nichols & Knobe 2007, 675)

Nichols and Knobe divided their subjects into four groups.

- Two of these groups received Rapist. Subjects in the first group were told that it took place in a deterministic universe where everything Bill did was determined by prior causes outside of his control. Subjects in the second group received the information that the case occurred in an indeterministic universe where Bill's actions were not fully causally determined.
- The two remaining groups received Tax Cheat. Again, participants in the first of these groups were told that Mark acted in the deterministic universe where what he did was completely causally determined. In the second group, subjects were informed that Mark acted in an indeterministic universe.

On Explanation 1, the pattern of judgements should not differ between Rapist and Tax Cheat. After all, both cases were concrete. On Explanation 2, however, there should be a significant difference because the two cases varied in emotional charge. The following matrix shows what Nichols and Knobe found (table 3.2).

These results support Explanation 2.[52]

- In Tax Cheat, there was a discrepancy between the deterministic and indeterministic scenarios. A total of 89 percent of subjects who assumed that Mark's actions were not determined judged that he acted freely. In contrast, only 23 percent of those who assumed that Mark's actions were fully determined attributed free will to him.
- In Rapist, which was more emotionally charged than Tax Cheat, there was a markedly different pattern of judgements. Here, a majority of 95 percent and 64 percent of subjects, respectively, judged that the rapist Bill acted freely.

The explanation that Nichols & Knobe (2007) give for their data appears convincing and elegant. But it, too, has its problems.

Firstly, Explanation 1 cannot be entirely ruled out by these findings. The data merely suggest that it cannot explain the judgements of philosophical laypersons by itself.

Secondly, other research teams have meanwhile run further experiments that cast doubt on the hypothesis that Nichols & Knobe (2007) put forward. Feltz et al. (2009), for example, conducted an experiment with 52 students of Florida State University using the same descriptions of the deterministic and indeterministic universes as did Nichols & Knobe (2007). They also used the same cases. However, unlike Nichols and Knobe, Feltz et al. (2009) presented their participants with *both* cases. As they report, most participants chose either the compatibilist option (25 percent) or the incompatibilist option (67 percent) in both cases. Only 8 percent chose different options in the two scenarios. On the explanation that Nichols & Knobe (2007) proposed, one should have expected that participants would choose different options, namely, the incompatibilist one in Tax Cheat and the compatibilist in Rapist. Feltz et al. (2009) conclude from this that

> whatever the explanation, it is clear that when participants are given both the high and low affect conditions, not many people succumb to the affective performance error identified by Nichols and Knobe. (Feltz et al. 2009, 10)

Table 3.2. Rapist vs. Tax Cheat

	Indeterministic universe	Deterministic universe
Rapist	95%	64%
Tax Cheat	89%	23%

This suggests that Explanation 2 favoured by Nichols & Knobe (2007) can only explain a small part of folk judgements about cases related to free will, if any.[53]

Thirdly, Cova et al. (2012) found evidence that emotional processes probably do not cause compatibilist judgements. In a very original study, they tested the judgements of patients who have frontotemporal dementia. This is a neurodegenerative condition which reduces the patients' ability to process emotional information in the brain. Because, according to Nichols and Knobe's Explanation 2, emotional reactions are the cause of compatibilist judgements, the number of subjects choosing the compatibilist option should go down significantly in a group of patients with frontotemporal dementia. Cova et al. (2012), however, were not able to confirm this prediction. They tested the Supercomputer case by Nahmias et al. (2005, 2006) and the concrete scenario in which Bill murders his family (Nichols & Knobe 2007). In both cases, most participants reported compatibilist intuitions.

Fourthly, Nahmias & Murray (2011) propose a plausible error theory that explains incompatibilist intuitions as the result of a basic confusion.[54] They argue that most persons who form incompatibilist judgements misinterpret the idea of determinism. They say that

> most laypersons who respond that agents do not have FW [free will; NM] and MR [moral responsibility; NM] in deterministic universes are in fact expressing only "apparent incompatibilist intuitions" because they misunderstand determinism to involve bypassing. (Nahmias & Murray 2011, 193)

As we discussed in section 3.4.1, determinism is merely the claim that the entire course of the world is predetermined, with necessity, by the initial conditions of the universe and the laws of nature. It is not the thesis that the convictions, desires, and decisions of human agents do not play a causal role. Nahmias & Murray (2011) call the latter notion "bypassing." On their error theory, persons who are inclined to form incompatibilist judgements in deterministic scenarios suppose that the mental states of the respective agent are causally "bypassed" and do not affect the course of the world.[55]

This error theory also allows testable predictions, and Nahmias & Murray (2011) did, of course, test them. They ran an experiment with the aid of 249 students of Georgia State University in Atlanta. In it, subjects were asked to judge scenarios in which the agent's behaviour was determined. Nahmias and Murray controlled whether study participants interpreted the deterministic aspect as "bypassing." To this end, they asked them to consider and judge the following statements.[56]

Decisions

In Universe [A/C] a person's decisions have no effect on what they end up being caused to do.

Wants

In Universe [A/C] what a person wants has no effect on what they end up being caused to do.

Believes

In Universe [A/C] what a person believes has no effect on what they end up being caused to do.

No Control

In Universe [A/C] a person has no control over what they do.

Past Different

In Universe [A/C] everything that happens has to happen, even if what happened in the past had been different. (Nahmias & Murray 2011, 202)

As Nahmias & Murray (2011) report, subjects affirmed these statements more frequently when they encountered the abstract question from Nichols & Knobe (2007). As the authors argue, this suggests that the formulation of the question led them to misinterpret determinism as bypassing. This misinterpretation would, in turn, explain why a great majority of subjects in Nichols' & Knobe's (2007) study seemed to have incompatibilist intuitions. If Nahmias and Murray are correct, this appearance is deceptive, and the results reported by Nichols and Knobe merely show that most people think bypassing and free will are incompatible. This finding, however, does not tell us anything about the intuitive compatibility of free will and determinism.

Now, what should we conclude from the x-phi studies on free will? At this stage, it seems clear that we cannot draw any definite conclusions from the debate. I think it is undeniable, however, that x-phi studies have led to interesting conceptual innovations and exciting new hypotheses which, in all likelihood, could not have been produced through armchair reflection alone. Unlike armchair philosophers have hitherto assumed, incompatibilism may not be the most intuitive interpretation of the concept of free will. Following the contributions of Nahmias et al. (2005, 2006) and other researchers which we considered in this section, we should be open to the possibility that compatibilism could, in fact, be the more intuitive position.

3.4.4 Recent Developments

Like the other areas of x-phi we have considered in this chapter, the experimental philosophy of free will has seen a number of interesting developments in recent years. Among them, the contribution by Feltz & Millan (2015) is surely noteworthy. These authors have proposed yet another error theory, maintaining that the experimental arguments of Nahmias and his colleagues are incomplete. Feltz and Millan concede that these researchers have provided evidence that ordinary folk, who seem to be natural incompatibilists, confuse bypassing and determinism. In their view, however, this does not support the claim, also endorsed by Nahmias and colleagues, that the folk are, instead, natural compatibilists. In their study, Feltz and Millan seek to show that the latter claim is, in fact, mistaken. In other words, they seek to support an error theory for compatibilist intuitions.

Their strategy is as follows. In a first step, they assume, rather plausibly, that a person should be categorised as a natural compatibilist only under specific conditions. Firstly, she should judge that an agent has free will in cases where genuine compatibilists would do so. Secondly, she should deny free will in a case where genuine compatibilists would reject this possibility. But when would genuine compatibilists ascribe free will, and when would they deny it? Feltz and Millan argue that they would distinguish between deterministic and fatalistic scenarios. In a *deterministic scenario*, all that happens is, as we have discussed, determined by prior causes and natural laws. However, an agent's thoughts, beliefs, desires, and plans can be causally relevant. In the words of Nahmias & Murray (2011), the agent's mental states are not "bypassed," at least not necessarily. Here, a genuine compatibilist would judge that free will is possible. In contrast, in a *fatalistic scenario*, things happen no matter what. That is, the agent's thoughts, beliefs, desires, and plans play no causal role. They are, indeed, "bypassed" such that compatibilists should deny the possibility of free will.[57] In a second step, Feltz and Millan gather data in a series of experiments. As their statistical analysis shows, many of their participants who judged that free will and determinism were compatible seemed not to be sensitive to their distinction between deterministic and fatalistic scenarios. In fact, their tendency to affirm free will in a fatalistic scenario predicted their tendency to affirm free will in a deterministic scenario. Feltz and Millan conclude from this that Nahmias & Murray (2011) likely made a mistake when they concluded that the majority of their participants had compatibilist intuitions. They suggest that many of these subjects simply had "free will not matter what" intuitions (FWNMW intuitions). Since they do not recognise distinctions that genuine compatibilists would draw, they should not be regarded as natural compatibilists.

Now, a proponent of X-Phi$_p$ might be interested to draw conclusions for the first-order philosophical debate about free will. So what can we conclude from Feltz's and Millan's data? Nahmias et al. (2005, 2006), recall, have argued that compatibilism is the more intuitive view and that it should, hence, be considered the default position. It should have "squatter's rights." In view of their findings, Feltz and Millan beg to differ, saying that "nobody has squatter's rights; everybody [in the debate about free will; NM] shoulders some argumentative burden of proof" (Feltz & Millan 2015, 550).

Does this mean that experimental arguments cannot be used to shift the burden of proof to incompatibilists? It seems that we should conclude this if Feltz's and Millan's argument is sound. Andow & Cova (2016), however, have doubted this. They point towards an issue with Feltz's and Millan's interpretation of the data. The problem is that a case can fulfil Feltz's and Millan's criteria for fatalistic scenarios without involving bypassing.[58] To illustrate, Andow and Cova use the following scenario.

Car

> Mr Green wants Mr Jones, the security guard, to steal Mrs Green's car at 12:00 am on 7 October. However, Mr Green doesn't entirely trust Mr Jones to do the job, so he has taken some extraordinary measures. Mr Green has consulted neuroscientists who have implanted a device in Mr Jones's brain without Mr Jones's knowledge. This device has isolated the "decision-making" neurons in Mr Jones's brain and is programmed to send, at exactly 12:00 am, impulses that will certainly cause Mr Jones to decide to steal the car just then. However, as it happens, at exactly 12:00am, Mr Jones decides on his own to steal the car and does it. Since Mr Jones decides on his own to steal the car, the impulses from the device were ineffectual because the decision-making neurons were activated by the decision-making process of Mr Jones himself. However, if Mr Jones had not, just then, decided on his own to steal the car, the device would have activated his decision-making neurons, and Mr Jones would have decided to steal the car anyway (Andow & Cova 2016, 557).

This is a fatalistic scenario. Jones's mental states made no difference to what happened in that situation. He would have stolen the car no matter what. Accordingly, Feltz and Millan seem committed to saying that genuine compatibilists have to reject the possibility that Jones acted from his own free will. As Andow and Cova argue, however, some compatibilists, which they call *source compatibilists*, would judge that Jones acted freely. These compatibilists would distinguish between actual control and regulative control (Fischer 1986). In the scenario at hand, Jones has *actual control* in the sense that his mental states are the causal drivers behind his actions. Green, in contrast, has *regulative control*. He could step in at any point but chooses not to. Now, as Andow and Cova explain, a source compatibilist can ascribe free will to Jones based on his actual control. His mental states were the source of his actions and, accordingly, not bypassed.

Based on this reasoning, Andow and Cova arrive at a testable hypothesis, namely, that many of Feltz's and Millan's participants, who seemed to report FWNMW intuitions, viewed the agent in the fatalistic scenario as having actual control and regarded the situation, accordingly, as involving no bypassing. In that case, it would make sense, from the perspective of a source compatibilist, to judge that the agent acted freely. To test this possibility, Andow and Cova ran an experiment in which they used Feltz's and Millan's cases and replicated their results. They also asked additional questions, however, to find out whether their subjects interpreted the situation as involving bypassing. From these questions, they computed a bypassing score. Analysing their data, they found that this bypassing score was a much better predictor of participants' willingness to ascribe free will than the fact that a given scenario was, on Feltz's and Millan's definition, fatalistic. In addition, they constructed a fatalistic scenario in which they made it absolutely clear that the relevant mental states of the agent were bypassed. Here, only a very small minority of subjects affirmed free will. Accordingly, Andow and Cova conclude that Feltz and Millan mistakenly dismiss Nahmias' and colleagues' suggestion that ordinary folk are natural compatibilists. In addition, they propose that the folk are likely source compatibilists, who believe that free will requires actual control but no alternate possibilities.

Andow's and Cova's results, hence, seem to rehabilitate the idea that compatibilism is intuitive. More trouble, however, might be lurking around the corner. In a recent paper, Lim & Chen (2018) doubt that we may conclude from Nahmias' and colleagues' data that ordinary folk intuitively agree with compatibilism. They do so, however, for reasons that are different from Feltz's and Millan's. First, they note that there is a tension in the available data. Some studies suggest that the folk think we live in an indeterminist universe (Nichols & Knobe 2007), and others find that they believe in a deterministic universe. Lim & Chen (2018) believe that this has to do with the way questions are posed. Specifically, they think it has to do with whether or not human decision-making is involved. When participants are asked, in the abstract, whether it is possible to build a machine that can predict future events with 100 percent accuracy, they may agree that this is possible (though Lim's and Chen's own data do not confirm this). However, when they are asked whether it is possible to predict human actions, they may reject this because the choices of humans tend to be regarded as an exception. As Lim and Chen note, this poses a problem for the interpretation of data that are drawn from experiments in which participants are asked to imagine that it is possible to predict human actions with 100 percent certainty. It is possible, they say, that subjects simply reject this instruction and judge human actions as though they were not determined. In that case, their answers would confirm the intuitiveness of compatibilism only superficially. Now, according to Lim and Chen, we have reason to suspect that this is precisely so. They used an interesting method to support this claim. Not only did they give participants vignettes, as is standard practice in x-phi. They supplemented this technique with qualitative methods, namely, interviews, which are much less common in x-phi research.[59] Citing conversations with participants, they argue it is likely that subjects have trouble supposing that human actions are determined and are unable to form intuitions based on that idea.

Now, there is obviously a problem with the qualitative approach that Lim & Chen (2018) use. The amount of data they can process this way is limited, and the data gathering and analysis is much more subjective. That said, qualitative analysis can certainly be useful in uncovering interesting hypotheses which can, in turn, guide further research. Lim's and Chen's contribution, I believe, illustrates this. However, we should be sceptical about their hypotheses until rigorous and controlled quantitative experiments have confirmed them. Accordingly, we should conclude by noting that it is a task for further research in the x-phi of free will to determine whether Lim's and Chen's conjectures hold water.[60]

3.5 SUMMARY

In this chapter, we discussed influential x-phi studies from *epistemology*, the *philosophy of language*, the *philosophical theory of action*, and the *philosophy of mind*.

We began with the classic studies by Weinberg et al. (2001) and Swain et al. (2008) that express, as we determined, a view of x-phi that matches X-Phi$_N$. Weinberg et al. (2001) point towards the demographic variability of epistemic intuitions, while Swain et al. (2008) report on experiments which suggest that epistemic intuitions are liable to order effects. Both teams of authors draw relatively far-reaching conclusions from their data. They maintain that these findings show the central MAP to be unreliable, and they propose to reject it – at least in epistemology. Our discussion yielded the result that these conclusions are, for all we know, premature. Important results on which they rest could not be replicated. Also, a comprehensive intercultural study (Machery & Stich et al. 2015) was recently able to show that at least certain epistemic intuitions are stable across cultural barriers. Moreover, some important exponents of X-Phi$_N$ no longer reject MAP outright but merely call for a "reboot" (Machery 2017). Nevertheless, we reasoned, the debate that Weinberg et al. (2001) and Swain et al. (2008) initiated was not in vain. After all, it did put the conventional armchair method of theorising in epistemology on a more secure foundation. Moreover, we said, the results are, from the perspective of X-Phi$_C$, interesting in their own right because they give us an insight into the workings of the human mind as regards epistemic matters.

In the area of the philosophy of language, x-phi studies have had a more pervasive effect. Machery et al. (2004) investigated intuitions about the reference of proper names that are central to the debate between adherents of Russell's theory of definite descriptions and proponents of the causal-historical view. They were able to show that important thought experiments, such as Kripke's famous Gödel case, are judged differently across cultures. This finding, which has been replicated multiple times in the meanwhile, is interesting because it casts doubt on the metaphilosophical underpinnings of the methodical use of intuitions (MAP) in the analytic philosophy of language. Unlike in epistemology, where experimental findings have tended to support MAP, experimental data about linguistic intuitions have encouraged X-Phi$_N$, which is critical of MAP.

In the area of the philosophy of action, we looked at the Knobe effect, which is an interesting judgement asymmetry about intentional action. Joshua Knobe found that his subjects were significantly more likely to judge that an unintended side effect of an action was brought about intentionally if the side effect was morally bad. This result, which seems robust and has been replicated across cultures, appears to discredit the so-called simple view, namely, the idea that the side effects of an action are to be viewed as intentional if and only if the agent intended them. The Knobe effect shows that most people seem to have different ideas. From the perspective of X-Phi$_C$, this result is philosophically interesting in and of itself. Whether it is important from the perspective of X-Phi$_P$ and X-Phi$_N$ depends in large part on its explanation. If it turned out that the Knobe effect is based on a performance error in the application of the concept of intentional action, this might rehabilitate the simple view. It would also make the effect much less interesting philosophically. If, on the other hand, it were shown that the effect gives us a genuine insight into the folk concept of intentional action, as Joshua Knobe suspects, this would substantiate the case against the simple view and would presumably suggest new directions for theorising in the philosophy of action. At this stage, it is unclear, however, which explanation of the Knobe effect is preferable since none of the hypotheses discussants have hitherto proposed can account for all the data that are currently available.

Finally, we discussed a number of x-phi studies that have given the philosophical debate about free will new and interesting impulses. First, we identified two central questions about free will – one conceptual, and the other one substantive. The substantive question is the issue whether we do, in fact, possess free will. The conceptual question is the problem of spelling out what it means to have free will. The latter question is commonly discussed against the background of the problem of determinism, which is the thesis that the entire course of the world is predetermined by the initial conditions of the universe and the laws of nature. Incompatibilists negate the possibility of free will, given the truth of determinism. Compatibilists, in contrast, affirm it. The incompatibilist position has traditionally been viewed as the more intuitive one. We discussed a study by Nahmias et al. (2005, 2006) that found no evidence for this claim. These authors report, rather, that their subjects were inclined to ascribe free will to agents even if those agents' behaviours were assumed to be fully determined by prior causes which, by stipulation, were outside of the agents' control. Hence, Nahmias et al. (2005, 2006) concluded that compatibilism should be regarded as the more intuitive default position. At this point, it is uncertain whether these authors' assessment is tenable. At the very least, however, we can record that their contributions gave the debate about free will fresh impulses that would have been hard to conceive of in the absence of the experimental data they provided. It seems plausible to suggest that incompatibilism has lost its initial plausibility as the "default view," even more so if we take Nahmias' & Murray's (2011) interesting error theory for incompatibilist intuitions into account. According to them, incompatibilist intuitions are the result of a basic confusion between the idea of determinism and what they call "bypassing." To shift the burden of proof back to the middle, incompatibilists would have to show that an error theory can explain the data from Nahmias et al. (2005, 2006) and subsequent studies. Feltz & Millan (2015) have tried this. However, it is doubtful, given the criticisms of Andow & Cova (2016), that they have succeeded. In contrast, Lim & Chen (2018) were more successful in poking holes into Nahmias' and colleague's arguments. Their criticisms, at any rate, have not been answered yet. At this point, it is therefore hard to construct a coherent view that can explain the extant data in the x-phi of free will.

In summary, we can record, therefore, that experimental philosophers have not been able to provide definite results in any of the four areas of philosophy we have looked at in this chapter. But in all fields, they have been able to contribute interesting new ideas and possibilities that would have been hard to think up from the armchair. Their contributions have also given rise to new and exciting problems that can now be tackled using both experimental and traditional philosophical means. I think it is undeniable, therefore, that experimental philosophy has, in a short time, accomplished quite a considerable feat. But it has also received criticisms. In the next chapter, we will consider some of them.

NOTES

1. See appendix A for brief discussions of further areas of x-phi research, namely, ethics (A.1), metaphysics (A.2), the philosophy of science (A.3), and logic and rationality (A.4).

2. We briefly encountered the study by Haidt et al. (1993) in section 2.4.

3. In addition, John Turri has made a number of interesting contributions to experimental epistemology which lie outside the scope of issues presently discussed. See, however, section 3.1.5 for one example as well as Turri's (2016) work on knowledge and the norm of assertion.

4. As Kim & Yuan (2015) point out, the study by Nagel et al. (2013) is not suitable, however, as a replication study because Nagel et al. (2013) gave their subjects various different cases. Accordingly, it is not clear whether this induced order effects in the subjects' assessment of the Car Case. However, Kim & Yuan (2015) arrive at a similarly critical evaluation of Weinberg et al. (2001). The same is true for Seyedsayamdost (2015). Knobe (2015b) has summarised the findings from various different experimental studies in epistemology in a helpful blog post.

5. The effect that subjects say what the experimenter wants to hear is a common phenomenon that plays a great role in the psychological research literature. It goes by the name "experimenter bias" or "experimenter demand" (Rosenthal et al. 1963; 1964). We will come back to it in section 4.2.2.

6. Joachim Horvath and Clayton Littlejohn also express this view in their comments about a blog post by Knobe (2015a).

7. In section 1.7, we already pointed out that the methodology of analytic armchair philosophers may, in fact, be justified using experimental means. In epistemology, it seems, they can in fact point to the results that the experimental debate has yielded so far and interpret them as an argument for their methodological views. Mortensen & Nagel (2016) pursue such an approach.

8. In addition, Turri et al. (2017) report further interesting findings about the folk concept of belief. In some of their experiments, they found, for example, that their participants tended to ascribe voluntary belief more readily to strong-willed individuals than to weak-willed individuals. They were also more inclined to judge that a belief was held voluntarily when it was based on inference rather than perception.

9. For a comprehensive discussion in ethics, see Mukerji (2016).

10. Wittgenstein (1953/1999) puts forward a particularly influential critique of it.

11. A similar distinction that seems to be more common today is that between *extension* and *intension*.

12. Donnellan (1966) has given a further influential critique.

13. For an influential critique of the Kripkean causal-historical view of proper names, see Evans (1973).

14. Lam (2010) is an exception in that regard. Machery et al. (2010) critically discuss his contribution.

15. Ludwig (2007) and Ichikawa et al. (2012) also put forward this objection. Sytsma and Livengood (2011) advance a similar objection.

16. Saul Kripke has pointed out the difference between the speaker meaning and semantic meaning in his influential paper "Speaker's reference and semantic reference" (Kripke 1977). A congeneric distinction in the philosophy of language is the distinction between logic and pragmatics (Grice 1989). The former is interested in the context-independent meaning of statements and their implications. The latter analyses the meaning of statements in a given context. It is interested in the components of meaning that go beyond semantic content, for example, in the form of so-called implicatures.

17. Note, however, that recent findings may complicate the picture. Domaneschi et al. (2017) have found that Deutsch's concern may still be warranted, albeit in a different domain: People tend to assign the semantic meaning to proper names of persons (e.g. "Marco Salvi") and tend to go with the speaker meaning in the case of geographical proper names (e.g. "Yalmo"). Similarly, Vignolo & Domaneschi (2018) have recently argued that previous experiments, which sought to disentangle semantic and speaker meaning, may not have been successful.

18. Note, however, that there are further points of criticism about Machery et al. (2004), which we have set aside. As Devitt (2011) points out, for example, the wording of their vignettes might be biased against descriptivism. On the descriptivist view, it would be strange for someone who thinks that, say, "bachelor" refers to an unmarried man to suppose, say, that bachelors in Iceland were married. Similarly, it seems strange for Machery et al. to say: "suppose that Gödel was not the author of this theorem" (Machery et al. 2004, B6).

19. As Mallon et al. (2009) note, arguments from reference are also used, for example, in debates about eliminativism in the philosophy of mind, between realists and anti-realists in the philosophy of science, and naturalists and anti-naturalists in metaethics.

20. See appendix C.2 on formal methods for a fuller discussion of Carnap's method of explication and how it may be linked with x-phi.

21. Carnap demands that the explicatum be *similar* to the explicandum, *exact*, *fruitful*, and *simple*. These criteria are modelled after the conceptual requirements that are common in the exact sciences. For our purposes, we can leave open what they demand exactly. For a discussion, see Carnap (1950/1962, 7–8).

22. He also uses Churchland's (1981) argument for eliminativism in the philosophy of mind for further illustration.

23. Note, however, that a number of different scholars have argued for a methodological combination of Carnapian explication and experimental testing (Schupbach 2017; Shepherd & Justus 2015). If their arguments are sound, then any defence of an argument from reference will have to be based on experimental evidence. See appendix C.2 for further discussion.

24. Natural kind concepts are obviously philosophically interesting because, as Putnam (1975) has proposed, the causal-historical theory of reference that Kripke suggests for proper names may be extended to them.

25. Barnard & Ulatowski (2017) and Ulatowski (2018), for example, investigate the folk concept of *truth*. Arico & Fallis (2013) investigate the folk concept of *lying*.

26. We have already discussed Knobe's main result in section 1.3.

27. O'Shaughnessy (1973), for example, explicates the concept of an intentional$_A$ action using the concept of *trying*. Audi (1986) thinks of it in terms of acting *for reasons*.

28. As of 31 August 2018, Knobe's paper has 833 citations, according to Google Scholar. Weinberg et al. (2001) is in second place at 746 citations.

29. See, for example, Knobe (2004), Knobe & Mendlow (2004), Tannenbaum et al. (2007), and Young et al. (2006).

30. Cova & Naar (2012) tested the Knobe effect with French participants. Knobe & Burra (2006) used persons whose mother tongue was Hindi. Michelin et al. (2010)

and Pellizzoni et al. (2009) worked with Italians and Dalbauer & Hergovich (2013) with Germans.

31. Cova (2016) gives a comprehensive overview of the debate.

32. A similar explanation was proposed by Nadelhoffer (2004b). For discussions of it, see Knobe & Mendlow (2004) and Nadelhoffer (2004a). For a later reply by Fred Adams, see Adams (2006).

33. The distinction between pragmatic and logical inferences is famously discussed by Grice (1989), as noted in footnote 16 (this chapter). We will come back to it in section 4.2.2.

34. Knobe (2004) also proposed a test. Adams & Steadman (2004b) rejected it, however.

35. Figure 3.1 is a reproduction of a figure from Knobe (2008).

36. Pettit & Knobe (2009) point out that judgement asymmetries like the Knobe effect are not confined to the concept of intentional$_A$ action. They also affect, for example, the notion of desire. They do not, then, propose their hypothesis only as an explanation of the Knobe effect but as an explanation of all these judgement asymmetries.

37. Note that it is, strictly speaking, lose talk to say that one is *indifferent to something* because indifference is a relational attitude. I shall sidestep this issue here. See however Mukerji (2018), where I discuss how such lose talk can be made sense of in the case of indifference to truth.

38. McIntyre (2014) recently made a further interesting point. She stresses that the doctrine of double effect has been appealing to ethicists partly because it seemed to serve as an "evaluatively neutral basis for moral judgments." However, if Knobe is correct, then the concept of intentional action, which is at the core of the doctrine, is not evaluatively neutral after all. This, it may be argued, reduces the doctrine's appeal as a moral principle.

39. For a brief discussion of the difference between the standard x-phi methodology and experimental economics, see appendix C.3.

40. There is, by the way, reason to think that blaming and praising groups can be justified philosophically. For a brief discussion of the issues involved, see Mukerji & Luetge (2014).

41. For a helpful introduction to the topic, see Kane (2005).

42. Experimental results suggest that most people believe that determinism is false (Knobe 2014b; Nichols & Knobe 2007). This seems to hold across cultures (Sarkissian et al. 2010).

43. For this reason, libertarism is usually portrayed as the combination of the first two theses.

44. Nahmias et al. (2006) present examples from the literature, for example, assertions by Ekstrom (2002), Strawson (1986), and Pink (2004).

45. The latter position is often referred to as "hard determinism."

46. Notable historical exponents of compatibilism are, for example, Thomas Hobbes, John Locke, David Hume, and John Stuart Mill.

47. For this reason, Dennett's book *Elbow Room* (1984) has the apt subtitle *The Varieties of Free Will Worth Wanting*.

48. This also fits the argumentation that Björnsson & Pereboom (2016) put forward.

49. In section 4.2.2, we will discuss why this is important in the experimental design of an x-phi study.

50. In section 3.3.3, we already considered this type of error theory, namely, the one due to Malle & Nelson (2003). However, these authors intended it to explain the Knobe effect, not judgements about free will.

51. In this connection, contributions by Andow & Cova (2015), Bear & Knobe (2016), de Brigard et al. (2009), Feltz & Millan (2014), Knobe (2014b), Mandelbaum & Ripley (2012), Murray & Nahmias (2014), Nahmias et al. (2007), Nahmias & Murray (2011), and Nahmias & Thompson (2014) are worth mentioning. Feltz & Cova (2014) conduct a meta-analysis of the debate and Sarkissian et al. (2010) an intercultural study. Björnsson & Pereboom (2016) give a current overview of the armchair philosophical and experimental approaches to the free will debate.

52. Joshua Knobe seems to have abandoned this position. At any rate, his reply to a blogpost on Thomas Nadelhoffer's Blog *Experimental Philosophy* seems to suggest as much (http://bit.ly/1TZDUfZ, accessed 31 August 2018).

53. There is, of course, an alternative explanation for this result. Perhaps, when given both scenarios, subjects who otherwise would have fallen for the performance error described by Nichols & Knobe (2007) did not succumb to it because they realised that their two judgements were in tension with one another.

54. See, also, Murray & Nahmias (2014) and Nahmias & Thompson (2014).

55. As Andow & Cova (2016) helpfully point out, the error theories proposed by Nichols & Knobe (2007) and Nahmias & Murray (2011) are of different types. The former holds that the error lies with the participants. Despite their belief that free will and determinism are incompatible, participants judge in high-affect cases that they are compatible because the strong affective component interferes with their thinking. In contrast, the latter error theory says, in effect, that experimenters who conclude that laypeople are natural incompatibilists fail to analyse their data properly. The mistake is in large part theirs because they do not realise that their subjects conflate determinism and bypassing.

56. These questions were supplemented with a description of a Universe A and Universe C, both of which were deterministic.

57. Note that the idea Feltz & Millan (2015) call "fatalism" is not what many other philosophers refer to when they use that term. It does, however, seem to line up with what at least some philosophers have said, for example, John Stuart Mill. According to him, the fatalist believes what the determinist believes, namely, that "whatever is about to happen, will be the infallible result of the causes which produce it." However, in addition to that, the fatalist believes "that there is no use in struggling against it; that it will happen however we may strive to prevent it" (Mill 1882/1976, IV, ii, §3). In other words, it seems fair to characterise Mill as thinking that fatalism is the view that certain things will happen, as Feltz and Millan put it, "no matter what."

58. Cases of this type can be traced back to Harry Frankfurt's seminal paper "Alternate Possibilities and Moral Responsibility" (1969) and are, therefore, commonly referred to as "Frankfurt cases." We will briefly discuss his contribution in section 4.3.5.

59. For a brief discussion of qualitative methods in x-phi, see appendix C.6.

60. I could have discussed many further interesting studies about the x-phi of free will but had to exclude them for lack of space. One example is Bear's & Knobe's (2016) interesting finding that ordinary folk seem significantly more likely to judge that a given behaviour is compatible with determinism if it is *passive*, that is, if the agent simply "goes with the flow," as it were. For an overview over current research on the x-phi of free will, see the PhilPapers database at https://bit.ly/2NaoZkX (accessed 31 October 2018).

Chapter 4

Objections

In chapter 3, we discussed influential x-phi studies from different areas of philosophy, and we addressed important aspects of the debates that these contributions initiated. In this chapter, I would like to focus on some of the objections that critics of x-phi have put forward against these studies as well as against the experimental approach to philosophising as a whole.

It seems well advised to start with some principled considerations. So we will, first of all, clarify which forms criticisms of x-phi might take and how far they, respectively, reach (section 4.1). On this basis, we will then address the various kinds of objections as well as counter-arguments to them (sections 4.2 and 4.3). In the final section, we will summarise and conclude (section 4.4).

4.1 THE SCOPE OF OBJECTIONS

Which possible forms of objections to x-phi are there, and how far do these objections reach? To answer these questions, we should once more call to memory the distinction between different metaphilosophical views that might underlie experimental research in philosophy. We discussed them in chapter 1. They were $X\text{-Phi}_C$, $X\text{-Phi}_P$, and $X\text{-Phi}_N$. In our discussion, we noticed a categorical difference between $X\text{-Phi}_C$, on the one hand, and both $X\text{-Phi}_P$ and $X\text{-Phi}_N$, on the other.

- Those who adhere to $X\text{-Phi}_C$ believe that philosophical questions go beyond the classical philosophical problems (e.g. the problem of knowledge). The latter can, according to armchair philosophers, be answered using only a priori means. In addition to these questions, proponents of $X\text{-Phi}_C$ believe

philosophy should investigate how people think about the classical philosophical issues and why they think what they think. They, hence, interpret experimental philosophy as the cognitive science of philosophy, which complements armchair philosophy by investigating these additional empirical questions. To them, these issues are philosophically interesting in and of themselves.
- Adherents of positive and negative experimental philosophy – X-Phi$_P$ and X-Phi$_N$ – also want to find out how people judge philosophical questions. However, to them, this is not an end in itself. Rather, they are interested in their findings as evidence for certain philosophical or metaphilosophical conclusions.

In chapter 2, we looked at various argumentation schemes that allow us to draw philosophically relevant inferences from experimental data. They are used, however, only by those who base their experimental research on X-Phi$_P$ or X-Phi$_N$. In studies that build on X-Phi$_C$, these schemes do not play a role at all. As we will see shortly, this immunises experimental research based on X-Phi$_C$ against one class of objections that critics commonly press against x-phi.

All objections that are specifically directed at X-Phi$_P$ and X-Phi$_N$ can be interpreted as objections to one or more of the argumentation schemes that we identified in chapter 3. As we discussed in section 2.3, these schemes are specific instances of a general form of argument. It looks as follows:

The Argument from Reliability

(P1) Our intuition that p possesses the empirical property E. (Empirical premise)

(P2) If an intuition possesses the empirical property E, then it is *pro tanto* (un)reliable. (Bridging premise)

(C) Our intuition that p is *pro tanto* (un)reliable. (Philosophically relevant conclusion)

It is possible to generalise this scheme even further to include arguments that follow the reasoning we discussed in section 2.5. In that section, we concluded that experimental evidence about the philosophical intuitions of laypersons might help us to determine the adequate interpretations of philosophical questions in the context of our lifeworld. If it can be shown, for example, that the folk prefer a compatibilist notion of free will, then this constitutes a good reason for philosophers to base their discussions on this concept. The reasoning follows this general scheme:

The Argument from Relevance

(P1) Most people favour interpretation *I* of concept *C*. (Empirical premise)
(P2) If most people favour a particular interpretation of a concept, then philosophers have a good reason to base their philosophical discussions on this interpretation of the concept. (Bridging premise)
(C)   Philosophers have a good reason to base their philosophical discussions on interpretation *I* of concept *C*. (Meta-/Philosophical conclusion)

As the aforementioned considerations illustrate, both arguments share a common structure:

- Their first premise, P1, states an *empirical finding*.
- The second premise, P2, has in each case the function of bridging the logical gap between the empirical finding from P1 and a (meta-)philosophical conclusion, C. P2 connects P1 and C in the form of a conditional, where the former is the antecedent and the latter the consequent.
- The conclusion, C, is in each case a (meta-)philosophical proposition.

Therefore, we can deduce a general scheme for x-phi arguments which subsumes all instances we considered in chapter 2. It is the following:

General Scheme for X-Phi Arguments

(P1) The empirical fact E obtains
(P2) If the empirical fact E obtains, then the (meta-)philosophical conclusion P follows
(C)   P

Now, how can objectors critique arguments that follow this general scheme? To answer this question, we should note that the scheme itself is *logically valid*. It is usually said that logically valid arguments can only be challenged by establishing that their premises are false. This is, indeed, one possibility. In section 4.3.5, we will see, however, that this is not the only option. Before that, however, we will confine ourselves to critiques of the premises.

Since the General Scheme for X-Phi Arguments has two premises, it makes sense to distinguish between two forms of criticism. The first focuses on P1 and the second on P2. We will call objections against P1 *methodological objections*. There are two reasons for this. Unlike armchair philosophers, experimental philosophers never simply postulate P1 in their arguments. There is always an experiment (or a series of experiments) that supports this premise, namely, that the fact E obtains. Philosophers who seek to criticise the argument by criticising P1 have to explain why they doubt that the experimental evidence that supporters of the argument point to does not allow us to infer, with sufficient probability, that fact E actually obtains. A radical way to do this is to question the reliability of empirical evidence in general. However, this possibility seems ridiculous, given the enormous success of the scientific enterprise. Furthermore, it is not my aim to discuss general scepticism. Hence, we will ignore objections from general scepticism. Instead, we will confine ourselves to a second possibility, namely, the claim that experimental philosophers have committed errors in their application of experimental research methods.

Critics who are prepared to concede that there are empirical facts that might allow (meta-)philosophical conclusions do not utter fundamental philosophical concerns about x-phi. They merely question whether the facts from which (meta-)philosophical conclusions follow have, in fact, been established. In contrast, philosophers who raise fundamental philosophical objections do not only question that the empirical facts in question have been established. They doubt, rather, that anything of philosophical interest follows from them. Hence, the criticisms they raise are, I believe, aptly called *philosophical objections*.

Based on the distinction between methodological and philosophical objections against x-phi, we can consider the question how far these criticisms, respectively, reach. At the beginning of the chapter, I remarked that a particular class of objections does not affect $X\text{-Phi}_C$. By this, I meant the class of philosophical objections. These criticisms attack the bridging premise in x-phi arguments. In other words, they rest on doubts about the possibility of deducing from an empirical claim any conclusion that is relevant to a classical philosophical question. Those who practice x-phi based on $X\text{-Phi}_C$ do not, however, say that this is possible. Their research is open, if any, to methodological objections, which allege mistakes in the application of experimental research methods. Proponents of $X\text{-Phi}_P$ and $X\text{-Phi}_N$ do maintain, however, that there are bridging premises that can take us from an empirical fact to a (meta-)philosophical conclusion. Their contributions are, hence, open to philosophical objections as well. Let us record, then, the following:

- Methodological objections affect all forms of x-phi, while philosophical objections can only be used against $X\text{-Phi}_P$ and $X\text{-Phi}_N$.
- By the same token, every type of objection that can be a valid criticism of $X\text{-Phi}_C$ can also be a valid criticism of $X\text{-Phi}_P$ and $X\text{-Phi}_N$. The reverse does not hold, however.

Table 4.1 summarises these points.

In section 4.2, we shall consider a small number of methodological objections that may represent valid criticisms of all forms of x-phi. In

Table 4.1. Objections to X-Phi and Their Reach

	X-Phi$_C$	X-Phi$_P$	X-Phi$_N$
Open to methodological objections?	Yes	Yes	Yes
Open to philosophical objections?	No	Yes	Yes

section 4.3, we will discuss philosophical objections that target only X-Phi$_P$ and X-Phi$_N$.

4.2 METHODOLOGICAL OBJECTIONS

We can divide methodological objections into two classes. Those in the first class represent very general criticisms. Philosophers who put them forward claim that the experimental research methods are generally unsuitable for making meaningful contributions to philosophical inquiry. Some remarks of the x-phi critic Herman Cappelen might be interpreted as falling into the category of general methodological objections. He doubts that experiments can add anything to philosophy because philosophical practice is so vastly different from what subjects are asked to do in experimental studies:

> Doing philosophy is thinking about and then giving reasons for a judgment about a case and the judgment is evaluated based on the quality of the reasons given. No part of philosophy is like responding to survey questions about vignettes. (Cappelen 2014, 283)

This point is surely important and should be addressed in a more comprehensive study of x-phi. However, it would go beyond the scope of this study and, hence, we shall put it aside.[1] Instead, we will confine ourselves to a different form of critique that is not based on such a fundamental scepticism.[2] It claims, merely, that x-phi violates certain principles of good empirical research practice.

We can divide objections of that second type further by using the important distinction between questions of *external validity* and questions of *internal validity*.[3] One kind of criticism claims that the studies of experimental philosophers are not externally valid, another maintains that they lack internal validity. In what follows, we will first address the former (section 4.2.1) and then the latter (section 4.2.2).

4.2.1 External Validity

Empirical studies investigate a particular object and try to support a hypothesis about it. More often than not, such studies can only capture a few data points about its object. Nevertheless, they seek to make a rather general claim. In an x-phi study, this is the case as well. Experimental philosophers, for example, Weinberg et al. (2001) and Machery et al. (2004), are interested, among other things, in finding out which intuitions people from different cultures have when they reflect on a particular philosophically relevant case. Others look for differences between genders (e.g. Buckwalter & Stich 2014; Seyedsayamdost 2014). And yet others investigate which intuitions persons with certain neurological conditions have and how their intuitions differ from those of other people (e.g. Cova et al. 2012). In an experimental study, it is not possible, however, to examine all intuitions of all members of such a group. Researchers have to settle for a small *sample*. They can only survey a small number of persons. Then, they draw a conclusion about the entire group. Such a generalising conclusion is only justified if the sample of persons is *representative* of the group as a whole. Only in that case does the study possess *external validity*.

To discuss the aspect of external validity in depth, we would have to address the sampling process in detail. Doing this would go beyond the scope of our present study. For this reason, we will confine our attention to one very simple example that should suffice to make many important points about the problems that can arise in data collection.[4]

Let us suppose we are considering an experimental study in order to find out how people in Germany think about a particular philosophical thought experiment. Call it T. To this end, we set up a simple questionnaire that consists of just one question about T and two possible reply options. We publish this questionnaire on the website of the philosophy department of the University of Munich, where everyone can access it and answer our question. To recruit volunteers for our study, we print posters and put them up at the department building.

Now, suppose we have collected some data through the online questionnaire, and let us assume we find that 90 percent of participants chose option A over B. We conclude that almost everybody in Germany favours answer A over answer B in thought experiment T. Is this conclusion warranted, or does it violate the idea of external validity?

If you have doubts about our inference, you are correct. The sample we have drawn does not seem to allow us to draw the conclusion we have drawn. It is not *representative*. There are at least two problems here.

Firstly, we should expect that our subjects came almost exclusively from a particular *socioeconomic background*. After all, we published our questionnaire on a university website where persons with high socioeconomic status are much more likely to find it. It is very doubtful whether their judgements about T are representative of the German population as a whole.

However, the pattern of responses is perhaps not even representative of people with high socioeconomic status in Germany. After all, participation was voluntary, and that may have led, secondly, to a *self-selection problem*. That means that persons with a keen interest in philosophy were presumably more likely to take the test than individuals who do not take an interest in philosophy. It is by no means guaranteed that those who find philosophy uninteresting and who did not participate in our study would respond in the same way as our participants. Hence, there are at least two reasons to be sceptical about the external validity of our study.

How could we improve our study? There are at least two possibilities. The first is, as it were, a "quick fix." We could simply adjust our research question to ensure that we do not overgeneralise. We could ask, for example, how German students with an interest in philosophy judge T. It seems that our experiment may be sufficient to draw a conclusion regarding that question.

If, however, we seek to draw a more general conclusion, we have to adjust our data collection process. To this end, we should certainly gather the data in a more neutral place where we would encounter persons from different socioeconomic backgrounds. Joshua Knobe conducted his first x-phi studies in a public Manhattan park (Knobe 2003 & 2004). We should also make sure that we *select people at random* and *in sufficient numbers*. The first aspect is important because we do not want our selected sample to be biased in favour of a particular group, for example, people with an extroverted and curious personality.[5] The second aspect is crucial because we want to reduce the likelihood to select an unrepresentative sample by accident.

This improved data collection procedure would mitigate the first issue, that is, the problem that we are likely to draw a sample from a particular socioeconomic group. It would not, however, solve our self-selection problem. We may conduct our experiment in a neutral place. However, we are still much more likely to select people who are interested in the topic of our discussion than individuals who are not. This is because everybody can opt out. So our sample is not necessarily representative of all people, and our study may still not be externally valid. Now, how can we solve this problem? One way to do this is to get people to commit to participating in the experiment first, perhaps by providing a small financial incentive, and to reveal the exact nature of the experiment only after that. By proceeding in this way, we would ensure that people who, if it were not for the little incentive, would not take part in the study are still represented in our sample.

Having introduced the basic idea behind external validity, we can now examine which arguments can be derived from it, and we can analyse whether they generally speak in favour of x-phi or against it. At first glance, the aspect of external validity seems to weigh in favour of x-phi rather than against it.

Experimental philosophers often motivate their research by pointing out that armchair philosophers assume, without any empirical evidence, that the folk share their intuitions. Thomas Nadelhoffer and Eddy Nahmias, for example, say the following:

> Philosophers are a rarefied and self-selected group, with a highly distinctive, largely shared educational history. It is not at all obvious that the intuitions they report will offer an accurate representation of the intuitions of non-philosophers. (Nadelhoffer & Nahmias 2007, 125)

In short, the argument is the following: armchair philosophers have hitherto supposed that their intuitions are representative of a larger group, and they have, therefore, assumed that other people share them. This assumption, however, seems unjustified because most philosophers are WEIRD, that is, "*W*estern," "*E*ducated," "*I*ndustrialised," "*R*ich," "*D*emocratic" (Stich 2010). Hence, we should not assume that their intuitions are shared by people who are not WEIRD. The inference, it seems, would be a *hasty overgeneralisation*, a conclusion that is not externally valid. The aim of proponents of X-Phi$_p$ (like Nadelhoffer and Nahmias) consists, then, in enlarging the data set that philosophers use in their work. By doing this, they want to help them to draw conclusions which are externally valid. They want to find out, for example, whether there is a consensus or disagreement on a particular intuition between different groups. Regarding the aspect of external validity, their studies seem to be a step in the right direction.

However, on occasion, x-phi studies have been criticised for an apparent lack of external validity. These criticisms have come both from exponents of empirical psychology and from analytic armchair philosophers.

Let us consider a critique of the first kind, which was put forward by the empirical psychologist Robert Woolfolk. As he points out, experimental philosophers criticise armchair philosophers for not seeking out empirical evidence for their empirical claims. As Woolfolk observes, some x-phi studies do, however, fall short of this standard themselves. He says:

> But rather ironically, the experiments conducted by experimental philosophers frequently fail to meet the methodological standards that are articulated by the experts on research design in those fields they would emulate. (Woolfolk 2013, 80)

In particular, Woolfolk points out that experimental philosophers often use so-called *opportunity samples*, which are available without much hassle (see textbox 4.1). These samples are drawn, for example, in lectures and seminars because this eliminates the need for recruiting volunteers. As Woolfolk reminds us, they are not necessarily representative of society as a whole.

Also, sample sizes in x-phi studies have often been quite small. This applies especially to the early studies. Small sample sizes are problematic because the probability of drawing a sample that is not representative of the larger group is comparatively higher. In fact, small sample sizes may explain why, for example, subsequent research did not replicate the early results by Weinberg et al. (2001), as we discussed in sections 3.1.2 and 3.1.4.[6]

TEXTBOX 4.1 OPPORTUNITY SAMPLES IN X-PHI RESEARCH

A large part of x-phi research relies on opportunity samples, which contain mostly university students. This is problematic to the extent that opportunity samples make empirical generalisations to other demographic groups difficult. It should be noted, however, that experimental philosophers can be partly excused for their practice of using opportunity samples. This method for obtaining data is, after all, commonplace in many well-established experimental research areas that involve human subjects. As Henrich et al. (2010, 61) point out, "Western, and more specifically American, undergraduates . . . form the bulk of the database in the experimental branches of psychology, cognitive science, and economics, as well as allied fields."

How should experimental philosophers react to this critique? We already have considered two possibilities.

Firstly, they might *restrict the conclusions* that they have drawn from their findings. They might concede that the results they have reported are only valid for a narrow group of persons, for example, only for American and Asian students at American universities. Some of the findings would still be interesting and philosophically suggestive, even under this more restrictive interpretation. In this connection, the conclusion that American and Asian students appear to have significantly different intuitions about the reference of proper names (Machery et al. 2004 and Mallon et al. 2009) is, perhaps, a suitable example. Though this result may not allow us to draw farther-reaching inferences about the linguistic intuitions of Americans and Asians in general, the observed disagreement does call into question the philosophical underpinnings of theories that presuppose a consensus about certain thought experiments. Moreover, experimental philosophers should proportion the strength of their conclusions to the size of their samples. When samples are small, they are well advised to qualify their results as empirically informed conjectures, rather than established research findings.[7] In addition, philosophers should, as John Doris cautions them, not "lean too heavily on any one study, or one series of studies, in theory construction" (Doris 2015, 49).

Secondly, experimental philosophers should try to confirm their earlier findings by using improved methods of data gathering. If successful, their findings would stand; if not, they would have to retract their conclusions. However, even in the latter case, they would still have made a significant contribution to the philosophical enterprise.

The second form of critique comes from proponents of *analytic armchair philosophy*. It is directed at experimental philosophers who favour X-Phi$_N$. They have tried to show that certain philosophical intuitions which are central to the arguments of analytic philosophers spring from cognitive errors. In section 3.1.3, we considered the contribution by Swain et al. (2008). They argue that epistemic intuitions are liable to order effects. Already in section 3.1.4, we pointed out that the conclusions that Swain et al. (2008) draw from their data are too far-reaching. They only tested some particular intuitions about a narrow range of cases but suggest sceptical conclusions about epistemic intuitions in general. By doing that, they seem to overgeneralise.

Analytic philosophers often use a similar argument to defend themselves against the critiques that experimental philosophers have levelled at them. It is the so-called *expertise reply* or *expertise defence*.[8] This argument is, perhaps, one of the most influential arguments against x-phi. It rejects the premise that data about the reliability of folk judgements can tell us anything about the reliability of philosophers' judgements. Philosophers, after all, are experts in the appraisal of thought experiments. The fact that laypersons judge these cases in a particular way does not tell us anything about the way philosophers think about them.[9]

This, at any rate, is what the argument says. Now, how can experimental philosophers react to it? First, we should point out that they should, of course, take the charge of overgeneralisation seriously. Those who have followed the x-phi debate from the start should have noticed that experimental philosophers have sometimes tended to overstate their claims and to draw conclusions that were too general. Jennifer Nado comments on this:

> There is, then, a take-home message for experimental philosophers here: don't draw conclusions about 'intuition' as a whole on the basis of studies of e.g. moral judgment. (Nado 2016, 786)

Results about the empirical properties of particular intuitions do not warrant, then, the conclusion that *all* intuitions have these properties. Experimental philosophers would seem to be well advised, therefore, to heed Bertrand Russell's lesson, which has become a methodological cornerstone of analytic philosophy. Russell pointed out that philosophical problems are best divided into small pieces and then solved bit by bit: "Divide and conquer," he said, "is the maxim of success here as elsewhere" (Russell 1918/2004, 87). This principle can help protect oneself against hasty conclusions and overgeneralisations. Moreover, of course, it also applies to the issue at hand. The fact that the intuitions of laypersons are liable to cognitive errors does not establish, in and of itself, that the intuitive verdicts of professional philosophers are also vulnerable to the same errors. Those who assume this without providing further evidence overgeneralise. To that extent, the expertise reply is, at least prima facie, a plausible counter-argument.

However, we can call the expertise reply into question once we make a simple observation: the intuitive verdicts of professional philosophers differ from each other. Sometimes they are diametrically opposed to one another. That, in turn, means that they cannot all be reliable.[10] Results about the patterns of thinking in laypersons suggest how this phenomenon might be explained: when professional philosophers think about philosophical thought experiments, they might commit errors similar to those of laypersons. Their intuitions might, for example, be guided by the theories they favour (Balaguer 2016, Prinz 2010).[11]

Of course, this is but one explanation. However, it is a plausible one, and there is some empirical evidence that supports it. A team of researchers led by the American philosopher Eric Schwitzgebel has conducted interesting studies which indicate that professional philosophers may, in fact, be even more prone to committing cognitive errors than the folk.[12] If true, this would seem to weaken the expertise reply considerably.

To sum up, then, let us record that the aspect of external validity is a major factor in the debate about x-phi. The quality of experimental studies stands or falls with the quality of the data gathering techniques. Also, experimental philosophers should take care to check which conclusions plausibly follow from their data sample and which conclusions may be overgeneralisations. That holds particularly for those experimental philosophers who have tried to show that certain philosophical intuitions are vulnerable to cognitive errors. The fact that laypersons commit certain errors does not, in and of itself, allow us to conclude that professional philosophers commit these errors as well. However, there is some evidence which suggests that this might, in fact, be so. To establish this more or less reliably, however, further research is surely needed.

4.2.2 Internal Validity

As we have seen in the previous section, x-phi studies should be externally valid, and experimental philosophers should attempt to use representative samples. In addition, their studies should be *internally valid*. That means that experimental philosophers have to make sure that their results are not subject to *confounding factors*. Again, I have to emphasise that we cannot, of course, discuss this issue in much depth. Rather, we will merely consider some aspects that will allow us to understand the basic idea behind internal validity. To this end, let us revisit the example that we focused on in the previous section.

We want to find out how people in Germany judge our thought experiment T. To this end, we have selected a sufficiently large sample of participants at random. Hence, we can justifiably presume that our group of participants is representative of the population at large. We present our subjects with T and find that 90 percent favour option A and that 10 percent favour option B. Are we warranted, then, in concluding that most people in Germany favour A?

Not necessarily. As Robert Woolfolk points out, "Once participants are recruited, how they are handled is crucial to our ability to draw sound inferences from our data analyses" (Woolfolk 2013, 83). We should ask a number of critical questions. In the following, we will discuss three of the most important ones.

Question 1

> Is it possible that our judgement about our thought experiment has affected our participants' judgements?

This question focuses on the so-called *experimenter bias* (Rosenthal 1976). What is it exactly?

We know from research in social psychology that the judgements and attitudes of the person who conducts an experiment can affect its outcome. Rosenthal & Fode (1963) illustrated this in a classic experiment. They asked their participants to carry out an experiment. In this experiment, subjects had to have rats run through a labyrinth and record the time. The rats were randomly divided up into two groups. One group was labelled "bright" and the other "dull." Those experimenters who conducted their trials with supposedly bright rats reported significantly better results than those experimenters who were handling what they thought were dull rats. Their expectations about the outcome of their experiment had obviously biased their results.

Rosenthal and Fode drew a methodological conclusion from their finding, namely, that the persons who would conduct experiments should not know the hypotheses that the experiments were designed to test. In medical research, this has been an established practice for a long time. The randomised double-blind, placebo-controlled trial is an essential part of the methodological inventory. In the course of such an experiment, neither the experimenters nor the participants are allowed to know whether a participant is getting a potentially effective substance or a placebo. A similar procedure has been adopted in the review process of research papers. When a paper is submitted to a journal, the editor passes it on to a referee who is asked to assess whether it is fit for publication. Importantly, the referee cannot know the identity of the author. Moreover, the author cannot know the identity of the referee. The process is double-blind. This is to ensure that the expectations of the referee do not affect the outcome of her review and that the author is not able to influence the referee in any way.[13]

Question 2

Is it possible that our participants have misinterpreted the thought experiment?

This question seems legitimate for at least two reasons. The first lies in the fact that philosophers use *philosophical jargon* that laypersons cannot be expected to understand. Importantly, even terms that are part of the folk vocabulary can have a special meaning when philosophers use them. Therefore, it is not necessarily reasonable to assume that participants did, in fact, report their intuitions about the thought experiment in question.[14]

There is a second reason why this might be so. When we consider a philosophical thought experiment, we should pay close attention to the details. We should be very precise because every detail might count. Importantly, we should not read more into the description of a case than its description explicitly states. Philosophical laypersons cannot necessarily be expected to understand this. They might be inclined to draw pragmatic conclusions that are not logically sound like they would in everyday life. In sections 3.2.3 and 3.3.3, we have already discussed this.

Question 3

Is it possible that our participants have fallen prey to a cognitive error when examining our thought experiment?

If we answer this third question in the affirmative, then it is plausible that the intuitive judgements our subjects have reported are not a genuine expression of their judgement but, instead, the product of a cognitive error in the application of their judgement.[15] To illustrate, we have already considered, in section 3.4.3, one possible source of such a cognitive error that may play a part in the philosophical debate about free will, namely, emotions. We discussed a study by Nahmias et al. (2005, 2006) which suggests that most people have compatibilist intuitions. Nichols & Knobe (2007) objected to this idea that the scenarios Nahmias et al. (2005, 2006) had used in their experiments may have induced emotional reactions which may, in turn, have distorted participants' judgements. Nahmias & Murray (2011) then proposed another error theory, which focused on another factor, namely, conceptual confusions.

Before we have given a satisfactory answer to at least those three critical questions, we cannot justifiably presume that our experiment possesses internal validity. Though it may give us a hint that most people in Germany prefer answer A to answer B in thought experiment T, this conclusion can still be subject to reasonable doubt.

As it turns out, then, it is far from easy to generate experimental data that are really reliable. At this point, we may ask how thorough experimental philosophers have been when it comes to ensuring the internal validity of their experiments. Of course, we cannot give an all-encompassing answer to this question. We have to confine ourselves to some important aspects that have to do with the three critical questions that we have discussed earlier.

How thorough have experimental philosophers been in answering question 1? Have they, by and large, ensured that their expectations and hypotheses would not influence their subjects' replies? In this connection, we should observe that experimental philosophers have, in fact, thought about this question. Justin Sytsma and Jonathan Livengood, for example, address it in their book *The Theory and Practice of Experimental Philosophy* (2016, 177–78). In it, they discuss what experimenters can do to avoid experimenter bias. However, they do not give their readers the advice to make their experiments double-blind. As Robert Woolfolk points out, this is a deficit that is characteristic of experimental research in philosophy more broadly:

> I have yet to read an experimental philosophy study explicitly stating that administrators or scorers of questionnaires were blind to the participants' assignment to conditions or to the experimental hypotheses.[16] (Woolfolk 2013, 83)

One could argue, however, that this objection carries little weight when it is brought up against experimental philosophy. In psychological experiments, one might argue, the issue of experimenter bias plays an important role because the experimenter often directly interacts with study participants. Philosophical experiments, however, are mostly conducted using questionnaires. There is little interaction between the experimenter and the subject of her study. In computer-based and online studies, this interaction is practically zero.

At first glance, this counter-argument appears to be reasonable. Upon further consideration, however, it only addresses one possible mechanism through which experimenter bias might work. There are others.

Strickland & Suben (2012) showed, for example, that the research hypothesis can affect the formulation of the questionnaires which, in turn, might affect the experimental results. They recruited 19 students of Yale

University who were asked to design an experiment. The experiment focused on a question that had been posed by Knobe & Prinz (2008): Under which circumstances do philosophical laypersons find it appropriate to ascribe mental attributes to collectives of persons? Knobe and Prinz expected that there would likely be an asymmetry. Philosophical laypersons, they thought, would be comparatively more inclined to accept the ascription of intentional states (e.g. convictions and intentions) to collectives and comparatively less inclined to accept the ascription of phenomenal states (e.g. suffering or love). Knobe and Prinz were successful in establishing this through their experiments. Strickland and Suben had their students re-examine this hypothesis by using the research design from Knobe & Prinz (2008). To this end, they had to formulate eight sentences. These sentences had to include the noun "Acme Corporation" which referred to a company. Also, it should include one of eight verbs that described a mental state. The first four verbs ("believe," "intend," "want," "know") described intentional states, the rest ("experience," "suffer," "love," "feel") phenomenal states. The crucial point was that Strickland & Suben (2012) divided the 19 students up into two groups that would receive different information about the research hypothesis. They told the nine students in the first group that the hypothesis was as follows:

Hypothesis 1 ("feeling condition")

Participants will find the feeling mental state ascription more acceptable than the non-feeling mental state ascriptions.

This hypothesis was contrary to Knobe's & Prinz's (2008) hypothesis. The ten students in the second group ("non-feeling condition") were told that the research hypothesis was the following, which was, in fact, proposed by Knobe and Prinz.

Hypothesis 2 ("non-feeling condition")

Participants will find the non-feeling mental state ascription more acceptable than the feeling mental state ascriptions.

Strickland & Suben (2012) then used the formulations of all 19 students and presented them to subjects of an online experiment. The latter were asked to rate on a scale from 1 to 7 how natural the sentences sounded (1 = very unnatural, 7 = very natural). The results were stunning. Experiments that were conducted using the sentences devised in the non-feeling condition (Hypothesis 2) were successful in replicating Knobe's and Prinz's results. In each of the ten cases, participants agreed comparatively more, on average, with sentences containing intentional verbs. In the other group ("feeling condition"), the results were inconclusive. Here, Knobe's and Prinz's result was found only in five out of nine cases.

Strickland & Suben (2012) were, hence, able to show that experimenter bias can be a serious problem for experimental philosophy, too. Just like Robert Woolfolk, they call for appropriate measures to address it. The use of online questionnaires, which are already widely adopted, surely goes a long way because this method takes away the necessity to blind experimenters to the hypotheses being tested. However, as Strickland's and Suben's results show, biases may still be introduced at an even earlier stage, namely, in the wording of the questions. In the past, at least some authors have, in fact, lamented that x-phi researchers use biased questionnaires, for example, Devitt (2011).[17] As an anonymous reviewer for Rowman & Littlefield has pointed out, however, it is hard to see how this problem can be fixed. After all, researchers, who devise their questionnaires, cannot be blinded to their own hypotheses. This is correct. Strickland and Suben, however, do show us a way out: Those who formulate the hypotheses need not be those who formulate the questionnaires, and the latter can be blinded. It is not entirely clear, though, whether this is a practicable approach. An easier solution, perhaps, would be to encourage "adversarial cooperation," that is, joint projects of researchers who disagree about the hypotheses to be tested.[18]

How thorough are experimental philosophers when it comes to question 2? How meticulous are they in ascertaining that their experimental subjects do in fact understand the questions they are asked? Giving a general answer is hard. We should point out, however, that experimental philosophers are aware of this problem. In connection with the debate about the freedom of the will, for example, Nahmias et al. (2006) point out that

> the descriptions of determinism cannot require untrained participants to understand the more technical aspects (e.g., modal operators) of the philosophical definitions of determinism. Nor can they describe determinism in ways that may mask any effects of determinism itself. (Nahmias et al. 2006, 40)

Nichols & Knobe (2007) go on record making similar statements:

> Of course, any attempt to translate complex philosophical issues into simpler terms will raise difficult questions. It is certainly possible that the specific description of determinism used in our study biased people's intuitions in one direction or another. Perhaps the overall rate of incompatibilist responses would have been somewhat higher or lower if we had used a subtly different formulation. (Nichols & Knobe 2007, 668)

Pragmatic factors also play a great role in x-phi debates. Weinberg et al. (2001) already discuss them. As we discussed in section 3.1.2, they were interested whether the epistemic intuitions of different demographic groups would differ significantly. To investigate this, they asked participants to judge a number of epistemological thought experiments. In particular, subjects were requested to assess whether a person really knows a particular proposition or merely believes it. The options participants could select were "Really Knows" and "Only Believes." Weinberg et al. (2001) comment on this as follows:

> It is certainly possible that some of our subjects were interpreting the "Really Know" option as a question about subjective certainty.

However, they go on to justify their conviction that this did not substantially affect their results.

> But there is reason to think that this did not have a major impact on our findings. For all of our subject groups (W, EA, and SC in the ethnic studies and high and low SES in the SES study) we included a question designed to uncover any systematic differences in our subjects' inclination to treat mere subjective certainty as knowledge. (Weinberg et al. 2001, 450)

At this point, we may leave aside whether this answer by Weinberg et al. (2001) is, in fact, satisfactory. It suffices to record that they are aware of, take seriously, and discuss the problem of pragmatic factors in x-phi studies.

The same holds for Machery et al. (2004). They studied the semantic intuitions of Asian and American participants and found that they were significantly different in certain cases. However, they qualify their results by saying that

> our experiment does not rule out various pragmatic explanations of the findings. Although we found the effect on multiple different versions of the Gödel case, the test question was very similar in all the cases. Perhaps the test question we used triggered different interpretations of the question in the two different groups. (Machery et al. 2004, B8)

As we pointed out already in section 3.2.3, Deutsch (2009) would later pick up on this point. He hypothesised that of the supposedly different intuitions are due to different interpretations of the questions that subjects were asked. In collaboration with Deutsch, Machery, & Sytsma et al. (2015) tested this hypothesis and rejected it as improbable.[19]

We can record, then, that the problem associated with question 2 seems, largely, to have been addressed in the x-phi debate. Experimental philosophers do try to ensure that study participants actually understand the thought experiments that they are asked to consider. In particular, they do seem to be aware of potential pragmatic inferences that subjects might draw. These are usually controlled for in x-phi studies. That does not mean, of course, that all x-phi studies sufficiently control for such factors. However, there does seem to be an overall awareness in the debate that ensures a satisfactory level of scrutiny.

Question 3 focuses on cognitive errors. How careful are experimental philosophers to avoid the possibility that their results are biased by cognitive errors? Do they really make sure that the intuitions their subjects report are the expression of their judgement and not an error in the application of their mental faculties?

Once more, it seems hard to give a general answer to this question. We should observe, however, that there is, again, evidence that experimental philosophers are, by and large, aware of the problem. At any rate, the fact that many studies try to explain widespread intuitions away suggests this. As we discussed in section 2.3, Joshua Greene (2008) and Peter Singer (2005) have argued in the normative-ethical debate, for example, that typical deontological intuitions are based on affective processes and are, to that extent, less reliable than consequentialist intuitions. In the debate about free will that we discussed in section 3.4, Nahmias & Murray (2011) argued for an error theory which indicates that seemingly incompatibilist folk intuitions, namely, that free will and determinism are irreconcilable, are based on confusions. These are just two examples. There are, hence, exponents of the x-phi debate that certainly do question whether study participants report their genuine intuitions. The fact that some researchers do this does not ensure, of course, that each study controls for the possibility of cognitive errors to a sufficient degree. However, it does increase the probability that the research community will, sooner or later, find out whether a purported intuition is genuine or merely the product of a cognitive error.

4.2.3 Conclusions

In the two previous sections, we discussed methodological objections against x-phi. In our discussion, we distinguished between two important aspects that allow us to assess the quality of experimental studies, namely, external and internal validity. In summary, we can draw the following conclusions from our investigation.

The aspect of external validity is, as we pointed out, Janus-faced. On the one hand, it can be called upon to criticise AC-Phi from the perspective of x-phi. Armchair philosophers, it could be argued, are not careful enough to ensure that the intuitions they use as premises in their arguments are representative. In contrast, the argument may proceed, those who practice x-phi do take care to ensure this. On the other hand, x-phi itself may, as we have seen, be criticised for its lack of external validity when its practitioners draw conclusions that are hasty and too far-reaching.

Concerning the internal validity of experimental studies, we focused on three points. We found, for instance, that such studies have to avoid experimenter bias. We also found that they have to ensure participants understand the questions they are asked. Furthermore, they have to ascertain that the answers subjects give are not biased by cognitive errors. Experimental philosophers who do not pay sufficient attention to these three points can legitimately be criticised. As we concluded, there might be a problem regarding the first point. It is unclear, however, how best to address experimenter bias in the wording of questionnaires. Concerning the second and third points, x-phi seems to be in quite good shape overall. It is unlikely, we concluded, that the findings proponents of x-phi have hitherto gathered can be explained away by assuming that study participants have fallen prey to pragmatic miscomprehensions of philosophical questions and cognitive errors. That said, we should, of course, note that experimental philosophers have, over time, become much more sophisticated methodologically (Bickle 2018), and they have increasingly opened up to further research methods (see appendix C, for a rough overview). Hence, many of the problems mentioned earlier have become less and less of an issue in recent years.

4.3 PHILOSOPHICAL OBJECTIONS

As we have already discussed, philosophical objections differ from methodological objections. If someone raises a philosophical objection to x-phi, she does not doubt the empirical premises that experimental philosophers use in their arguments. Rather, she doubts that these premises can play a role in the debate about a philosophical issue. In the following, we will consider arguments whose champions seek to establish that experimental findings are simply out of place in discussions about philosophical problems.

4.3.1 Philosophy Is Not a Popularity Contest

A first objection consists in a simple observation: In philosophy, we attempt to find out whether there are sufficiently good reasons to believe a given claim. This picture of philosophy seems to be in stark contrast with what experimental philosophers do in their investigations. They use questionnaires because they are interested to find out what laypersons think about the issues that philosophers discuss. This enterprise, it appears, can only have a philosophical relevance if we assume that philosophical debates are no longer adjudicated by looking at the arguments but, rather, by a popularity contest.

This seems to be a preposterous notion. Therefore, Max Deutsch, who is an avowed critic of x-phi, says:

> Majority opinion does not determine the truth, or constitute the primary source of evidence in philosophy, and despite appeals to 'what we would say' about cases, majority opinion has never been thought to play these roles in philosophical argument. (Deutsch 2009, 465)

Now, what are we to make of this objection? Not much, I believe. There are at least two reasons for this. Firstly, experimental philosophers have clarified on multiple occasions that they do not share the picture of philosophy that is attributed to them by objectors who press the aforementioned point. Nahmias et al. (2006), for example, write that

> it is important to keep in mind that we are not suggesting that any philosophical theory would be demonstrably confirmed (or disconfirmed) just because it aligns with (or conflicts with) folk intuitions and practices. After all, such intuitions and practices may be mistaken or contradictory and hence in need of elimination or revision. (Nahmias et al. 2006, 34)

Other experimental philosophers have made similar statements. Knobe & Nichols (2008), for example, say the following regarding the same issue:

> Philosophical inquiry has never been a popularity contest, and experimental philosophy is not about to turn it into one. (Knobe & Nichols 2008, 6)

Opponents of x-phi who, despite such statements, affirm that experimental philosophers want to replace philosophical argumentation by a popularity contest have to back up their claims with evidence. They have to point to particular utterances in the x-phi literature which indicate that experimental philosophers misunderstand what they are doing. If they cannot provide such evidence, they clearly violate the principle of charity and merely resort to a straw man argument.

Secondly, we have already discussed in sections 2.4 and 2.5 which types of arguments experimental philosophers actually put forward. In this connection, we discussed framing effects, order effects, irrelevant factors, and the issue of determining the most relevant questions in philosophy. Experimentally informed arguments that tap into these aspects resort to data that stem from questionnaires. However, these data are used because there is the hope that they might allow us to draw philosophically relevant conclusions. These concern either the credibility of philosophical intuitions or the interpretations of philosophical questions. In other words, experimental philosophers never simply appeal to majority opinion.

To this, one might object that there is at least one argumentation scheme that seems to suggest the opposite. It is, of course, the following.

The Argument from Agreement

(P1) There is agreement on the intuition that p.
(P2) If there is agreement on the intuition that p, then this intuition is *pro tanto* reliable.
(C) The intuition that p is *pro tanto* reliable.

Does the Argument from Agreement support the strong claim that experimental philosophers take philosophy to be a popularity contest? Not quite. For those who resort to the Argument from Agreement do not argue that this particular argument can settle a philosophical issue *conclusively*. It merely states that agreement about a particular intuition is one factor that counts in favour of accepting p as a premise, which can then be used in an argument. That is the meaning of the term "pro tanto" that qualifies both the premise P2 and the argument's conclusion C. In other words, experimental philosophers would not exclude the possibility that under some circumstances a widely agreed-upon intuition will nevertheless be rejected as unreliable. It might turn out, for example, that this intuition contains an internal contradiction or that it stems from an unreliable cognitive process. Both possibilities would, if they proved to be actual, discredit the intuition in question, widespread agreement about it notwithstanding.

We can conclude, then, that the first objection is merely a straw man argument. It supposes that experimental philosophers make a blatantly absurd assumption even though they clearly do not.

4.3.2 Philosophical Problems Are Not Empirical Problems

According to the first objection, experimental philosophers regard the debate about a philosophical problem as a popularity contest. As we pointed out in the previous section, however, this is false. In fact, none of them hold the view that a simple empirical consensus on a philosophical question can settle it conclusively. Critics of x-phi may react to this counter-argument by weakening the objection. Perhaps, they might concede, experimental philosophers do not use crude empirical agreement on the answer to a philosophical question as a criterion of adequacy. However, they may insist, these philosophers do use an empirical test. This indicates that they misunderstand the nature of philosophical problems, which are, after all, not empirical problems.

As the journalist Christopher Shea reports, this objection was raised, for example, by the acclaimed American philosopher Judith Jarvis Thomson:

> A philosophical problem is not an empirical problem," writes Judith Jarvis Thomson, the noted MIT moral philosopher, in an e-mail message to The Chronicle, "so I don't see how their empirical investigations can be thought

to have any bearing on any philosophical problem – much less help anyone to solve a philosophical problem. (Shea 2008)

I have already mentioned this kind of criticism of x-phi in the introduction. As I said there, it involves a basic misstep in thinking. It may be true that philosophical questions differ in their nature from empirical questions.[20] However, this does not imply that the latter are always irrelevant for the former. For example, whether a person has acted with premeditation is an empirical issue about the psychology of that person. However, it may be relevant for the answer to a legal question. The question which properties a given building material has is a physics question. However, it may be economically relevant. In like manner, an empirical issue may be of interest to a philosophical problem.[21]

By now, we possess the conceptual and theoretical resources to understand better both the objection and my reply to it. To employ these resources, we should, first of all, relate the argument to the general argumentation scheme that we introduced in section 4.1. In that connection, the following observation is helpful: Philosophers who put forward the objection at issue would presumably concede that philosophical and empirical questions *exist*. Accordingly, it should be possible to answer at least some of them. In other words, there should exist theses of the same kind as E and theses of the same kind as P. The objection does not seem, then, to be directed at P1, which merely states E. Rather, it appears to target the bridging premise P2, which establishes a connection between E and P. However, two interpretations of the critique can be distinguished.

On the first interpretation, it is merely a *challenge*. The objection then says that experimental philosophers should make it clear how the logical gap between an empirical question and a philosophical question can plausibly be bridged. In reply, experimental philosophers can simply reprise what we said in sections 2.4 and 2.5. In these parts of our discussion, we considered four argumentation schemes that explain why and how empirical findings can be relevant in answering classical philosophical questions.

There is, however, a second interpretation of the objection. It is bolder. On this interpretation, the objection says that there is simply *no bridging premise* that can establish a plausible connection between an empirical finding and the answer to a classical philosophical question. For this version of the objection to hold water, all instances of all argumentation schemes from sections 2.4 and 2.5 would have to be unsound. This much stricter reading could, as far as I can see, only be supported in two ways, namely, firstly, by offering principled considerations[22] and, secondly, by examining all argumentation schemes that we have discussed up to this point.

Principled considerations could be offered, for example, based on a Wittgensteinian perspective. On this outlook, philosophy's role consists in "dissolving" philosophical problems by addressing linguistic confusions through a priori analysis. This AC-Phi view may have been influential historically. However, as far as I can see, it does not – *pace* Peter Hacker – play a major role in the contemporary debate. In this investigation, we cannot assess, of course, how plausible it is in its own right. Hence, for our purposes, it shall suffice to point out that this particular way of rendering the objection appears to put the objector into a weak dialectic position, at least in the context of contemporary discourse. The view of philosophy on which it is based would, it seems, not convince many philosophers today. This does not show, of course, that there are no other principled objections that could be made plausible. I believe, however, that the burden of proof resists on the objector here. That is, anyone who alleges that it can be shown, on principled grounds, that there is no way to bridge the gap between an empirical premise and a philosophical conclusion has to be prepared to support this idea with an argument.

The second strategy, which is based on a consideration of all the individual argumentation schemes, is confronted with two problems. Those who choose it have to show that the bridging premises of all argumentation schemes are false or at least implausible. That is a tall order. For, as we have seen, these premises do seem rather plausible. However, even if that undertaking were successful, a further problem would remain. Even if it were shown that none of the bridging premises we have considered are plausible, this would not show, conclusively, that there cannot be a plausible argumentative connection between an empirical finding and a philosophical claim. For this reason, even staunch critics of x-phi make it clear that they do not want to argue for that latter view. Timothy Williamson, for example, who in his influential book *The Philosophy of Philosophy* (2007) offers a defence of the view that philosophy is an armchair discipline, says the following:

> This book raises no objection to the idea that the results of scientific experiments are sometimes directly relevant to philosophical questions. (Williamson 2007, 6)

Let us record, then, that the objection we have considered in this section seems to be untenable. Even if philosophical problems are not empirical problems, this does not show that empirical and, in particular, experimental findings are never philosophically relevant.

4.3.3 What Is an Intuition Anyway?

According to a further objection, experimental philosophy is to be criticised because, upon reflection, it is unclear what its subject matter even is. Experimental philosophers aim to investigate philosophical intuitions of laypersons to draw philosophically relevant conclusions from their findings. To do this, they have to make clear what they mean when they say "intuition." Doing this is, however, harder than it first appears. In section 2.2, I remarked that the notion of an intuition is quite contested in philosophical discourse. As Nado points out, there is no single property of mental states that all philosophers would accept as characteristic of an intuition (Nado 2016). Williamson believes, therefore, that philosophers should give up the idea entirely. "Philosophers," he says, "might be better off not using the word 'intuition' and its cognates" (Williamson 2007, 220).

At this point, we shall not discuss whether and to which extent the notion of intuition can be clarified. Let us concede that the diagnosis may be correct and that it is, perhaps, entirely unclear what an intuition is. Would it be possible to make a sound case against x-phi based on that supposition? Before we can address this point, it is necessary to remind ourselves of the distinction between the three types of x-phi that we have drawn in chapter 1. For the answer seems to depend on whether we are talking about X-Phi$_C$, X-Phi$_P$, or X-Phi$_N$.

Let us consider X-Phi$_C$ first. Its proponents want to find out which intuitions laypersons have when they consider philosophical thought experiments. They also want to investigate the cognitive mechanisms that are causally connected to these intuitions. To this end, they use questionnaires that they then analyse using statistical methods. Is this enterprise threatened by the fact that the notion of an intuition is unclear?

That does not appear to be the case because there seems to be an easy way for proponents of X-Phi$_C$ to dodge the objection.[23] To this end, all they need to do is to re-describe their research project while avoiding the concept of intuition. This seems possible. All they need to say is that they are interested in how people judge philosophical thought experiments and why. After that, they can carry on with their research exactly as they did before.

Proponents of X-Phi$_P$ want to make a positive contribution to a philosophical debate. They try to accomplish this by investigating the credibility of intuitions about thought experiments that philosophers commonly use as premises in their arguments. As we discussed in section 2.4, there are various argumentation schemes they can use to bridge the gap between the empirical and philosophical sphere. They can investigate whether there is agreement or disagreement on a given intuition, whether the order in which thought experiments are presented affects the intuitions subjects report, and whether there is evidence of cognitive errors when people report their intuitions. It seems that proponents of X-Phi$_P$ can do all these things even if we suppose that "intuition talk" is problematic. Just like champions of X-Phi$_C$, they can replace this problematic concept by the more general notion of a *judgement*. In other words, they can say that they are interested in finding out how reliable a particular judgement about a given thought experiment is. X-Phi$_P$, then, also seems to be unscathed by the objection under consideration.

The same cannot be said, however, in regard to X-Phi$_N$. As we just saw, proponents of X-Phi$_C$ and X-Phi$_P$ can reformulate their research projects without using the problematic idea of an intuition. Why should this not be possible for adherents of X-Phi$_N$? To understand this, we should observe that those experimental philosophers who subscribe to X-Phi$_N$ have a more general objective than those who adhere to X-Phi$_C$ and X-Phi$_P$. The latter two are primarily interested in investigating how philosophical laypersons judge particular thought experiments – either for its own sake (X-Phi$_C$) or because they seek data that are relevant to a classical philosophical question (X-Phi$_P$). Though experimental philosophers who practice X-Phi$_N$ also investigate how philosophical laypersons judge individual thought experiments, they try to support a general claim, namely, that the MAP is flawed. According to this approach, we test philosophical claims by comparing their implications about thought experiments with our intuitions about these cases. Those who dismiss this idea have to be able to explain *what* exactly they are criticising. They have to be able to say what it means to reject the methodical use of intuitions about thought experiments. The latter idea only has meaning if proponents of X-Phi$_N$ can explain what they mean by "intuition."[24]

4.3.4 Experimental Philosophy Leads to Scepticism

Perhaps philosophers who advocate X-Phi$_N$ can tackle the challenge we have discussed in the previous section by pointing towards a paradigmatic case of an intuition. Perhaps they could use the judgement most of us make in the Gettier case as an example and say that an intuition is any verdict about a case that is similar to that judgement in relevant respects.[25] This strategy may seem promising, but it is also problematic. For it appears to lead to an unattractive and encompassing kind of scepticism. Let us find out why.[26]

First, let us recapitulate the thought experiment we discussed earlier to illustrate Gettier's argumentative strategy. It served to cast doubt on the standard analysis of knowledge as justified true belief. If that analysis were correct, it would be impossible to construct a case in which a person has a justified and true belief that *p* but does not know that *p*. Our thought experiment (Thought Experiment 2, section 1.2) showed, however, that such situations can occur. We assumed a *hypothetical scenario* in which Anna consults her watch, which displays 2:51 pm. Hence, Anna believes that it is 2:51 pm. It is, in fact, 2:51 pm. However, the watch has stopped working yesterday at exactly the same time. Anna is not aware of this. Most people who are confronted with this scenario would judge, it appears, that Anna has a true and justified belief that it is 2:51 pm without knowing that it is 2:51 pm.

Accordingly, we can conclude that knowledge cannot be analysed as justified true belief. After all, if knowledge were justified true belief, cases in which a person has a justified true belief but no knowledge could not occur. As our hypothetical example shows, however, such cases seem to be possible, which contradicts the standard analysis.

As Williamson (2007) shows, it is possible to show this, however, without using a hypothetical case. Instead of a hypothetical scenario, he explains, we can employ an *actual scenario*.

> For example, I have begun a lecture by apologizing for not giving a power-point presentation; I explained that the only time I gave a power-point presentation it was a complete disaster. Since my listeners had no reason to distrust me on a claim so much to my discredit, they acquired through my testimony the justified belief that the only time I gave a power-point presentation it was a complete disaster. They competently deduced that I had never given a successful power-point presentation. Thus they acquired the justified belief that I had never given a successful power-point presentation. That belief was true, but the reason was that I had never given a power-point presentation at all (and still do not intend to). My assertion that the only time I had given a power-point presentation it was a complete disaster was a bare-faced lie. Thus they were basing their justified true belief that I had never given a successful power-point presentation on their justified false belief that the only time I had given a power-point presentation it was a complete disaster. Consequently, they did not know that I had never given a successful power-point presentation. (Williamson 2007, 192)

This real-life case shows, just like the hypothetical case which Gettier used, that there can be situations in which justified true belief and knowledge come apart. It, too, can disprove the standard analysis of knowledge.

This fact seems to confront proponents of X-Phi$_N$ with a dilemma. They have to decide whether they want to categorise the judgement about the actual scenario as an intuition. If they opt against it, then they cannot criticise Gettier's methodology using their experimental results because intuitions are then inessential to his argumentative strategy. If, instead, they include judgements about real-life cases among the class of intuitions, then the experimental critique would threaten to generalise to all these cases. Hence, adherents of X-Phi$_N$ would commit themselves to a global form of scepticism. Williamson calls it *judgement scepticism*.[27] It differs from other types of scepticism by the object of doubt. Sceptics about perception doubt our sense data. Sceptics about memory doubt our recollections. In like manner, judgement sceptics doubt that we are reliable when we apply concepts, for example, the concept of knowledge, to form judgements.

If the objection were sound, it would seem to constitute a serious criticism of X-Phi$_N$ – at least for two reasons. Firstly, judgement scepticism is a very far-reaching form of scepticism that seems philosophically unattractive. It would, for example, encompass science because scientists gain insights by systematising our observation through the application of concepts, that is, by judging. Secondly, a judgement scepticism that applies to scientific practice might undermine X-Phi$_N$ itself. For X-Phi$_N$ is itself based on empirical-scientific methods which involve the application of concepts (Bealer 1992).

How can proponents of X-Phi$_N$ defend their views against Williamson's criticism? There seems to be only one way: They have to demonstrate that their objection to the use of intuitions in philosophy does not generalise into an encompassing form of judgement scepticism. Weinberg (2007) seeks to make this idea plausible. To do this, he proposes a new criterion that we can use to evaluate whether a source of knowledge is epistemically legitimate. It is the property of *hopelessness*.

Hopelessness implies unreliability, but not *vice versa*. A hopeless source of knowledge is unreliable. However, an unreliable source may be hopeful to the extent that we can identify and correct its errors. This correction is possible, for example, by comparing its deliverances with data from different sources.[28] Our visual sense is an example of a source of knowledge that is, on occasion, unreliable but, nevertheless, hopeful. Visual data can, after all, be checked against other sense data (e.g. auditory data). According to Weinberg (2007), even intuitions can be hopeful. In particular, he thinks that the intuitions we employ in our scientific practice fall into that category.

> We have had a long and fairly well-documented history of trying out different norms to guide our inquiries, and we can learn from our historians which norms have been active when and what results they seem to have yielded. And we can use our best information about the structure of investigative communities both past and present, as well as what we know about the human agents who operate within them, to speculate counterfactually about what results various sorts of norms might or might not generate for us today. I am willing to place some confidence in our intuitions about the norms that govern justification, for example, because I expect that where we need to we can appeal to something outside of those intuitions themselves. (Weinberg 2007, 339)

Because we can check the intuitions we use in our scientific practice independently, they can be hopeful. Now, what about the intuitions that we use in our philosophical investigations? These, argues Weinberg, are largely hopeless since they are not embedded into a practice of inquiry that allows for independent validation. There simply are no other sources of knowledge against which we can check our philosophical intuitions. We cannot, therefore, correct potential errors as we can do in science. This, at any rate, is Weinberg's reasoning.

If this argument were sound, it would show that X-Phi$_N$ does not necessarily lead to a global and self-undermining scepticism. So, is it? This is not easy to assess. There is, in fact, quite a bit of controversy about this in the literature.[29] In the context of our investigation, it would not be possible to adjudicate it thoroughly. Hence, we will leave the question open.

4.3.5 Intuitions Are Irrelevant in Philosophy

Williamson's criticism of x-phi, which we discussed in the previous section, seeks to defend the MAP against experimentally informed objections. Before we proceed to the last objection to x-phi, it is worthwhile to reflect on the logical structure of Williamson's criticism. As we recorded in section 4.1, objections to x-phi can be categorised using a general argumentation scheme which is logically valid. Hence, any criticism of a particular version of it cannot target the logical transition from the premises to the conclusion. It is, however, possible to attack the two premises. However, as I pointed out earlier, this is not the only option, as Williamson's objection illustrates. He questions neither the empirical premise nor the bridging premise of any X-Phi$_N$ argument. With his demur, Williamson directly targets the conclusion. He points out that those who accept it commit themselves to a problematic form of scepticism which, as he sees it, is absurd. Accordingly, Williamson reasons, we have to resist the conclusion that adherents of X-Phi$_N$ want us to draw.

Now, there is a further argument against x-phi that is directed at the conclusions that experimental philosophers draw. However, this argument is different from Williamson's. Its adherents do not try to show that these conclusions are false. Rather, they seek to establish their philosophical irrelevance. This type of argument, which we find in the contributions of Cappelen (2012, 2014) and Deutsch (2009, 2010, 2015a, b, 2016, 2017), is designed to show that experimental philosophers misunderstand the role that intuitions play in philosophy. In fact, argue Cappelen and Deutsch, intuitions play no role at all in philosophical arguments. Accordingly, empirical findings regarding their properties, though perhaps interesting in and of themselves, do not have any bearing on philosophical practice.

Before we examine this objection more closely, we should clarify which forms of experimental philosophy it targets. The two previous arguments concerned only X-Phi$_N$. To be sure, Cappelen's and Deutsch's arguments also target this version of x-phi. Proponents of X-Phi$_N$ seek to show that the MAP is untenable. According to Cappelen and Deutsch, however, no philosopher uses this method. Hence, experimental criticisms misfire.

However, Cappelen's and Deutsch's arguments might also concern X-Phi$_P$. Those who practice this form of x-phi use empirical data to make a substantive contribution to the debate about a classical philosophical question. To this end, they devise experiments that are designed to test the reliability of our philosophical intuitions which, as they suppose, are used as premises in philosophical arguments. As we have seen in section 3.4, Nahmias et al. (2005, 2006) seek to show that most people intuitively disagree with incompatibilism. They then argue, based on this finding, that the burden of proof shifts to the incompatibilists. On Cappelen's and Deutsch's view, however, whether incompatibilism is intuitive or not is neither here nor there, at least when it comes to its philosophical credentials. In other words, the experimental results that X-Phi$_P$ theorists like Nahmias and colleagues use to contribute to the philosophical debate are irrelevant. Let us record, then, that Cappelen's and Deutsch's critique of x-phi concerns both X-Phi$_P$ and X-Phi$_N$.

Having discussed the status and target of their critique, we can examine its substance. To this end, we shall confine ourselves to the version that is put forward by Max Deutsch, which is, as Jennifer Nado has recently commented, "a wonderful instance of something . . . far too rare in philosophical practice – a bold, skeptical examination of a thesis that the majority of the field simply takes as given"[30] (Nado 2017, 387). Despite what so many authors have explicitly claimed in the past (e.g. Joel Pust, Alvin Goldman, George Bealer, Laurence Bonjour, and Frank Jackson), Deutsch dares to say that philosophers practically never use intuitions as premises in their arguments. Bolder yet, he claims that analytic philosophers who beg to differ are *methodologically confused*.

> Sometimes they are confused to the point that, even when explicitly addressing the question of how philosophy is done, they mischaracterize their own methods. I think Pust, Goldman, Bealer, Bonjour, and Jackson are all guilty of this confusion. (Deutsch 2015b, 39)

We may object that when we consider typical philosophical thought experiments (e.g. Gettier's or Kripke's), we find that the conclusions philosophers draw from them are, indeed, very intuitive. So intuitiveness does seem to play an argumentative role, does it not? Again, Deutsch begs to differ. As he says,

> Gettier's and Kripke's arguments do not, and do not need to, appeal to the intuitiveness of the counterexamples they involve; the arguments would (or could) be successful refutations, even if the counterexamples were highly counterintuitive, or if intuition were agnostic with respect to them. (Deutsch 2015b, 40)

Deutsch believes, then, that judgements about thought experiments can support philosophical positions even if these judgements are completely counter-intuitive. To him, their intuitiveness is not the issue. What counts is, rather, that they *genuinely* back up the positions they are meant to support. According to Deutsch, Gettier's thought experiment, for example, genuinely supports the view that the standard analysis of knowledge is false. In like manner, Kripke's Gödel case genuinely supports the view that Russell's theory of definite descriptions for proper names is false.

So far, so good. But how, if not based on intuition, can we determine whether a thought experiment genuinely supports a philosophical position? Deutsch thinks that we have to look for *arguments*. He says that "when it comes to providing evidence for judgments about thought experiments and cases, philosophy trades in arguments, not intuitions"[31] (Deutsch 2015b, 57). On its face, this answer seems naïve. For it appears only to reallocate the problem.[32] Even if the judgement about a given thought experiment rests on an argument, the argumentation has to stop somewhere. Where should it stop? Evidently, it should stop with a judgement that is intuitively appealing rather than intuitively unappealing.

Deutsch is well aware of this problem, which he calls the "relocation problem." He answers it in his book (see Deutsch 2015b, 122–27). At this point, we shall not consider his answer, however. For our purposes, I believe, it suffices to make two remarks that are independent of Deutsch's reply to the relocation problem.

My first comment starts from a simple observation, namely, that it would actually be a good sign for Deutsch if his argumentation did, in fact, run into the relocation problem. For this would mean that he has cleared at least one argumentative hurdle. It would mean that he has, in fact, shown that analytic philosophers argue for their judgements about thought experiments. Many philosophers have denied this.[33] Deutsch attempts to make this plausible using a case that he takes from Harry Frankfurt's influential papers "Alternate Possibilities and Moral Responsibility" (1969). In it, Frankfurt examines whether it is justifiable to ascribe moral responsibility to an agent even if she had no other way of acting than the way in which she actually did act. Frankfurt thinks that it is and offers the following scenario to support it.

> Suppose someone – Black, let us say – wants Jones to perform a certain action. Black is prepared to go to considerable lengths to get his way, but he prefers to avoid showing his hand unnecessarily. So he waits until Jones is about to make up his mind what to do, and he does nothing unless it is clear to him (Black is an excellent judge of such things) that Jones is going to decide to do something other than what he wants him to do. If it does become clear that Jones is going to decide to do something else, Black takes effective steps to ensure that Jones decides to do, and that he does do, what he wants him to do. Whatever Jones's initial preferences and inclinations, then, Black will have his way. . . . Now suppose that Black never has to show his hand because Jones, for reasons of his own, decides to perform and does perform the very action Black wants him to perform. In that case, it seems clear, Jones will bear precisely the same moral responsibility for what he does as he would have borne if Black had not been ready to take steps to ensure that he do it. (Frankfurt 1969, 835–36)[34]

In this thought experiment, Jones does not have a choice. He has to do what Black wants him to do. Nevertheless, we should, according to Frankfurt, attribute to him a moral responsibility for his action. Deutsch quotes the following passage, in which Frankfurt explains this judgement (Deutsch 2015, xv).

> It would be quite unreasonable to excuse Jones for his action or withhold the praise to which it would normally entitle him, on the basis of the fact that he could not do otherwise. This fact played no role at all in leading him to act as he did. He would have acted the same even if it had not been a fact. Indeed, everything happened just as it would have happened without Black's presence in the situation and without his readiness to intrude into it. (Frankfurt 1969, 836)

Now, Deutsch believes that this second passage contains an *argument* that supports Frankfurt's judgement about Jones that is contained in the latter parts of the first quote from Frankfurt (1969). As Deutsch claims, the same goes for other passages that he does not explicitly mention, however. He asks, therefore: "What do these arguments have to do with who intuits what?" And he answers his own question thus: "In a word: nothing" (Deutsch 2015, xv).

It seems, therefore, that Deutsch is successful in demonstrating that Frankfurt argues for his central judgement and does not justify it based on its intuitiveness. If this were correct, it would constitute a partial victory for him. However, if we consider the respective passages from Frankfurt more closely, it is far from obvious that Deutsch's interpretation of their logical status is correct.

The passage consists of four sentences. In the first sentence, Frankfurt says that it would be quite unreasonable not to regard Jones as morally responsible for his action merely because he could not have acted differently. This first sentence simply expresses Frankfurt's central judgement about his own thought experiment. Deutsch claims that it is not justified with an intuition but, rather, with an argument. On Deutsch's interpretation, this argument has to appear in the second, third, or fourth sentence of the passage because these are the only sentences he cites. There, Frankfurt says that the fact that Jones could not have acted differently made no difference in this situation, that he would have acted the same way even if he had had a different option, and that everything happened exactly the way it would have happened had Black not been present and not ready to intervene. I, for one, am at a loss when it comes to making sense of Deutsch's claim that these considerations represent an argument.[35] After all, an argument would have to contain new information that is not already contained in the description of the thought experiment. In the second, third, and fourth sentences of the second passage, Frankfurt, however, merely makes points that he has already made in the first passage that Deutsch quotes. From a logical point of view, his remarks are redundant, and we should, hence, not regard them as constituting an argument. I believe that it is most reasonable to interpret them as having a *rhetorical function*. They serve to highlight the main aspects of the case such that we can judge it more easily. We do the latter, I believe, by consulting our intuitions.[36]

Now, as Deutsch points out, an anonymous reviewer for MIT Press criticised his treatment of the Gettier case, which he also uses to make his point, in a similar way. He or she said that "every premise of the argument is *nothing more* than Gettier repeating some *fact* about the case he just presented" (quoted by Deutsch 2015, 174; emphasis in the original). Deutsch has a response to this that he would, I presume, also give to what I just said about Frankfurt's case. He would say that I illegitimately "assume that the premises of the argument can't *also* be features or facts" of the Frankfurt case itself. To this, he responds that

> the most likely place to find the premises of an argument supporting a judgment about a thought experiment is right there in the specification of the details of the thought experiment or case itself – where else? (Deutsch 2015, 174; emphasis in the original)

Note, then, that I am not saying the assumed circumstances of the case cannot be used as premises of an argument. What I am saying is that these premises do not, by themselves, constitute an argument, at least not one that is worthy of much consideration. Let me explain.

Remember what Frankfurt wants to accomplish. He disagrees, recall, with the principle that moral responsibility requires alternate possibilities and wants to disprove it. Formally, this principle is a universally quantified conditional of the form: For all cases, C, if there is moral responsibility, then there are, also, alternate possibilities. Such a conditional is disproven by pointing to a case, C', in which the antecedent is true (there is moral responsibility) and the consequent false (there are no alternate possibilities). Frankfurt tries to do this. He constructs such a case in the thought experiment we considered earlier. He *assumes* certain circumstances, including the lack of alternate possibilities for the agent. To complete his case, he cannot simply suppose, in addition to that, that the agent is responsible if he is in the envisioned situation. Doing this would merely beg the question against someone who believes in the principle Frankfurt seeks to disprove. Such a person would, after all, deny precisely this additional assumption. Therefore, if Frankfurt wants, indeed, to make a respectable case for his position, he has to establish, first, that *if said circumstances obtain, then it is at least plausible to conclude that there is, nevertheless, moral responsibility*. This task cannot be achieved by merely pointing to said circumstances, as Deutsch seems to suggest. To claim otherwise would be tantamount to saying that I can prove reading philosophy books makes you go blind simply by pointing to people reading philosophy books.[37]

If this is correct, then it is at least doubtful that Deutsch can claim partial victory. In that case, any further discussion of the relocation problem would be moot. Nevertheless, let us suppose, contrary to what we just established, that Deutsch's diagnosis was correct and that, indeed, analytical philosophers never used the intuitiveness of a judgement as a consideration that counts in its favour. Would this constitute an objection against x-phi? My second remark addresses this question.

Earlier, we recorded that the objection from irrelevance, which Cappelen and Deutsch press against x-phi, attacks both X-Phi$_P$ and X-Phi$_N$. The latter rejects MAP. If, however, analytic philosophers do not use this method, as Cappelen and Deutsch maintain, then X-Phi$_N$'s claim is irrelevant for the way these scholars go about their business. Critics of x-phi can use a similar argument against X-Phi$_P$. Proponents of this version of x-phi try to assess the reliability of important philosophical intuitions by running experiments. However, if these intuitions play no role in the arguments of analytic philosophers, as Cappelen and Deutsch believe, then this variant of x-phi also makes claims that are irrelevant for philosophical practice. I believe, though, that experimental philosophy could play an indirect role, even in that case.[38]

To explain this, we should begin with an observation. Cappelen and Deutsch merely say that intuitions are irrelevant for the justification of a philosophical judgement. They do not deny that intuitions can serve as explanations that elucidate why philosophers hold the views that they do.[39] The distinction I am driving at is, of course, that between the *context of justification* and the *context of discovery* (see Reichenbach 1938/1983). My claim is, hence, that X-Phi$_P$ can play an indirect role in the assessment of philosophical propositions that is mediated through the context of discovery.

At first glance, it is far from clear how this claim can be justified. Philosophers, after all, commonly accept that issues which have to do with the context of justification are to be strictly separated from matters that concern the context of discovery. Causal explanations, which elucidate why a person holds a particular view (or how she came to believe it), belong to the context of discovery. By themselves, they do not tell us anything about the justification of the view in question. To judge the latter issue, we need to examine whether there are sufficiently good reasons to support it. These reasons belong to the context of justification. Let us assume, for example, that Jones and Smith are colleagues. Jones believes that Smith does not deserve to be paid a bonus this year. Now, this belief might be causally explained by the fact that Jones is jealous. Jones's jealousy is a fact that belongs to the context of discovery. It plausibly explains why Jones holds the view that he does. Whether his standpoint is justified, however, depends only on the reasons for and against it, which belong to the context of justification. If we want to know whether Jones's view about Smith's bonus is justified, we should, hence, consider only the reasons he presents in favour of it. If we reject these reasons simply by pointing towards Jones's jealousy, then we use what may be called a *psychoanalytic argument*, which is a special case of the *genetic fallacy*. We dismiss a consideration because it is causally connected to a particular psychological state. This would justifiably be regarded as problematic.

However, we should not make a mistake and disregard psychological considerations entirely. On occasion, it can be reasonable to assess the credentials of a proposition based on the psychological properties of those who hold it. Imagine that we have to form a judgement about an issue. We are unable to judge the arguments on the table directly, for example, due to a lack of time, resources, or information. But we know that an expert supports a particular view about the question we are interested in. Should we believe her? The fact that she is an expert speaks in favour of it. However, should we learn that she stands to gain if we accept her view, then this should incline us to doubt what she says. It is, after all, well known that self-interest can bias a person's judgement.[40] For that to be the case, there does not even have to be ill intent. This is why scientific publishers, for example, routinely ask their authors to declare possible conflicts of interest. In other words, the source of an argument may, under certain circumstances, be relevant to the assessment of its reliability.

This having said, we should ask whether such circumstances obtain in the philosophical debate. That might be the case. Anyone who has attended a philosophical conference knows this. When philosophers argue with each other, they typically do not act impartially. They do not behave like impartial judges who neutrally balance the reasons on all sides. In all likelihood, they have a dog in the fight, namely, a philosophical thesis that constitutes part of their self-image. And they defend this thesis like attorneys.[41] That is, they focus primarily on considerations that support their views and on arguments that cast doubt on contrary standpoints. (The author of this book is surely no exception in that regard.)

Now, this is not necessarily a problem for the profession as a whole if there is a *sufficient diversity of views*. Different philosophers usually differ in the views they hold about the subjects they study such that arguments on many sides of an issue get a fair hearing. However, this is not necessarily the case in every situation. There might be debates in which particular views are not expressed such that the arguments in their favour are not drawn to our attention. This situation might arise for several reasons.

One likely candidate that should play a role in the context of discovery is the *intuitiveness of a philosophical idea*, as both Cappelen and Deutsch acknowledge. If that is true, counter-intuitive views should, in comparison, be expressed much less frequently than more intuitive views, and arguments that support them would tend not to get an ear. However, if, as Cappelen and

Deutsch maintain, the intuitiveness of a philosophical position does not give us any clue as to their credibility, then this means that the differences in the intuitiveness of competing philosophical views can lead to an imbalance. In that case, it could be that positions which are true are not recognised as such because nobody bothers to argue for them, due to their counter-intuitiveness. Following this logic, we should be especially careful when it comes to philosophical ideas that are very intuitive because we may assume that philosophers have spent less time and energy on refuting them.[42] This reasoning would radically contradict the logic of the Argument from Agreement and the Argument from Disagreement that we discussed in section 2.4.1. Nevertheless, it would show, contrary to Cappelen's and Deutsch's claims, that empirical and, in particular, experimental research has a role to play in philosophy. Let us record, then, that X-Phi$_P$ would, for all it seems, still be in a position to contribute indirectly to philosophical debate even if it turned out that the intuitiveness of a philosophical idea is irrelevant to its justification.[43]

4.3.6 Conclusions

In the five previous sections, we discussed philosophical objections to x-phi and examined possible answers for which its adherents might opt. In doing that, we took care to distinguish between X-Phi$_P$ and X-Phi$_N$. For, as it turned out, many objections only seem to pose a threat to X-Phi$_N$ but not to X-Phi$_P$.

While we rejected the first two criticisms of x-phi in regard to both X-Phi$_P$ and X-Phi$_N$, we found that the third, fourth, and fifth objections seem to be more problematic for X-Phi$_N$ than for X-Phi$_P$. In fact, it is not even clear that these objections concern the latter at all. As we found, X-Phi$_P$ does not depend on a precise notion of intuition. Furthermore, it does not appear to entail a global form of judgement scepticism. In the case of X-Phi$_N$, these issues have to be taken more seriously. Also, we can give, as we did in the previous section, an indirect motivation for X-Phi$_P$ that applies even if intuitions do not play a justificatory role in philosophy, as Max Deutsch and Herman Cappelen believe. In contrast, X-Phi$_N$, which rejects the use of intuitions about thought experiments in philosophy, evidently becomes irrelevant if intuitions do not, in fact, play a justificatory role in philosophy. Accordingly, we can condense the findings of our discussion into a tentative conclusion, namely, that X-Phi$_N$ seems to be quite problematic, while X-Phi$_P$ does not.

Our conclusion is not very surprising. X-Phi$_N$, after all, makes a rather far-reaching claim. It says, essentially, that there are no unobjectionable applications of the MAP. This is a negative existential statement. From a logical point of view, it is hard to make it plausible, but easy to reject. To lend it any credibility, we would have to gather a large sample of data which confirms X-Phi$_N$'s rejection of MAP more or less unanimously. To demolish it, we merely need a few examples which suggest that the application of MAP is unproblematic. Regarding X-Phi$_P$, the opposite is true. X-Phi$_P$ only supposes that experimental findings can play a role in the debate about a philosophical issue. In this case, those who deny it subscribe to a negative existential statement. They say that no bridging premise can plausibly connect an experimental result (as the argument's premise) with a philosophical thesis (as the argument's conclusion). This idea is hard to support, but rather easy to discredit. To do the latter, all we need is one example which shows that experimental results can support a philosophical thesis. Hence, in addition to the considerations discussed earlier, there does seem to be an a priori reason for our tentative conclusion that X-Phi$_P$ is rather unobjectionable, while X-Phi$_N$ is more problematic.

4.4 SUMMARY

In this chapter, we discussed important objections to x-phi. To this end, we first categorised them and determined the potential reach of the various forms of criticism.

As a first step, we introduced a General Scheme for Experimental Arguments that could encompass all x-phi argumentation schemes we had considered up until this point. This scheme had two premises and a (meta-)philosophical conclusion. The first premise is an empirical statement of fact, while the second bridges the gap between the empirical and the philosophical sphere. Since the argument is formally valid, we concluded that arguments against x-phi might concern the first premise, which is empirical, and the second premise, which links the empirical with the philosophical sphere. We called arguments of the first kind methodological objections and arguments of the second kind philosophical objections.

We observed that methodological objections have a high potential reach as they can affect X-Phi$_C$, X-Phi$_P$, and X-Phi$_N$ simultaneously. They are, however, comparatively unproblematic. Experimental philosophers address them simply by conforming to empirical research standards.

Philosophical objections, on the other hand, have a more limited reach. They target only those forms of x-phi that attempt to make a positive contribution to philosophical or metaphilosophical questions. That is, they target only X-Phi$_P$ and X-Phi$_N$. However, they are considerably more severe than methodological objections because, unlike the latter, they concern the philosophical underpinnings of these branches of x-phi.

Having categorised the two variants of critique, we first turned our attention to methodological objections. Our discussion began with a fundamental distinction between two types of arguments, namely, those that allege a lack of external validity and those that problematise a lack of internal validity.

Critics who scold x-phi for lack of external validity object that the conclusions experimental philosophers draw are too far-reaching. If, for example, they conduct their studies only with educated participants who happen to have a keen interest in philosophy, then they get a biased sample, and their conclusions cannot be generalised.

Armchair philosophers often propose one particular argument against x-phi that picks up on the notion of external validity. It is the expertise reply. Those who use it criticise x-phi because its proponents usually recruit philosophical laypersons for their studies. The outcomes of these studies, therefore, do not tell us anything about professional philosophers, whose mental life can be expected to differ vastly from those of laypersons. Or so they say. As we have seen, however, when professional philosophers get tested, their results suggest that they commit the same cognitive errors as ordinary folk. In fact, they might commit even graver ones than the folk.

By and large, we concluded that the aspect of external validity appears to be Janus-faced for x-phi. On the one hand, x-phi seems to be in a better position than AC-Phi and A-Phi because armchair philosophers tend not to take care to obtain samples of intuitions that are representative of the population as a whole. On the other hand, however, there do seem to be legitimate criticisms of x-phi because some of its proponents have tended to overgeneralise. This applies, however, much more to the early work than it does to recent studies.

X-phi can be criticised for lack of internal validity if the results of experimental studies are likely to have been caused by confounding factors. We went into three issues that have to do with this point.

Firstly, we discussed the so-called experimenter bias, where the outcome of a trial can be partly explained by the attitude of the experimenter who conducted it. This aspect, we concluded, seems to play a smaller role than it does, for example, in experimental psychology. Nevertheless, we should not neglect it. In fact, experimental philosophers, too, are well advised to take appropriate measures to rule out any experimenter bias. The hardest problem to solve is, perhaps, the problem of potential biases in the wording of questionnaires.

Secondly, we talked about the problem that philosophical laypersons, who make up the lion's share of participants in x-phi experiments, may misunderstand the questions they are asked. As we observed, however, experimental philosophers seem to be well aware of this problem and try to address it by taking suitable measures.

Thirdly, we spoke about the possibility that the answers x-phi subjects give are not an expression of their linguistic competence but, rather, based on cognitive errors in its application. This is a serious problem of which experimental philosophers are well aware. In fact, unlike armchair philosophers, they are in a unique position to tackle this difficulty, and they have done it in multiple studies. In the x-phi debate, it is, in fact, more likely than in the AC-Phi debate that a judgement which is based on a cognitive error will be recognised as such.

Towards the end of section 4.2.3, we concluded that methodological objections to x-phi do not pose a serious threat to X-Phi_C, X-Phi_P, or X-Phi_N. Experimental philosophers can always address them by adopting improved research methods. In recent times, it has been proposed that x-phi should adopt even more methods from the empirical sciences (for a brief overview, see appendix C).

Philosophical objections, on the other hand, might be more problematic. We considered five philosophical objections, three of which seemed legitimate. According to the first one, x-phi does not even have a subject matter to study. Experimental philosophers say they study philosophical intuitions. However, it is not even clear what it means for a mental state to be an intuition. On the second objection, x-phi leads to a rather sweeping form of scepticism that is philosophically unattractive. Finally, those who press the third objection declare x-phi as irrelevant because intuitions do not, as these critics believe, play the role that experimental philosophers think they do. Accordingly, their studies of intuitions do not have any bearing on the debate about any philosophical issue. Based on our distinction between X-Phi_P and X-Phi_N, we recognised that all these objections seem to concern only X-Phi_N. This variant of x-phi appears, then, to be more controversial than X-Phi_P. An a priori reasoning eventually took us to the same conclusion. However, our discussion was, of course, too incomplete to draw any definite conclusions from it.

NOTES

1. Perhaps, this point can be answered, at least partly, by pointing out that experimental philosophers have further research methods at their disposal, for example, qualitative methods (for a brief discussion, see appendix C.6). These methods enable x-phi researchers to extract much more information from their subjects than a simple "yes" or "no." They can, for example, ask them about the reasons for their judgements.

2. It may seem as though Cappelen's point is an instance of the general scepticism that we have already addressed. But Cappelen is surely not a general sceptic about empirical methods. He does not deny that it is possible to apply empirical research techniques to empirical questions. He does not even deny that certain empirical methods might be called for in the discussion of a philosophical issue (see, in

particular, his remarks in Cappelen 2018, 120–21). He denies only that specific forms of empirical evidence about intuitions are relevant to philosophy. His scepticism is, hence, much less general than the general scepticism about empirical research methods. Nevertheless, it seems to me to be too general for us to address here.

3. By focusing on these two aspects, we avoid more fundamental issues that would require a more formal treatment, such as the selection of statistical methods. On this issue, see Sytsma & Livengood (2016, Part II).

4. The properties of our example case ensure that we avoid certain problems. They arise, in particular, when it comes to the justification of causal inferences in quasi-experiments. In a quasi-experiment, the explanatory variable is fixed before the experiment and cannot be randomised (e.g. sex). A comprehensive assessment of x-phi studies would have to address these aspects as well.

5. For a review of studies that investigate the link between personality and philosophical judgement, see Feltz & Cokely (2016).

6. Stephen Stich, who is one of the co-authors of Weinberg et al. (2001), shares this view. He pointed this out to me in personal communication.

7. Small sample sizes are sometimes inevitable, for example, when experiments are conducted with very atypical subjects. As we discussed in section 3.4.3, Cova et al. (2012) investigated how patients who have frontotemporal dementia judge particular cases that are relevant to the free will debate. Accordingly, the sample Cova et al. (2012) had to work with was very small.

8. The expertise defence and similar replies have been discussed rather intensely in the x-phi debate. See, for example, Cappelen (2014), Deutsch (2015b), Goldman (2007), Hales (2006, 2012), Kauppinen (2007), Ludwig (2007), Tobia et al. (2012), Weinberg et al. (2010), and Williamson (2011). Alexander (2016) provides an instructive overview of the debate about the expertise defence.

9. The notion of expertise is central to a further, similar objection. It says that the judgements of laypersons are simply philosophically irrelevant when it comes to answering philosophical questions because laypersons lack the required expertise (Ludwig 2007).

10. To my mind, there are only two ways to avoid this conclusion: we might, firstly, endorse a variant of *truth relativism*. That is, we might subscribe to the idea that there are multiple answers to a philosophical question that are each true with respect to some standard of truth. We might, secondly, opt for *dialetheism*, which claims that there are true contradictions (Priest 1995/2002). I am indebted to Georgios Karageorgoudis, who called the second option to my attention.

11. To be sure, many philosophers are completely aware that this might be so. The consequentialist moral philosopher Alastair Norcross writes, for example: "I am all too aware that non-consequentialists' intuitions diverge radically from my own" (Norcross 2008, 66).

12. See, for example, Schwitzgebel & Cushman (2012, 2015). These authors examined how far framing effects and, in particular, order effects affected philosophers' judgements about moral issues. For further studies that used philosophers as subjects, see Machery (2012) on reference and Sytsma & Machery (2010) on consciousness.

13. Note, however, that the review process differs between disciplines. In the natural sciences, for example, single-blind reviewing is the norm. The author of a paper does not know the identity of the reviewer. The reviewer, however, knows the identity of the author. This is commonly justified by pointing out that the identity of the author is very easy to infer based on the paper's content.

14. Kauppinen (2007), for example, has uttered an objection of that type.

15. Noam Chomsky's seminal contributions to linguistics have presumably played a big role in making philosophers aware of this hypothesis. Chomsky distinguishes between *linguistic performance* and *linguistic competence*. He clarifies that to "study actual linguistic performance, we must consider the interaction of a variety of factors, of which the underlying competence of the speaker-hearer is only one" (Chomsky 1965, 4).

16. Robert Woolfolk could be correct at least insofar as prominent x-phi publications, such as the collections by Knobe & Nichols (2008, 2014), do not explicitly discuss the blinding of hypotheses.

17. See footnote 18 (chapter 3).

18. For an example, see Machery & Sytsma et al. (2015).

19. A further example which illustrates that pragmatic factors are taken seriously in the x-phi debate is the discussion between Knobe (2003, 2004) and Adams & Steadman (2004a,b). We discussed it in section 3.3.3.

20. In this investigation, we can leave aside the question how vast the essential differences between philosophy and the empirical sciences really are. I shall merely point out that this is itself a contested issue. Important naturalist philosophers (e.g. Quine) have held that there is merely a gradual difference between the sphere of philosophy and the empirical sciences.

21. Regarding this point, see also Angner's (2013) instructive discussion, which shows how empirical research can inform philosophical conclusions in the context of the philosophical debate about well-being.

22. In Mukerji (2015), I have discussed one specific version of such a principled objection. It is directed at a particular version of x-phi, namely, experimental ethics and consists in the allegation that, necessarily, an experimental ethics would, firstly, violate the Is-Ought-dichotomy and, secondly, commit the naturalistic fallacy.

23. This should not surprise us. As we said in sections 4.1, it seems that philosophical objections do not affect X-Phi$_C$.

24. However, the same objection would, it seems, apply to those who support the general use of MAP. They, too, have to explain how the class of intuitions can be demarcated from all other mental states.

25. In sections 1.2, 2.2, and 3.1.1, we have discussed Gettier's thought experiment.

26. In what follows, we shall confine ourselves to a variant of the scepticism objection that is put forward by Williamson (2007). Note, however, that other authors have uttered similar objections, for example, Hales (2012) and Sosa (2007).

27. For a brief formulation of this objection, see Williamson (2016).

28. Weinberg states three further criteria that can be used to assess how hopeful a source of knowledge is (Weinberg 2007, 330–31). For reasons of scope, we shall not discuss them here, however.

29. A number of authors have followed up on Weinberg's arguments. Grundmann (2010) and Ichikawa (2012), for example, criticise it. Nado (2015) proposes a new variant of the argument that is designed to avoid a number of criticisms. An interesting exchange of arguments can also be found in Weinberg (2009) and Williamson (2009).

30. Cappelen puts forward his position in Cappelen (2012, 2014). Interesting exchanges followed in the course of two symposia on his book *Philosophy Without Intuitions* (2012), whose proceedings were published in *Analytic Philosophy* (Issue 55/4, 2014) and *Philosophical Studies* (Issue 171/3, 2014). In an interesting discussion, Nado (2016) distinguishes various arguments by Cappelen and Deutsch and proposes answers from an x-phi perspective.

31. Deutsch discusses this thesis against the background of his analysis of Gettier's case (see Deutsch 2015b, chapter 4 and Deutsch 2016).

32. For discussions of this problem, see Chalmers (2014), Nado (2016, 2017), and Weinberg (2014).

33. For a recent example, see Colaço & Machery (2017). These authors also accuse Deutsch of cherry-picking his examples by ignoring large chucks of the history of analytic philosophy, and they criticise his characterisation of the MAP as viciously circular. Deutsch (2017) responds to their arguments.

34. Deutsch (2015b, ix) directly refers to this passage and quotes it in his own text.

35. This point has been discussed, for example, by Colaço & Machery (2017) and Machery (2017, 177–80).

36. Note that I do not want to argue that philosophers never argue for their judgements about cases. My point is, rather, that it is possible to find examples in the literature which show that philosophers do consult their intuitions about cases and then use them with argumentative intent. In my view, the passage from Frankfurt (1969), which Deutsch (2015b) quotes, shows this clearly.

37. If this is not obvious, note that the claim I use to illustrate my point is also a conditional. It says that, *if you read philosophy books, then you go blind*. Simply pointing to people reading philosophy books is not an argument for that claim.

38. Nado (2016, 2017) makes similar points. Deutsch (2017) responds to them.

39. In fact, both of them concede this point explicitly. Max Deutsch says: "Various arguments in philosophy . . . may 'rely,' or 'depend,' on intuition, but only causally, not inferentially or evidentially" (Deutsch 2010, 453). And Cappelen says:

> I have said nothing about whether something that some philosophers would label 'intuition' could play a significant role in the context of discovery. It is not implausible that something reasonably labeled 'intuitive' can serve as a creative starting point for many cognitive activities, including philosophizing. (Cappelen 2012, 230)

40. This type of bias is an instance of the general phenomenon of *motivated reasoning*.

41. I borrow this comparison from Kramer & Messick (1996). They do not use it, however, to describe the behaviour of philosophers. Rather, they are interested in managers.

42. In statistics, it is common to use correction methods, for example, when the likelihood of getting a statistically significant result is increased by the fact that

multiple comparisons are made within the same data set (e.g. Bonferroni correction). We might need analogous, although presumably less precise, methods in philosophy to correct for the asymmetry between the intuitiveness of various philosophical positions. These methods would reduce the weight of arguments for intuitive claims and increase the weight of arguments for counter-intuitive ideas. If we can expect that the likelihood of finding a supporting argument goes up as the intuitiveness of the respective claim increases, this correction might seem reasonable.

43. Colaço & Machery (2017) have also argued that Deutsch's main argument against x-phi can be rejected even if philosophers do not, in fact, rely on intuitions for evidence (see, also, Machery 2017). They use an analogy to illustrate their point:

> "If scientists discover that different researchers obtain different measurements, and if for all they know these scientists are equally competent at measuring, then they ought to suspend judgment about the temperature of the sample" (Colaço & Machery 2017, 417).

In like manner, we have reason to suspend judgement if individuals, who seem equally competent at judging philosophical cases, arrive at different judgements – whether they come from intuition or not. Accordingly, Deutsch's focus on intuition is a red herring, and he does not demonstrate that x-phi is philosophically irrelevant.

Conclusion

In this study, we discussed three variants of x-phi, namely, X-Phi$_C$, X-Phi$_P$, and X-Phi$_N$, and investigated how they could be distinguished from traditional armchair philosophy (AC-Phi) and, in particular, its analytic version (A-Phi). Furthermore, we examined how it is possible to bridge the gap between an empirical research finding and a philosophical conclusion. Moreover, we considered a number of x-phi studies in various branches of philosophy. Finally, we addressed a set of significant objections to x-phi and considered possible replies from the perspectives of X-Phi$_C$, X-Phi$_P$, and X-Phi$_N$. I hope that this discussion has convinced you that x-phi is an exciting new movement in philosophy, which is able to deliver interesting results and initiate fruitful debates.

In my experience, traditionally minded philosophers have a hard time accepting these conclusions. Many of them still have strong reservations about x-phi. Timothy Williamson, whom we have come to know as a staunch x-phi critic, is a good example. He said, bluntly, that experimental philosophers are just "philosophy-hating philosophers" (Williamson 2010).[1] Why, we should ask, do traditionalists react to x-phi like that?

I would imagine that fear of loss is at least partly responsible. Perhaps traditionalists are afraid that x-phi might make them obsolete? Perhaps they think that x-phi aims to obviate the need for the armchair, which they take to be the quintessential symbol of this discipline? I believe, as I have argued elsewhere (Mukerji 2014), that both fears are based on a misconception.

Firstly, x-phi hardly threatens any of the traditional methods of philosophy. Experimental philosophers who practice X-Phi$_C$ and X-Phi$_P$ do not have the slightest intention to replace any of the classic techniques by experiments. They understand what they contribute merely as a supplement. Adherents of X-Phi$_N$ do, admittedly, attack methods of analytic armchair philosophy.

However, as I remarked in section 1.2, they have a rather idiosyncratic conception of what these methods are. It comprises only a small part of the instruments that analytic philosophers would typically count among their methodological arsenal.[2] In addition, one can, as we found in section 1.7, be open to experimental findings while staying true to AC-Phi and, more particularly, A-Phi. One may, after all, to expect experimental results to turn out such that they lend further support to traditional armchair methods.[3]

Secondly, x-phi does not diminish classical armchair reflection. I would, in fact, go so far as to claim that it increases its status! For one thing, x-phi methods can be combined with traditional methods (see, e.g., appendix C on formal methods). Also, x-phi creates new questions for philosophers to think about in the armchair. The latter point is, in fact, easy to see. Philosophical experiments do not fall into our laps. Before we can conduct them, we have to identify a research desideratum. To this end, we have to study philosophical theories and discussions, and we have to interpret them and draw conclusions from them. It is only in this way that we can arrive at philosophically relevant empirical hypotheses that we can then put to the test. In addition, test instruments have to be carefully designed to ensure that our experiments do, in fact, test what they are supposed to test. Finally, the experimental data have to be analysed with an eye towards philosophical conclusions. All of these are tasks that philosophers can take up, all of these are new tasks, and all of these are tasks that can be pursued from the armchair! In fact, I do not know of a better place from which to pursue them. Hence, the fear that experimental philosophy might make armchair reflection superfluous seems to me to be absolutely baseless.

I would very much welcome it if traditionally minded philosophers, too, would discover the tools of experimental research methodology for their own work. At the same time, I do not want to be unrealistic. In classical philosophical training, these tools do not play a role yet. Hence, it will surely take a long time until the experimental approach to philosophy will have the same status as, say, the method of logical analysis. The influence of x-phi would have to grow considerably until philosophers would consider replacing the motto that is inscribed over the doorways of their academies, until it says: "Let no one enter who is ignorant of the experimental method." However, if this would happen one day, I would be all for it. After all, it might be worth an experiment!

NOTES

1. Today's x-phi had, by the way, a historical precursor in the "experimental philosophy" of the early modern age, which gave birth, amongst other things, to what

would later develop into modern physics (Anstey & Vanzo 2016). Like x-phi, its early modern forerunner was met by considerable resistance because its experimental method did not conform to the rationalistic paradigm of the time. Nowadays, however, the use of experiments is a matter of course in empirical research methodology.

2. On this point, see Hanjo Glock's influential book *What Is Analytic Philosophy?* (2008), which covers many methods of analytic philosophy proponents of X-Phi$_N$ do not attack.

3. After the completion of my manuscript, Michael Strevens' new book *Thinking Off Your Feet* (2019) got published. It is a psychologically informed defence of armchair philosophy.

References

Adams, Ernest W. 2005. "What Is at Stake in the Controversy over Conditionals?" In: Kern-Isberner, Gabriele; Rödder, Wilhelm; Kulmann, Friedhelm (eds.), *Conditional, Information, and Inference*. Berlin: Springer, 1–11.

Adams, Fred. 2006. "Intentions Confer Intentionality upon Actions: A Reply to Knobe and Burra." *Journal of Cognition and Culture* 6(1–2): 255–68.

Adams, Fred; Steadman, Annie. 2004a. "Intentional Action and Moral Considerations: Still Pragmatic." *Analysis* 64(3): 268–76.

———. 2004b. "Intentional Action in Ordinary Language: Core Concept or Pragmatic Understanding?" *Analysis* 64(2): 173–81.

Alexander, Joshua. 2016. "Philosophical Expertise." In: Sytsma, Justin; Buckwalter, Wesley (eds.), *A Companion to Experimental Philosophy*, Oxford: Wiley-Blackwell, 557–67.

Alexander, Joshua; Mailon, Ron; Weinberg, Jonathan M. 2014. "Accentuate the Negative." In: Knobe, Joshua; Nichols, Shaun (eds.). *Experimental Philosophy* (Vol. 2). Oxford: Oxford University Press, 31–50.

Alexander, Joshua; Weinberg, Jonathan M. 2007. "Analytic Epistemology and Experimental Philosophy." *Philosophy Compass* 2(1): 56–80.

Alfano, Mark. 2013. "Identifying and Defending the Hard Core of Virtue Ethics." *Journal of Philosophical Research* 38: 233–60.

———. 2018. "A Plague on both your Houses: Virtue Theory after Situationism and Repligate." *Teoria* 38(2); 115–22.

Alfano, Mark; Loeb, Don; Plakias, Alexandra. 2018. "Experimental Moral Philosophy," In: Zalta, Edward N. (ed.), *The Stanford Encyclopedia of Philosophy* (Fall 2018), Stanford: The Metaphysics Research Lab, Center for the Study of Language and Information (Stanford University). URL: https://stanford.io/2vzrenQ (accessed 31 August 2018).

Alfano, Mark; Rusch, Hannes; Uhl, Matthias. 2018. "Ethics, Morality, and Game Theory." *Games* 9(2), 20.

Alicke, Mark; Rose, David; Bloom, Dori. 2011. "Causation, Norm Violation, and Culpable Control." *Journal of Philosophy* 108(12): 670–96.

Andow, James. 2015. "How 'Intuition' Exploded." *Metaphilosophy* 46(2): 189–212.

———. 2016. "Qualitative Tools and Experimental Philosophy." *Philosophical Psychology* 29(8): 1128–41.

———. 2017. "Do Non-Philosophers Think Epistemic Consequentialism Is Counterintuitive?" *Synthese* 194(7): 2631–43.

Andow, James; Cova, Florian. 2016. "Why Compatibilist Intuitions Are Not Mistaken: A Reply to Feltz and Millan." *Philosophical Psychology*, 1–17.

Angner, Erik. 2013. "Is Empirical Research Relevant to Philosophical Conclusions?" *Res Philosophica* 90(3), 365–85.

Anscombe, Gertrude E. M. 1957/2000. *Intention*. Cambridge, MA: Harvard University Press.

Anstey, Peter R.; Vanzo, Alberto. 2016. "Early Modern Experimental Philosophy." In: Sytsma, Justin; Buckwalter, Wesley (eds.), *A Companion to Experimental Philosophy*, Oxford: Wiley-Blackwell, 87–102.

Appiah, Kwame A. 2008. *Experiments in Ethics*. Cambridge, MA: Harvard University Press.

Arico, Adam; Fiala, Brian; Goldberg, Robert F.; Nichols, Shaun. "The Folk Psychology of Consciousness." *Mind & Language* 26(3): 327–52.

Ashton, Zoe; Mizrahi, Moti. 2018a. "Intuition Talk Is Not Methodologically Cheap: Empirically Testing the "Received Wisdom" about Armchair Philosophy." *Erkenntnis* 83(3): 595–612.

———. 2018b. "Show Me the Argument – Empirically Testing the Armchair Philosophy Picture." *Metaphilosophy* 49(1–2), 58–70.

Audi, Robert. 1986. "Acting for Reasons." *The Philosophical Review* 95(4): 511–46.

Balaguer, Mark. 2016. "Conceptual Analysis and X-Phi." *Synthese* 193(8): 2367–88.

Bardon, Adrian. 2005. "Performative Transcendental Arguments." *Philosophia* 33(1), 69–95.

Bealer, George. 1992. "The Incoherence of Empiricism." *Proceedings of the Aristotelian Society, Supplementary Volumes* 66: 99–138.

———. 1996. "'A Priori' Knowledge and the Scope of Philosophy." *Philosophical Studies* 81(2/3): 121–42.

———. 1999. "A Theory of the A Priori." *Philosophical Perspectives* 13: 29–55.

Bear, Adam; Knobe, Joshua. 2016. "What Do People Find Incompatible with Causal Determinism?" *Cognitive Science* 40, 2025–49.

———. 2017. "Normality: Part Descriptive, Part Prescriptive," *Cognition* 167: 25–37.

Beebe, James R; Undercoffer, Ryan. 2015. "Moral Valence and Semantic Intuitions." *Erkenntnis* 80(2): 445–66.

———. 2016. "Individual and Cross-Cultural Differences in Semantic Intuitions: New Experimental Findings." *Journal of Cognition and Culture* 16(3–4): 322–57.

Berker, Selim. 2009. "The Normative Insignificance of Neuroscience." *Philosophy and Public Affairs* 37(4): 293–329.

Berniūnas, Renatas; Dranseika, Vilius. 2016. "Folk Concepts of Person and Identity: A Response to Nichols and Bruno." *Philosophical Psychology* 29(1): 96–122.

Bickle, John. 2018. "Lessons for Experimental Philosophy from the Rise and "Fall" of Neurophilosophy." *Philosophical Psychology* 32(1): 1–22.

Blais, Michel J. 1987. "Epistemic Tit for Tat." *Journal of Philosophy* 84(7), 363–75.

Björnsson, Gunnar; Pereboom, Derek. 2016. "Traditional and Experimental Approaches to Free Will and Moral Responsibility." In: Sytsma, Justin; Buckwalter, Wesley (eds.), *A Companion to Experimental Philosophy*, Oxford: Wiley-Blackwell, 142–57.

Boh, Ivan. 1985. "Belief, Justification, and Knowledge – Some Late-Medieval Epistemic Concerns." *Journal of the Rocky Mountain Medieval and Renaissance Association* 6: 87–104.

Boyd, Kenneth; Nagel, Jennifer. 2014. "The Reliability of Epistemic Intuitions." In: Machery, Édouard; O'Neill, Elizabeth (eds.), *Current Controversies in Experimental Philosophy*. New York: Routledge, 109–27.

Braithwaite, Richard B. 1955. *Theory of Games as a Tool for the Moral Philosopher*. Cambridge: Cambridge University Press.

Brandeis, Louis D. 1914. *Other People's Money and How the Bankers Use It*. New York: Frederick A. Stokes Company Publishers.

Bratman, Michael. 1984. "Two Faces of Intention." *The Philosophical Review* 93(3): 375–405.

Bray, Dennis; von Storch, Hans. 2017. "The Normative Orientations of Climate Scientists." *Science and Engineering Ethics* 23(5): 1351–67.

De Brigard, Felipe, Eric Mandelbaum, and David Ripley. 2009. "Responsibility and the Brain Sciences." *Ethic Theory Moral Practice* 12(5): 511–24.

De Bruin, Boudewijn. 2005. "Game Theory in Philosophy." *Topoi* 24: 197–208.

———. 2010. *Explaining Games: The Epistemic Programme in Game Theory*. Dordrecht: Springer.

Buckwalter, Wesley, Stich, Stephen. 2014. "Gender and Philosophical Intuition." In: Knobe, Joshua; Nichols, Shaun (eds.), *Experimental Philosophy* (Vol. 2), Oxford: Oxford University Press, 307–46.

Buller, David J. 2005. *Adapting Minds*. Cambridge, MA: MIT Press.

Cappelen, Herman. 2012. *Philosophy without Intuitions*. Oxford: Oxford University Press.

———. 2014. "X-Phi without Intuitions?" In: Booth, Anthony R.; Rowbottom, Darrell P. (eds.), *Intuitions*, Oxford: Oxford University Press, 269–86.

Carnap, Rudolf. 1950/62. *Logical Foundations of Probability*. Chicago: The University of Chicago Press.

Chalmers, David J. 2011. "Verbal Disputes." *Philosophical Review* 120(4): 515–66.

———. 2014. "Intuitions in Philosophy: A Minimal Defense." *Philosophical Studies* 171(3): 535–44.

Chappell, Sophie Grace. 2013. "Plato on Knowledge in the *Theaetetus*." In: Zalta, Edward N. (ed.), *The Stanford Encyclopedia of Philosophy* (Winter 2013 Edition), Stanford: The Metaphysics Research Lab, Center for the Study of Language and Information (Stanford University). URL: https://stanford.io/2Stjmhh (accessed 31 October 2018).

Chomsky, Noam. 1965. *Aspects of the Theory of Syntax*. Cambridge, MA: MIT Press.

Churchland, Paul M. 1981. "Eliminative Materialism and the Propositional Attitudes." *Journal of Philosophy* 78(2): 67–90.

Cohen-Eliya, Moshe; Porat, Iddo. 2015. "The Knobe Effect, Indifference, and Constitutional Law." *Law & Ethics of Human Rights* 9(2): 229–47.

Cohnitz, Daniel; Haukioja, Jussi. 2015. "Intuitions in Philosophical Semantics." *Erkenntnis* 80: 617–41.

Colaço, David; Buckwalter, Wesley; Stich, Stephen; Machery, Édouard. 2014. "Epistemic Intuitions in Fake-Barn Thought Experiments." *Episteme* 11(2): 199–212.

Colaço, David; Machery, Édouard. 2017. "The Intuitive Is a Red Herring." *Inquiry* 60(4): 403–19.

Colombo, Matteo; Duev, Georgi; Nuijten, Michèle B; Sprenger, Jan. 2018. "Statistical Reporting Inconsistencies in Experimental Philosophy." *PLoS ONE* 13(4): e0194360.

Cosmides, Leda; Tooby, John. 1992. "Cognitive Adaptations for Social Exchange." In: Barkow, Jerome H.; Cosmides, Leda; Tooby, John (eds.), *The Adapted Mind: Evolutionary Psychology and the Generation of Culture*. New York: Oxford University Press, 163–228.

Cottingham, John. 2011. "The Role of God in Descartes' Philosophy," In: Broughton, Janet; Carriero, John (eds.), *A Companion to Descartes*. Oxford: Wiley-Blackwell, 288–301.

Cova, Florian. 2016. "The Folk Concept of Intentional Action: Empirical Approaches." In: Sytsma, Justin; Buckwalter, Wesley (eds.), *A Companion to Experimental Philosophy*, Oxford: Wiley-Blackwell, 121–41.

Cova, Florian; Bertoux, Maxime; Bourgeois-Gironde, Sacha; Dubois, Bruno. 2012. "Judgments about Moral Responsibility and Determinism in Patients with Behavioural Variant of Frontotemporal Dementia: Still Compatibilists." *Consciousness and Cognition* 21(2): 851–64.

Cova, Florian; Lantian, Anthony; Boudesseul, Jordane. 2016. "Can the Knobe Effect Be Explained Away? Methodological Controversies in the Study of the Relationship between Intentionality and Morality." *Personality and Social Psychology Bulletin* 42(10): 1295–308.

Cova, Florian; Naar, Hichem. 2012. "Side-Effect Effect without Side Effects: The Pervasive Impact of Moral Considerations on Judgments of Intentionality." *Philosophical Psychology* 25(6): 837–54.

Cova, Florian; Strickland, Brent; Abatista, Angela; Allard, Aurélien; Andow, James; Attie, Mario; Beebe, James; Berniūnas, Renatas; Boudesseul, Jordane; Colombo, Matteo; Cushman, Fiery; Diaz, Rodrigo; N'Djaye, Noah; van Dongen, Nikolai; Dranseika, Vilius; Earp, Brian D.; Gaitán Torres, Antonio; Hannikainen, Ivar; Hernández-Conde, José V.; Hu, Wenjia; Jaquet, François; Khalifa, Kareem; Kim, Hanna; Kneer, Markus; Knobe, Joshua; Kurthy, Miklos; Lantian, Anthony; Liao, Shen-yi; Machery, Édouard; Moerenhout, Tania; Mott, Christian; Phelan, Mark; Phillips, Jonathan; Rambharose, Navin; Reuter, Kevin; Romero,Felipe; Sousa, Paulo; Sprenger, Jan; Thalabard, Emile; Tobia, Kevin; Viciana, Hugo; Wilkenfeld, Daniel; Zhou, Xiang. Forthcoming. "Estimating the Reproducibility of Experimental Philosophy." *Review of Philosophy and Psychology*.

Cullen, Simon. 2010. "Survey-Driven Romanticism." *Review of Philosophy and Psychology* 1(2): 275–96.

Cummins, Robert. 1998. "Reflection on Reflective Equilibrium." In: DePaul, Michael R.; Ramsey, William M. (eds.), *Rethinking Intuition: The Psychology of Intuition and Its Role in Philosophical Inquiry*, Lanham: Rowman & Littlefield, 113–28.

Cushman, Fiery; Mele, Alfred R. 2008. "Intentional Action: Two-And-A-Half Folk Concepts?" In: Knobe, Joshua; Nichols, Shaun (eds.), *Experimental Philosophy* (Vol. 1), Oxford: Oxford University Press, 170–84.

Dalbauer, Nikolaus; Hergovich, Andreas. 2013. "Is What Is Worse More Likely? The Probabilistic Explanation of the Epistemic Side-Effect Effect." *Review of Philosophy and Psychology* 4(4): 639–57.
de Cruz, Helen. 2018. "Religious Beliefs and Philosophical Views: A Qualitative Study." *Res Philosophica* 95(3): 477–504.
Dennett, Daniel. 1984. *Elbow Room: The Varieties of Free Will worth Wanting*. Oxford: Clarendon Press.
Descartes, René. 1641/1996. *Meditations on First Philosophy*. Ed. by John Cottingham. Cambridge: Cambridge University Press.
Descartes, René. 1964–1974. *Oeuvres de Descartes*. Ed. by Charles Adam & Paul Tannery. Paris: Vrin/CNRS.
Deutsch, Max. 2009. "Experimental Philosophy and the Theory of Reference." *Mind and Language* 24(4): 445–66.
———. 2010. "Intuitions, Counter-Examples, and Experimental Philosophy." *Review of Philosophy and Psychology* 1(3): 447–60.
———. 2015a. "Kripke's Gödel Case." In: Haukioja, Jussi (ed.), *Advances in Experimental Philosophy of Language*. New York: Bloomsbury Academic, 7–30.
———. 2015b. *The Myth of the Intuitive: Experimental Philosophy and Philosophical Method*. Cambridge, MA: MIT Press.
———. 2016. "Gettiers Method." In: Nado, Jennifer (ed.), *Advances in Experimental Philosophy and Philosophical Methodology*, New York: Bloomsbury Academic, 69–98.
———. 2017. "Replies to Commentators." *Inquiry* 60(4): 420–42.
Devitt, Michael. 2011. "Whither Experimental Semantics?" *Theoria* 73: 5–36.
———. 2012. "The Role of Intuitions." In: Russell, Gillian; Fara, Delia Graff (eds.), *The Routledge Companion to Philosophy of Language*. New York and London: Routledge, 554–65.
Diaz, Rodrigo; Viciana, Hugo; Gomila, Antonio. 2017. "Cold Side-Effect Effect: Affect Does Not Mediate the Influence of Moral Considerations in Intentionality Judgments." *Frontiers in Psychology* 8 (295), 1–9.
Donnellan, Keith S. 1966. "Reference and Definite Descriptions." *The Philosophical Review* 75 (3): 281–304.
Doris, John. 1998. "Persons, Situations, and Virtue Ethics." *Noûs* 32(4): 504–30.
———. 2002. *Lack of Character – Personality and Moral Behaviour*. Cambridge: Cambridge University Press.
———. 2015. *Talking to Our Selves: Reflection, Ignorance, and Agency*. Oxford: Oxford University Press.
Douven, Igor. 2016. "Experimental Approaches to the Study of Conditionals." In: Sytsma, Justin; Buckwalter, Wesley (eds.), *A Companion to Experimental Philosophy*, Oxford: Wiley-Blackwell, 545–54.
Dretske, Fred I. 1970. "Epistemic Operators." *The Journal of Philosophy* 67(24): 1007–23.
Edwards, Allen. 1953. "The Relationship between the Judged Desirability of a Trait and the Probability That the Trait Will Be Endorsed." *Journal of Applied Psychology* 37(2): 90–93.
Ekstrom, Laura. 2002. "Libertarianism and Frankfurt-Style Cases." In: Kane, Robert (eds.), *The Oxford Handbook of Free Will*, Oxford: Oxford University Press, 309–22.

Elstein, Daniel; Jenkins, Caroline S. Forthcoming. "The Truth Fairy and the Indirect Epistemic Consequentialist." In: Pedersen, Nikolaj J. L. L.; Graham, Peter J. (eds.), *Epistemic Entitlement*. Oxford: Oxford University Press.

Evans, Gareth. 1973. "The Causal Theory of Names." *Proceedings of the Aristotelian Society, Supplementary Volumes* 47: 187–208.

Feltz, Adam; Cokely, Edward T. 2009. "Do Judgments about Freedom and Responsibility Depend on Who You Are? Personality Differences in Intuitions about Compatibilism and Incompatibilism." *Consciousness and Cognition* 18(1): 342–50.

———. 2016. "Personality and Philosophical Bias." In: Sytsma, Justin; Buckwalter, Wesley (eds.), *A Companion to Experimental Philosophy*. Oxford: Wiley-Blackwell, 578–89.

Feltz, Adam; Cokely, Edward T.; Nadelhoffer, Thomas. 2009. "Natural Compatibilism versus Natural Incompatibilism: Back to the Drawing Board." *Mind and Language* 24(1): 1–23.

Feltz, Adam; Cova, Florian. 2014. "Moral Responsibility and Free Will: A Meta-Analysis." *Consciousness and Cognition* 30: 234–46.

Feltz, Adam; Millan, Melissa. 2015. "An Error Theory for Compatibilist Intuitions." *Philosophical Psychology* 28(4): 529–55.

Fischer, Eugen; Curtis, Mark (eds.). 2019. *Methodological Advances in Experimental Philosophy*. London: Bloomsbury.

Frankfurt, Harry G. 1969. "Alternate Possibilities and Moral Responsibility." *The Journal of Philosophy* 66(23): 829–39.

Frege, Gottlob. 1892. "Über Sinn und Bedeutung." *Zeitschrift für Philosophie und Philosophische Kritik* 100(1): 25–50.

Gettier, Edmund L. 1963. "Is Justified True Belief Knowledge?" *Analysis* 23(6): 121–23.

Glock, Hans-Johann. 2008. *What Is Analytic Philosophy?* Cambridge: Cambridge University Press.

Goldman, Alvin I. 2007. "Philosophical Intuitions: Their Target, Their Source, and Their Epistemic Status." *Grazer Philosophische Studien* 74: 1–26.

Goodnick, Liz. 2016. "A De Jure Criticism of Theism." *Open Theology* 2, 23–33.

Graham, George; Horgan, Terry. 1994. "Southern Fundamentalism and the End of Philosophy." *Philosophical Issues* 5: 219–47.

Greene, Joshua D. 2008. "The Secret Joke of Kant's Soul." In: Sinnott-Armstrong, Walter (ed.), *Moral Psychology (Vol. 3): The Neuroscience of Morality – Emotion, Brain Disorders, and Development*. Cambridge, Massachusetts: MIT Press, 35–80.

———. 2014. "Beyond Point-and-Shoot Morality: Why Cognitive (Neuro)Science Matters for Ethics." *Ethics* 124(4): 695–726.

Greene, Joshua D.; Sommerville, R. Brian; Nystrom, Leigh N.; Cohen, Jonathan D. 2001. "An fMRI Investigation of Emotional Engagement in Moral Judgment." *Science* 293(5537): 2105–8.

Grice, Paul. 1989. *Studies in the Way of Words*. Cambridge, MA: Harvard University Press.

Griffiths, Paul E.; Machery, Édouard; Linquist, Stefan. 2009. "The Vernacular Concept of Innateness." *Mind and Language* 24(5): 605–30.

Griffiths, Paul E.; Stotz, Karola. 2008. "Experimental Philosophy of Science." *Philosophy Compass* 3/3 (2008): 507–21.

Griggs, Richard A.; Cox, James R. 1983. "The Effects of Problem Content and Negation on Wason's Selection Task." *Quarterly Journal of Experimental Psychology* 35(3), 519–33.

Grundherr, Michael. 2016. "Order Ethics and Situationist Psychology." In: Luetge, Christoph; Mukerji, Nikil (eds.), *Order Ethics – An Ethical Framework for the Social Market Economy*. Dordrecht: Springer, 79–92.

Grundmann, Thomas. 2010. "Some Hope for Intuitions: A Reply to Weinberg." *Philosophical Psychology* 23(4): 481–509.

Haidt, Jonathan; Koller, Silvia H.; Dias, Maria G. 1993. "Affect, Culture, and Morality, or Is It Wrong to Eat Your Dog?" *Journal of Personality and Social Psychology* 65(4): 613–28.

Hales, Steven D. 2006. *Relativism and the Foundations of Philosophy*. Cambridge, MA: MIT Press.

———. 2012. "The Faculty of Intuition." *Analytic Philosophy* 53(2): 180–207.

Harman, Gilbert. 1976. "Practical Reasoning." *The Review of Metaphysics* 29(3): 431–63.

———. 1999a. *Reasoning, Meaning, and Mind*. Oxford: Oxford University Press.

———. 1999b. "Moral Philosophy Meets Social Psychology: Virtue Ethics and the Fundamental Attribution Error." *Proceedings of the Aristotelian Society* 99: 315–31.

Heinzelmann, Nora. 2018. "Deontology Defended." *Synthese* 195(12): 5197–216.

Henrich, Joseph; Heine, Steven J.; Norenzayan, Ara. 2010. "The Weirdest People in the World?" *Behavioral and Brain Sciences* 33(2–3): 61–83.

Hertwig, Ralph; Ortmann, Andreas. 2001. "Experimental Practices in Economics: A Methodological Challenge for Psychologists?" *Behavioral and Brain Sciences* 24(3): 383–403.

Hintikka, Jaakko. 1999. "The Emperor's New Intuitions." *The Journal of Philosophy* 96(3): 127–47.

Hitchcock, Christopher; Knobe, Joshua. 2009. "Cause and Norm." *Journal of Philosophy* 106 (11): 587–612.

Hobbes, Thomas. 1651/1995. *Leviathan*. Oxford: Blackwell.

Hume, David. 1739–40/1960. *A Treatise of Human Nature*. Oxford: Clarendon Press.

———. 1757/2007. "The Natural History of Religion." (1757) In: Beauchamp, T.L. (ed.), *A Dissertation on the Passions, The Natural History of religion: A Critical Edition*. Oxford: Clarendon Press.

Ichikawa, Jonathan J. 2012. "Experimentalist Pressure against Traditional Methodology." *Philosophical Psychology* 25(5): 743–65.

Ichikawa, Jonathan J.; Maitra, Ishani; Weatherson, Brian. 2012. "In Defense of a Kripkean Dogma." *Philosophy and Phenomenological Research* 85(1): 56–68.

Jackson D Frank. 1998. *From Metaphysics to Ethics*. Oxford: Oxford University Press.

James, William. 1907/1921. *Pragmatism*. New York: Longmans, Green and Co.

Jauernig, Johanna. 2017. *Using Experiments in Ethics – an Inquiry into the Dark Side of Competition* (Manuscript). URL: https://bit.ly/2MYc71V (accessed 31 October 2018).

Jong, Jonathan. 2012. "Explaining Religion (Away?): Theism and the Cognitive Science of Religion." *Sophia 52*: 521–33.

Jong, Jonathan; Visala, Aku. 2014. "Evolutionary Debunking Arguments against Theism, Reconsidered." *International Journal for Philosophy of Religion* 76(3): 243–58.

Joyce, Richard. 2006a. *The Evolution of Morality*. Cambridge, MA.: MIT Press.

———. 2006b. "Metaethics and the Empirical Sciences." *Philosophical Explorations* 9(1): 133–48.

Kahane, Guy. 2010. "Evolutionary Debunking Arguments." *Noûs* 45(1): 103–25.

Kahneman, Daniel. 2003. "Maps of Bounded Rationality: Psychology for Behavioral Economics." *American Economic Review* 93(5): 1449–75.

Kane, Robert (ed.). 2002. *The Oxford Handbook of Free Will*. Oxford: Oxford University Press.

———. 2005. *A Contemporary Introduction to Free Will*. Oxford: Oxford University Press.

Kass, Leon R. 1997. "The Wisdom of Repugnance." *The New Republic* (02 June 1997), 17–26.

Kauppinen, Antti. 2007. "The Rise and Fall of Experimental Philosophy." *Philosophical Explorations* 10(2): 95–118.

Khalidi, Muhammad A. 2016. "Innateness as a Natural Cognitive Kind." *Philosophical Psychology* 29(3): 319–33.

Kim, Minsun; Yuan, Yuan. 2015. "No Cross-Cultural Differences in the Gettier Car Case Intuition: A Replication Study of Weinberg et al. 2001." *Episteme* 12(3): 355–61.

Knobe, Joshua. 2003. "Intentional Action and Side Effects in Ordinary Language." *Analysis* 63(3): 190–94.

———. 2004. "Intention, Intentional Action and Moral Considerations." *Analysis* 64(2): 181–87.

———. 2007a. "Experimental Philosophy." *Philosophy Compass* 2(1): 81–92.

———. 2007b. "Reason Explanation in Folk Psychology." *Midwest Studies in Philosophy* 31(1): 90–106.

———. 2008. "The Concept of Intentional Action." Knobe, Joshua; Nichols, Shaun (eds.), *Experimental Philosophy* (Vol. 1), Oxford: Oxford University Press, 129–48.

———. 2010. "A Return to Tradition." *The New York Times*. URL: http://nyti.ms/1ZhiAkY (accessed 31 October 2018).

———. 2014a. "Person as Scientist, Person as Moralist." In: Knobe, Joshua; Nichols, Shaun (eds.), *Experimental Philosophy (Vol. 2)*, New York: Routledge, 195–228.

———. 2014b. "Free Will and the Scientific Vision." In: Machery, Édouard; O'Neill, Elizabeth (eds.), *Current Controversies in Experimental Philosophy*. New York: Routledge, 69–85.

———. 2015a. "New Study: No Difference in Gettier Intuition across Cultures" (Blog-Post). URL: http://bit.ly/1tycVws (accessed 31 October 2018).

———. 2015b. "What Has Experimental Philosophy Discovered about Demographic Effects?" (Blog-Post). URL: http://bit.ly/1W1clCd (accessed 31 August 2018).

———. 2015c. "Philosophers Are Doing Something Different Now: Quantitative Data." *Cognition* 135: 36–38.

———. 2016. "Experiment Philosophy Is Cognitive Science." In: Sytsma, Justin; Buckwalter, Wesley (eds.), *A Companion to Experimental Philosophy*. Oxford: Wiley-Blackwell, 37–52.

Knobe, Joshua; Burra, Arudra. 2006. "The Folk Concepts of Intention and Intentional Action: A Cross-Cultural Study." *Journal of Cognition and Culture* 6(1–2): 113–32.

Knobe, Joshua; Mendlow, Gabriel S. 2004. "The Good, the Bad and the Blameworthy: Understanding the Role of Evaluative Reasoning in Folk Psychology." *Journal of Theoretical and Philosophical Psychology* 24(2): 252–58.

Knobe, Joshua; Nichols, Shaun. 2008. "An Experimental Philosophy Manifesto." Knobe, Joshua; Nichols, Shaun (eds.), *Experimental Philosophy* (Vol. 1), Oxford: Oxford University Press, 3–14.

Knobe, Joshua; Prinz, Jesse. 2008. "Intuitions about Consciousness: Experimental Studies." *Phenomenology and the Cognitive Sciences* 7(1): 67–83.

Knobe, Joshua; Samuels, Richard. 2013. "Thinking like a Scientist: Innateness as a Case Study." *Cognition* 126(1): 72–86.

Königs, Peter. 2018. "Two Types of Debunking Arguments." *Philosophical Psychology* 31(3): 383–402.

Kornblith, Hilary. 2007. "Naturalism and Intuitions." *Grazer Philosophische Studien* 74: 27–49.

Kramer, Roderick M.; Messick, David M. 1996. "Ethical Cognition and the Framing of Organisational Dilemmas: Decision Makers as Intuitive Lawyers." In: Messick, David M.; Tenbrunsel, Ann E. (eds.), *Codes of Conduct: Behavioral Research into Business Ethics*. New York: Russell Sage Foundation, 59–85.

Kripke, Saul. 1972/1980. *Naming and Necessity*. Cambridge, MA: Harvard University Press.

———. 1977. "Speaker's Reference and Semantic Reference." *Midwest Studies in Philosophy* 2(1): 255–76.

Kumar, Victor; Campbell, Richmond. 2012. "On the Normative Significance of Experimental Moral Psychology." *Philosophical Psychology* 25(3): 311–30.

Lam, Barry. 2010. "Are Cantonese-Speakers Really Descriptivists? Revisiting Cross-Cultural Semantics." *Cognition* 115(2): 320–29.

Lehrer, Keith. 1990. *Theory of Knowledge*. Boulder, CO: Westview Press.

Leslie, Alan M.; Knobe, Joshua; Cohen, Adam. 2006. "Acting Intentionally and the Side-Effect Effect." *Psychological Science* 17(5): 421–27.

Levin, Janet. 2005. "The Evidential Status of Philosophical Intuitions." *Philosophical Studies* 121(3): 193–224.

Lewis, David. 1973/2001. *Counterfactuals*. Oxford: Basil Blackwell.

———. 1983. *Philosophical Papers (Vol. 1)*. New York: Oxford University Press.

Li, Jincai; Liu, Longgen; Chalmers, Elizabeth; Snedeker, Jesse. 2018. "What Is in a Name?" *Cognition* 171: 108–11.

Libet, Benjamin. 2002. "Do We Have Free Will?" In: Kane, Robert (ed.), *The Oxford Handbook of Free Will*. Oxford: Oxford University Press, 551–64.

Linquist, Stefan. 2018. "The Conceptual Critique of Innateness." *Philosophy Compass* 13 (5): e12492.

Locke, John. 1710/1975. *An Essay Concerning Human Understanding*. Oxford: Clarendon Press.
Lombrozo, Tania. 2006. "The Structure and Function of Explanations." *Trends in Cognitive Sciences* 10(10): 464–70.
———. 2009. "Explanation and Categorization: How 'Why?' Informs 'What?'." *Cognition* 110 (2): 248–53.
Ludwig, Kirk. 2007. "The Epistemology of Thought Experiments: First Person versus Third Person Approaches." *Midwest Studies in Philosophy* 31(1): 128–59.
Luetge, Christoph; Mukerji, Nikil (eds.). 2016. *Order Ethics – An Ethical Framework for the Social Market Economy*. Dordrecht: Springer.
Luetge, Christoph; Rusch, Hannes; Uhl, Matthias (eds.). 2014. *Experimental Ethics: Toward an Empirical Moral Philosophy*. London: Palgrave Macmillan.
Machery, Édouard. 2012. "Expertise and Intuitions about Reference." *Theoria* 73(1): 37–54.
———. 2014. "What Is the Significance of the Demographic Variation in Semantic Intuitions?" In: Machery, Édouard; O'Neill, Elizabeth (eds.), *Current Controversies in Experimental Philosophy*. New York: Routledge, 3–16.
———. 2016. "Experimental Philosophy of Science." In: Sytsma, Justin; Buckwalter, Wesley (eds.), *A Companion to Experimental Philosophy*. Oxford: Wiley-Blackwell, 475–90.
Machery, Édouard; Cohen, Kara. 2012. "An Evidence-Based Study of the Evolutionary Behavioral Sciences." *The British Journal for the Philosophy of Science* 63: 177–226.
Machery, Édouard; Deutsch, Max; Mallon, Ron; Nichols, Shaun; Sytsma, Justin; Stich, Stephen. 2010. "Semantic Intuitions: Reply to Lam." *Cognition* 117(3): 361–66.
Machery, Édouard; Mallon, Ron; Nichols, Shaun; Stich, Stephen. 2004. "Semantics, Cross-Cultural Style." *Cognition* 92(3): B1–B12.
Machery, Édouard; Stich, Stephen; Rose, David; Chatterjee, Amita; Karasawa, Kaori; Struchiner, Noel; Sirker, Smita; Usui, Naoki; Hashimoto, Takaaki. 2015. "Gettier across Cultures." *Noûs (Early View)*.
Machery, Édouard; Sytsma, Justin; Deutsch, Max. 2015. "Speaker's Reference and Cross-Cultural Semantics." In: Bianchi, Andrea (ed.), *On Reference*, Oxford: Oxford University Press, 62–76.
Makel, Matthew C.; Plucker, Jonathan A.; Hegarty, Boyd. 2012. "Replications in Psychology Research: How Often Do They Really Occur?" *Perspectives on Psychological Science: A Journal of the Association for Psychological Science* 7(6): 537–42.
Malle, Bertram F.; Nelson, Sarah E. 2003. "Judging Mens Rea: The Tension between Folk Concepts and Legal Concepts of Intentionality." *Behavioral Sciences and the Law* 21(5): 563–80.
Mallon, Ron; Machery, Édouard; Nichols, Shaun; Stich, Stephen. 2009. "Against Arguments from Reference." *Philosophy and Phenomenological Research* 79(2): 332–56.
Mandelbaum, Eric; Ripley, David. 2012. "Explaining the Abstract/Concrete Paradoxes in Moral Psychology: The NBAR Hypothesis." *Review of Philosophical Psychology* 3(3): 351–68.

Mangan, Katherina. 2019. "Proceedings Start Against 'Sokal Squared' Hoax Professor." *The Chronicle of Higher Education* 18(65). URL: https://www.chronicle.com/article/Proceedings-Start-Against/245431.

McIntyre, Alison. 2014. "Doctrine of Double Effect." In: Zalta, Edward N. (ed.), *The Stanford Encyclopedia of Philosophy* (Winter 2014 Edition), Stanford: The Metaphysics Research Lab, Center for the Study of Language and Information (Stanford University). URL: https://stanford.io/2Mxmppw (accessed 31 October 2018).

Meehl, Paul E. 1992. "Cliometric Metatheory: The Actuarial Approach to Empirical, History-Based Philosophy of Science." *Psychological Reports* 71: 339–467.

———. 2002. "Cliometric Metatheory II: Criteria Scientists Use in Theory Appraisal and Why It Is Rational to Do So." *Psychological Reports* 91: 339–404.

———. 2004. "Cliometric Metatheory III: Peircean Consensus, Verisimilitude and Asymptotic Method." *British Journal for the Philosophy of Science* 55: 615–43.

Mele, Alfred R.; Cushman, Fiery. 2007. "Intentional Action, Folk Judgments, and Stories: Sorting Things Out." *Midwest Studies in Philosophy* 31(1): 184–201.

Michael, John A.; Szigeti, András. 2018. "The Group Knobe Effect: Evidence That People Intuitively Attribute Agency and Responsibility to Groups." *Philosophical Explorations* (Online first).URL: https://doi.org/10.1080/13869795.2018.1492007 (accessed 31 October 2018).

Michelin, Corinna; Pellizzoni, Sandra; Tallandini, Maria A.; Siegal, Michael. 2010. "Evidence for the Side-Effect Effect in Young Children: Influence of Bilingualism and Task Presentation Format." *European Journal of Developmental Psychology* 7(6): 641–52.

Mill, John Stuart. 1859. *On Liberty*. London: John W. Parker & Son.

———. 1882/1976. *A System of Logic Ratiocinative and Inductive. (Collected Works, Vol. 8)*. Ed. by J. M. Robson. Toronto: University of Toronto Press.

Mittelstadt, Brent; Floridi, Luciano. 2016. "The Ethics of Big Data: Current and Foreseeable Issues in Biomedical Contexts." *Science and Engineering Ethics* 22(2): 303–41.

Mizrahi, Moti. 2012. "Intuition Mongering." *The Reasoner* 6(11): 169–70.

Moser, Paul K. 1999. "Metaphilosophy." In: Audi, Robert (ed.), *The Cambridge Dictionary of Philosophy*, Cambridge: Cambridge University Press, 561–62.

Mortensen, Kaija; Nagel, Jennifer. 2016. "Armchair-Friendly Experimental Philosophy." In: Sytsma, Justin; Buckwalter, Wesley (eds.), *A Companion to Experimental Philosophy*. Oxford: Blackwell-Wiley, 53–70.

Mukerji, Nikil. 2014. "Intuitions, Experiments, and Armchairs." In: Luetge, Christoph; Rusch, Hannes; Uhl, Matthias (eds.), *Experimental Ethics: Toward an Empirical Moral Philosophy*, London: Palgrave Macmillan, 227–43.

———. 2015. "Experimentelle Ethik." In: Nida-Rümelin, Julian; Spiegel, Irina; Tiedemann, Markus (eds.), *Handbuch Philosophie und Ethik (Vol. 2): Disziplinen und Themen*. Ferdinand Schöningh: Paderborn, 93–101.

———. 2016. *The Case Against Consequentialism Reconsidered*. Dordrecht: Springer.

———. 2017. *Die 10 Gebote des gesunden Menschenverstands*. Heidelberg: Springer.

———. 2018. "What is Fake News?" *Ergo* 5(35), 923–46. http://dx.doi.org/10.3998/ergo.12405314.0005.035

Mukerji, Nikil. Luetge, Christoph. 2014. "Responsibility, Order Ethics, and Group Agency." *Archives for Philosophy of Law and Social Philosophy* 100(2): 176–86.

Mukerji, Nikil; Schumacher, Christoph. 2016a. "Order Ethics, Economics, and Game Theory." In: Luetge, Christoph; Mukerji, Nikil (eds.), *Order Ethics – An Ethical Framework for the Social Market Economy*. Dordrecht: Springer, 93–107.

———. 2016b. "Is the Minimum-Wage Ethically Justifiable? an Order-Ethical Answer." In: Luetge, Christoph; Mukerji, Nikil (eds.), *Order Ethics – An Ethical Framework for the Social Market Economy*. Dordrecht: Springer, 279–92.

Müller-Lyer, Franz C. 1889. "Optische Urtheilstäuschungen." *Archiv für Anatomie und Physiologie, Physiologische Abteilung 2 (Supplement)*: 263–70.

Murray, Dylan; Nahmias, Eddy. 2014. "Explaining Away Incompatibilist Intuitions." *Philosophy and Phenomenological Research* 88(2): 434–67.

Nadelhoffer, Thomas. 2004a. "Blame, Badness, and Intentional Action: A Reply to Knobe and Mendlow." *Journal of Theoretical and Philosophical Psychology* 24(2): 259–69.

———. 2004b. "On Praise, Side Effects, and Folk Ascriptions of Intentionality." *Journal of Theoretical and Philosophical Psychology* 24(2): 196–213.

Nadelhoffer, Thomas; Nahmias, Eddy. 2007. "The Past and Future of Experimental Philosophy." *Philosophical Explorations* 10(2): 123–49.

Nado, Jennifer. 2015. "Intuition, Philosophical Theorising, and the Threat of Scepticism." In: Fischer, Eugen; Collins, John (eds.), *Experimental Philosophy, Rationalism, and Naturalism: Rethinking Philosophical Method*. London: Routledge, 204–21.

———. 2016. "The Intuition Deniers." *Philosophical Studies* 173(3): 781–800.

———. 2017. "Demythologizing Intuition." *Inquiry* 60(4): 386–402.

Nagel, Jennifer; Juan, Valerie S.; Mar, Raymond A. 2013. "Lay Denial of Knowledge for Justified True Beliefs." *Cognition* 129(3): 652–61.

Nahmias, Eddy; Coates, Justin; Kvaran, Trevor. 2007. "Free Will, Moral Responsibility, and Mechanism: Experiments on Folk Intuitions." *Midwest Studies in Philosophy* 31: 214–42.

Nahmias, Eddy; Morris, Stephen G.; Nadelhoffer, Thomas; Turner, Jason. 2005. "Surveying Freedom: Folk Intuitions about Free Will and Moral Responsibility." *Philosophical Psychology* 18(5): 561–84.

———. 2006. "Is Incompatibilism Intuitive?" *Philosophy and Phenomenological Research* 73(1): 28–53.

Nahmias, Eddy; Murray, Dylan. 2011. "Experimental Philosophy on Free Will: An Error Theory for Incompatibilist Intuitions." In: Aguilar, Jesús H.; Buckareff, Andrei A.; Frankish, Keith (eds.), *New Waves in Philosophy of Action*, Basingstoke: Palgrave Macmillan, 189–216.

Nahmias, Eddy; Thompson, Morgan. 2014. "A Naturalistic Vision of Free Will." In: Machery, Édouard; O'Neill, Elizabeth (eds.), *Current Controversies in Experimental Philosophy*, New York: Routledge, 86–103.

Nichols, Shaun. 2014. "Process Debunking and Ethics." *Ethics* 124(4): 727–49.

Nichols, Shaun; Bruno, Michael. 2010. "Intuitions about Personal Identity: An Empirical Study." *Philosophical Psychology* 23(3): 293–312.

Nichols, Shaun; Knobe, Joshua. 2007. "Moral Responsibility and Determinism: The Cognitive Science of Folk Intuitions." *Noûs* 41(4): 663–85.

Nichols, Shaun; Ulatowski, Joseph. 2007. "Intuitions and Individual Differences: The Knobe Effect Revisited." *Mind and Language* 22(4): 346–65.

Nida-Rümelin, Julian. 1997a. *Economic Rationality and Practical Reason*. Dordrecht: Springer.
———. 1997b. "Why Consequentialism Fails." In: Holmström-Hintikka, Ghita; Tuomela, Raimo (eds.), *Contemporary Action Theory*. Dordrecht: Kluwer Academic Pub, 295–308.
———. 2009. *Philosophie und Lebensform*. Frankfurt: Suhrkamp.
———. 2016. *Humanistische Reflexionen*. Berlin: Suhrkamp.
———. 2018. *Structural Rationality and Other Essays on Practical Reason*. Dordrecht: Springer.
Nisbett, Richard E.; Peng, Kaiping; Choi, Incheol; Norenzayan, Ara. 2001. "Culture and Systems of Thought: Holistic Versus Analytic Cognition." *Psychological Review* 108(2): 291–310.
Nietzsche, Friedrich. 1878/1986. *Human, All-Too-Human: A Book for Free Spirits*. Cambridge: Cambridge University Press.
Norcross, Alastair. 2008. "Off Her Trolley? Frances Kamm and the Metaphysics of Morality." *Utilitas* 20(1): 65–80.
O'Shaughnessy, Brain. 1973. "Trying (as the Mental 'Pineal Gland')." *The Journal of Philosophy* 70(13): 365–85.
Ostermaier, Andreas; Uhl, Matthias. 2017. "Spot on for Liars! How Public Scrutiny Influences Ethical Behavior." *PLoS ONE* 12(7): e0181682.
Paulo, Norbert. Forthcoming. "In Search of Green's Argument." *Utilitas*.
Pellizzoni, Sandra; Siegal, Michael; Surian, Luca. 2009. "Foreknowledge, Caring, and the Side-Effect Effect in Young Children." *Developmental Psychology* 45(1): 289–95.
Perler, Dominik. 1998. *René Descartes*. München: C. H. Beck.
Pettit, Dean; Knobe, Joshua. 2009. "The Pervasive Impact of Moral Judgment." *Mind and Language* 24(5): 586–604.
Pfeifer, Niki. 2012. "Experiments on Aristotle's Thesis: Towards an Experimental Philosophy of Conditionals." *The Monist* 95(2): 223–40.
———. 2014. "Reasoning about Uncertain Conditionals." *Studia Logica*, 102(4): 849–66.
Pfeifer, Niki; Douven, Igor. 2014. "Formal Epistemology and the New Paradigm Psychology of Reasoning." *The Review of Philosophy and Psychology* 5(2): 199–221.
Pfeifer, Niki; Kleiter, Gernot D. 2010. "The Conditional in Mental Probability Logic." In: Oaksford, Mike; Chater, Nick (eds.), *Cognition and Conditionals: Probability and Logic in Human Thought*. Oxford: Oxford University Press, 153–73.
———. 2011. "Uncertain Deductive Reasoning." In: Manktelow, Ken; Over, David E.; Elqayam, Shira (eds.), *The Science of Reason: A Festschrift for Jonathan St B.T. Evans*. Hove: Psychology Press, 145–66.
Pfeifer, Niki; Pankka, Hanna. 2017. "Modeling the Ellsberg Paradox by Argument Strength." In: Gunzelmann, Glenn; Howes, Andrew; Tenbrink, Thora; Davelaar, Eddy (eds.). *Proceedings of the 39th Cognitive Science Society Meeting*, 925–30.
Pfeifer, Niki; Sanfilippo, Giuseppe. 2017. "Probabilistic Squares and Hexagons of Opposition under Coherence." *International Journal of Approximate Reasoning* 88: 282–94.

Pfeifer, Niki; Tulkki, Leena. 2017. "Conditionals, Counterfactuals, and Rational Reasoning: An Experimental Study on Basic Principles." *Minds and Machines* 27(1): 119–65.

Pinder, Mark. 2017. "The Explication Defence of Arguments from Reference." *Erkenntnis* 82: 1253–76.

Pink, Thomas. 2004. *Free Will: A Very Short Introduction*. Oxford: Oxford University Press.

Pinker, Steven. 2008. "The Stupidity of Dignity." *The New Republic* (28 May 2008).

Planck, Max. 1923. *Kausalgesetz und Willensfreiheit: Öffentlicher Vortrag gehalten an der Preussischen Akademie der Wissenschaften am 17. Februar 1923*. Berlin: Springer.

Plato. 1997. *Complete Works*. Ed. by Cooper, John M. Indianapolis, IN: Hackett.

Pluckrose, Helen; Lindsay, James A.; Boghossian, Peter. 2018. "Academic Grievance Studies and the Corruption of Scholarship." *Areo Magazine*. URL: https://areomagazine.com/2018/10/02/academic-grievance-studies-and-the-corruption-of-scholarship (accessed 31 Oct 2018).

Priest, Graham. 1995/2002. *Beyond the Limits of Thought*. Cambridge: Cambridge University Press.

Prinz, Jesse. 2008. "Empirical Philosophy and Experimental Philosophy." Knobe, Joshua; Nichols, Shaun (eds.), *Experimental Philosophy* (Vol. 1), Oxford: Oxford University Press, 189–208.

———. 2010. "Ethics and Psychology." In: Skorupski, John (ed.), *The Routledge Companion to Ethics,* New York: Routledge, 384–96.

Pust, Joel. 2014. "Intuition." In: Zalta, Edward N. (ed.), *The Stanford Encyclopedia of Philosophy* (Fall 2014 Edition), Stanford: The Metaphysics Research Lab, Center for the Study of Language and Information (Stanford University). URL: http://stanford.io/1XYnbLh (accessed 31 October 2018).

Rawls, John. 2003. *Justice as Fairness: A Restatement*. Cambridge: Harvard University Press.

Reichenbach, Hans. 1938/1983. *Erfahrung und Prognose: Eine Analyse der Grundlagen und der Struktur der Erkenntnis*. Braunschweig: Vieweg.

Ridge, Michael. 2015. "Naïve Practical Reasoning and the Second-Person Standpoint: Simple Reasons for Simple People?" *Journal of Value Inquiry* 49(1–2): 17–30.

Ripley, David. 2016. "Experimental Philosophical Logic." In: Sytsma, Justin; Buckwalter, Wesley (eds.), *A Companion to Experimental Philosophy*, Oxford: Wiley-Blackwell, 523–34.

Rodgers, Travis J.; Warmke, Brandon. 2015. "Situationism versus Situationism." *Ethical Theory and Moral Practice* 18(1): 9–26.

Rose, David; Danks, David. 2012. "Causation: Empirical Trends and Future Directions." *Philosophy Compass* 7(9): 643–53.

———. 2013. "In Defense of a Broad Conception of Experimental Philosophy." *Metaphilosophy* 44(4): 512–32.

Rosenthal, Robert. 1976. *Experimenter Effects in Behavioral Research*. New York: John Wiley & Sons.

Rosenthal, Robert; Fode, Kermit L. 1963. "The Effect of Experimenter Bias on the Performance of the Albino Rat." *Behavioral Science* 8(3): 183–89.

Rosenthal, Robert; Persinger, Gordon W.; Mulry, Ray C.; Vikan-Kline, Linda; Grothe; Mardell. 1964. "Changes in Experimental Hypotheses as Determinants of Experimental Results." *Journal of Projective Techniques and Personality Assessment* 28(4): 465–69.

Rosenthal, Robert; Persinger, Gordon W.; Vikan-Kline, Linda; Mulry, Ray C. 1963. "The Role of the Research Assistant in the Mediation of Experimenter Bias." *Journal of Personality* 31(3): 313–35.

Russell, Bertrand. 1905. "On Denoting." *Mind* 14(56): 479–93.

———. 1918/2004. *Mysticism and Logic*. Mineola, NY: Dover Publications.

———. 1948. *Human Knowledge – Its Scope and Limits*. London: George Allen & Unwin.

Ryle, Gilbert. 1949/2002. *The Concept of Mind*. Chicago: The University of Chicago Press.

Samuels, Richard; Stich, Stephen. 2004. "Rationality and Psychology." In: Mele, Alfred R.; Rawling, Piers (eds.), *The Oxford Handbook of Rationality*. Oxford: Oxford University Press, 279–300.

Sanfilippo, Giuseppe; Pfeifer, Niki; Over, David E.; Gilio, Angelo. 2018. "Probabilistic Inferences from Conjoined to Iterated Conditionals." *International Journal of Approximate Reasoning* 93: 103–18.

Sarkissian, Hagop; Chatterjee, Amita; de Brigard, Felipe; Knobe, Joshua; Nichols, Shaun; Sirker, Smita. 2010. "Is Belief in Free Will a Cultural Universal?" *Mind and Language* 25(3): 346–58.

Sartwell, Crispin. 1991. "Knowledge Is Merely True Belief." *American Philosophical Quarterly* 28(2): 157–65.

Schupbach, Jonah N. 2016. "Experimental Philosophy Meets Formal Epistemology." In: Sytsma, Justin; Buckwalter, Wesley (eds.), *A Companion to Experimental Philosophy*, Oxford: Wiley-Blackwell, 535–44.

———. 2017. "Experimental Explication." *Philosophy and Phenomenological Research* 94(3): 672–710.

Schwitzgebel, Eric; Cushman, Fiery. 2012. "Expertise in Moral Reasoning? Order Effects on Moral Judgment in Professional Philosophers and Non-Philosophers." *Mind and Language* 27(2): 135–53.

———. 2015. "Philosophers' Biased Judgments Persist Despite Training, Expertise and Reflection." *Cognition* 141: 127–37.

Searle, John R. 1983. *Intentionality: An Essay in the Philosophy of Mind*. Cambridge: Cambridge University Press.

———. 2007. *Freedom and Neurobiology: Reflections on Free Will, Language, and Political Power*. New York: Columbia University Press.

Segall, Marshall H.; Campbell, Donald T.; Herskovits, Melville J. 1966. *The Influence of Culture on Visual Perception*. Indianapolis: Bobbs-Merrill.

Seyedsayamdost, Hamid. 2014. "On Gender and Philosophical Intuition: Failure of Replication and Other Negative Results." *Philosophical Psychology* 28(5): 642–73.

———. 2015. "On Normativity and Epistemic Intuitions: Failure of Replication." *Episteme* 12(1): 95–116.

Shafer-Landau, Russ. 2006. "Ethics as Philosophy – A Defense of Ethical Non-naturalism." In: Horgan, Terry; Timmons, Mark (eds.), *Metaethics after Moore*. Oxford: Oxford University Press, 209–32.

Shea, Christopher. 2008. "Against Intuition." *The Chronicle of Higher Education* (3 Oct 2008): B8–B12.

Shepherd, Joshua; Justus, James. 2015. "X-Phi and Carnapian Explication." *Erkenntnis* 80(2): 381–402.

Sidgwick, Henry. 1907. *The Methods of Ethics*. London: Hackett Publishing.

Simons, Daniel J.; Chabris, Christopher F. 1999. "Gorillas in Our Midst: Sustained Inattentional Blindness for Dynamic Events." *Perception* 28: 1059–74.

Singer, Peter. 2005. "Ethics and Intuitions." *The Journal of Ethics* 9(3–4): 331–52.

Sinnott-Armstrong, Walter. 2008. "Framing Moral Intuitions." In: Sinnott-Armstrong, Walter (ed.), *Moral Psychology (Vol. 2): The Cognitive Science of Morality: Intuition and Diversity*. Cambridge, MA: MIT Press, 47–76.

Sokal, Alan. 1996. "Transgressing the Boundaries: Towards a Transformative Hermeneutics of Quantum Gravity." *Social Text* 46/47: 217–52.

Sokal, Alan; Bricmont, Jean. 1998. *Fashionable Nonsense: Postmodern Intellectuals' Abuse of Science*. New York: Picador.

Sorokowski, Piotr; Kulczycki, Emanuel; Sorokowska, Agnieszka; Pisanski, Katarzyna. 2017. "Predatory Journals Recruit Fake Editor." *Nature* 543(7646): 481–83.

Sosa, Ernest. 2007. "Experimental Philosophy and Philosophical Intuition." *Philosophical Studies* 132(1): 99–107.

Stern, Robert. 2000. *Transcendental Arguments and Skepticism*. Oxford: Oxford University Press.

Stevenson, Charles L. S. 1937. "The Emotive Meaning of Ethical Terms." *Mind* 46(181): 14–31.

———. 1938. "Persuasive Definitions." *Mind* 47(187): 331–50.

Stich, Stephen. 1990. *The Fragmentation of Reason*. Cambridge, Massachusetts: MIT Press.

———. 2001. "Plato's Method Meets Cognitive Science." *Free Inquiry* 21(2): 36–38.

———. 2010. "Philosophy and WEIRD intuition." *Behavioral and Brain Sciences* 33(2–3): 110–11.

Stich, Stephen; Tobia, Kevin P. 2016. "Experimental Philosophy and the Philosophical Tradition." In: Sytsma, Justin; Buckwalter, Wesley (eds.), *A Companion to Experimental Philosophy*, Oxford: Wiley-Blackwell, 5–21.

Stotz, Karola. 2009. "Experimental Philosophy of Biology: Notes from the Field." *Studies in History and Philosophy of Science* 40: 233–37.

Stotz, Karola. Griffiths, Paul E. 2004. "Genes: Philosophical Analyses Put to the Test." *History and Philosophy of the Life Sciences* 26 (2004): 5–28.

Stotz, Karola. Griffiths, Paul E.; Knight, Rob D. 2004. "How Scientists Conceptualize Genes: An Empirical Study." *Studies in History and Philosophy of Biological and Biomedical Sciences* 35(4): 647–73.

Strawson, Galen. 1986. *Freedom and belief*. Oxford: Oxford University Press.

Strevens, Michael. 2019. *Thinking off Your Feet: How Empirical Psychology Vindicates Armchair Philosophy*. Cambridge, MA: Harvard University Press.

Strickland, Brent; Suben, Aysu. 2012. "Experimenter Philosophy: The Problem of Experimenter Bias in Experimental Philosophy." *Review of Philosophy and Psychology* 3(3): 457–67.

Swain, Stacey; Alexander, Joshua; Weinberg, Jonathan M. 2008. "The Instability of Philosophical Intuitions: Running Hot and Cold on Truetemp." *Philosophy and Phenomenological Research* 76(1): 138–55.

Sytsma, Justin; Livengood, Jonathan. 2011. "A New Perspective Concerning Experiments on Semantic Intuitions." *Australasian Journal of Philosophy* 89(2): 315–32.

———. 2016. *The Theory and Practice of Experimental Philosophy*. Peterborough: Broadview Press.

Sytsma, Justin; Livengood, Jonathan; Sato, Ryoji; Oguchi, Mineki. 2015. "Reference in the Land of the Rising Sun: A Cross-Cultural Study on the Reference of Proper Names." *Review of Philosophy and Psychology* 6(2): 213–30.

Sytsma, Justin; Machery, Édouard. 2010. "Two Concepts of Subjective Experience." *Philosophical Studies* 151(2), 299–327.

Tannenbaum, David; Ditto, Peter H.; Pizarro, David A. 2007. "Different Moral Values Produce Different Judgements of Intentional Action." (Working Draft). URL: http://bit.ly/1ZTVpwB (accessed 31 October 2018).

Thaler, Richard; Sunstein, Cass. 2008. *Nudge – Improving Decisions about Health, Wealth, and Happiness*. New Haven: Yale University Press.

Tobia, Kevin; Buckwalter, Wesley; Stich, Stephen. 2012. "Moral Intuitions: Are Philosophers Experts?" *Philosophical Psychology* 26(5): 629–38.

Tsoi, Lily. 2016. "A Unified Versus Componential View of Understanding Minds." In: Sytsma, Justin; Buckwalter, Wesley (eds.), *A Companion to Experimental Philosophy*, Oxford: Wiley-Blackwell, 279–91.

Turri, John. 2013. "A Conspicuous Art: Putting Gettier to the Test." *Philosophers' Imprint* 13(10): 1–16.

———. 2016. *Knowledge and the Norm of Assertion – An Essay in Philosophical Science*. Cambridge: Open Book Publishers.

Turri, John; Rose, David; Buckwalter, Wesley. 2018. "Choosing and Refusing: Doxastic Voluntarism and Folk Psychology." *Philosophical Studies* 175(10): 2507–37.

Tversky, Amos; Kahneman, Daniel. 1981. "The Framing of Decisions and the Psychology of Choice." *Science* 211(4481): 453–58.

———. 1983. "Extensional Versus Intuitive Reasoning: The Conjunction Fallacy in Probability Judgment." *Psychological Review* 90(4): 293–315.

Tyler, Tom R., Mentovich, Avital. 2010. "Punishing Collective Entities." *Journal of Law and Policy* 19: 203–30.

Utikal, Verena; Fischbacher, Urs. 2014. "Attribution of Externalities: An Economic Approach to the Knobe Effect." *Economics and Philosophy* 30(2): 215–40.

Wallace, David F. 2003. *Everything and More: A Compact History of Infinity*. New York: W.W. Norton.

Wason, Peter C. 1968. "Reasoning About a Rule." *Quarterly Journal of Experimental Psychology* 20(3): 273–81.

Weinberg, Jonathan M. 2007. "How to Challenge Intuitions Empirically without Risking Skepticism." *Midwest Studies in Philosophy* 31(1): 318–43.

———. 2009. "On Doing Better, Experimental-Style." *Philosophical Studies* 145(3): 455–64.

———. 2014. "Cappelen between Rock and a Hard Place." *Philosophical Studies* 171(3): 545–53.

Weinberg, Jonathan M.; Gonnerman, Chad; Buckner, Cameron; Alexander, Joshua. 2010. "Are Philosophers Expert Intuiters?" *Philosophical Psychology* 23(3): 331–55.

Weinberg, Jonathan M.; Nichols, Shaun; Stich, Stephen. 2001. "Normativity and Epistemic Intuitions." *Philosophical Topics* 29(1–2): 429–60.

Wilkins, John S.; Griffiths, Paul E. 2013. "Evolutionary Debunking Arguments in Three Domains: Fact, Value, and Religion." In: Maclaurin, James; Dawes, Greg (eds.), *A New Science of Religion*. London: Routledge, 133–46.

Williams, Bernard. 1970. "The Self and the Future." *The Philosophical Review* 79(2): 161–80.

Williamson, Timothy. 2005. "Armchair Philosophy, Metaphysical Modality and Counterfactual Thinking." *Proceedings of the Aristotelian Society* 105: 1–23.

———. 2007. *The Philosophy of Philosophy*. Oxford: Blackwell Publishing.

———. 2009. "Replies to Ichikawa, Martin and Weinberg." *Philosophical Studies* 145(3): 465–76.

———. 2010. "Philosophy vs. Imitation Psychology." *The New York Times*. URL:http://nyti.ms/11YWJRh (accessed 31 October 2018).

———. 2011. "Philosophical Expertise and the Burden of Proof." *Metaphilosophy* 42(3): 215–29.

———. 2016. "Philosophical Criticisms of Experimental Philosophy." In: Sytsma, Justin; Buckwalter, Wesley (eds.), *A Companion to Experimental Philosophy*, Oxford: Wiley-Blackwell, 22–36.

Wittgenstein, Ludwig. 1953/1999. *Philosophical Investigations*. Oxford: Basil Blackwell.

Woolfolk, Robert L. 2013. "Experimental Philosophy: A Methodological Critique." *Metaphilosophy* 44(1–2): 79–87.

Wright, Jennifer Cole; Bengson, John. 2009. "Asymmetries in Judgments of Responsibility and Intentional Action." *Mind and Language* 24(1): 24–50.

Young, Liane; Cushman, Fiery; Adolphs, Ralph; Tranel, Daniel; Hauser, Marc. 2006. "Does Emotion Mediate the Relationship between an Action's Moral Status and Its Intentional Status? Neuropsychological Evidence." *Journal of Cognition and Culture* 6(1–2): 291–304.

Zalla, Tiziana; Leboyer. Marion. 2011. "Judgment of Intentionality and Moral Evaluation in Individuals with High Functioning Autism." *Review of Philosophy and Psychology* 2(4): 681–98.

Appendix A

This book mainly focuses on four areas within x-phi, namely, epistemology, the philosophy of language, intentional action, and free will. There are, however, numerous further areas of x-phi research. In the following, I very briefly and selectively review some of the most significant ones, namely, ethics, metaphysics, the philosophy of science, and logic and rationality.

A.1 ETHICS

Ethics is the theoretical study of morality. Ethical theories usually focus on what is right or permissible to do and offer criteria to determine this in concrete situations. Three families are most commonly distinguished, namely, consequentialist, deontological, and virtue-ethical theories. All of them have been subject to experimental investigation.[1]

Joshua Greene has famously argued, using fMRI studies (Greene et al. 2001; Greene 2008), that characteristically deontological judgements correlate with processes in areas of the brain that are associated with emotion processing. Deontological theories, which seek to account for such judgements, are therefore best regarded as mere rationalisations of emotional responses. (This, Greene holds, is "The Secret Joke of Kant's Soul," which is the title of his influential paper. Kant, the famous deontologist, claimed, after all, that his theory was based entirely on *reason*.) In contrast, characteristically consequentialist judgements, argues Greene, are not based on emotional processes and may, hence, be considered more rational. Greene's experimental research has prompted numerous responses, some critical (e.g. Berker 2009) and some supportive (e.g. Singer 2005). Greene, in turn, has responded to them (Greene 2014). (See Heinzelmann 2018, Mukerji 2014 and 2016, and Paulo forthcoming, for more recent discussions.)

Doris (1998, 2002) has taken on virtue ethics using empirical evidence from social psychology (for a similar contribution, see also Harman 1999b). Virtue ethics, roughly speaking, instructs the individual to develop the character of a virtuous person. Doris argues that this idea runs afoul of the important principle that "ought implies can," which states that an ethical theory cannot require the agent to do something that is impossible for her. As Doris explains, research in social psychology by and large supports, however, a view that is called "situationism." It holds that human agents act more or less uniformly in many situations. Doris thinks, therefore, that situationism shows, in conjunction with the principle that ought implies can, that virtue ethicists have largely made unjustifiable demands.

Like Greene's view, Doris's position has also led to much debate in ethics. See, for example, Annas (2005) for a critical rejoinder, Alfano (2013) for an overview, and Alfano (2018) for an up-to-date assessment. One conclusion some participants of the debate have drawn is that ethicists should focus on the choice environment in which people act rather than just the principles to be consciously applied by moral agents themselves (Grundherr 2016, Rodgers & Warmke 2015). This basic idea is behind what has come to be known as "nudging" (Thaler & Sunstein 2008). It is also a fundamental tenet of order ethics (Luetge & Mukerji 2016), which is an ethical approach that is commonly used in business ethics and public policy debates.

A.2 METAPHYSICS

Metaphysics is, to put it in very rough terms, the study of the fundamental nature of reality. Within metaphysics, there are various subfields that deal with different questions. Many of them have been addressed by experimental philosophers. Here is one example.

Wherein consists the *identity of a person*? Under which conditions should we say that A and B are the same person? When are they different persons? This problem has concerned philosophers throughout history. Locke has famously proposed a psychological account (Locke 1710/1975): A and B are the same if they are *psychologically continuous*, that is, if they have the same memories, personality traits, and so on. Locke substantiated this using his famous thought experiment of the cobbler and the prince. If the two were to swap "souls," as it were, such that the soul of the prince is in the body of the cobbler and vice versa, we would feel inclined to say, it seems, that the person who has the soul of the prince *is* the prince. As Williams (1970) has pointed out, however, this might all be a matter of perspective. If I am told I will be tortured tomorrow, I should be frightened. This holds even if I am told, also, that I will not remember this announcement. Here, the aspect relevant to me seems that the body which will be tortured will be *physically continuous* with me. What should we do with these two conflicting intuitions? Nichols & Bruno (2010) have approached this problem experimentally working on the supposition that intuitions should be given more weight the more robust they are. Depending on the framing of the question, they found evidence that the folk intuitively agree with the psychological and the physical account. However, once they pointed out that the two contradicted each other and forced their participants to choose, a significant majority (64 percent) sided with the psychological account. For a recent response to Nichols & Bruno (2010), see Berniūnas & Dranseika (2016).

Causation is a further major issue in metaphysics that has received attention from experimental philosophers. One influential study is the one by Hitchcock & Knobe (2009). They investigate the idea of *actual causation* (or token causation), which is commonly distinguished from the idea of the causal structure. The latter can be illustrated as follows. Consider three persons: A, B, and C. A poisons C's drink. C dies. However, if A had not poisoned C's drink, B would have, and C would have died anyway. We recognise this configuration of actual and possible events and counterfactual dependencies as the causal structure of the situation. Over and above that, however, we recognise that A *actually caused* C to die, while B did not. Now, Hitchcock and Knobe ask which purpose the idea of actual causation serves. The existence of this notion is somewhat puzzling. After all, if we know the causal structure of a situation, we know more than if we only know the patterns of actual causation. So why should we not go with the former idea and dispense with the latter? Hitchcock and Knobe seek to answer this question in part by surveying empirical findings on how ordinary folk determine causes. The folk do this, the authors claim, by identifying relevant counterfactuals which, in turn, are picked out by applying norms. For example, if A and B both do an act, ϕ, and ϕ causes event E, then people are most likely to identify ϕ as the cause if A was not supposed to do ϕ (by some social norm) or does not normally do ϕ (as a matter of statistical regularity). Then, they explain why this way of identifying causes seems helpful by showing that it guides us in determining the most suitable interventions for avoiding particular effects. For a critical rejoinder to Hitchcock & Knobe (2009), see Alicke et al. (2011). For a helpful overview of the literature, see Rose & Danks (2012).

A.3 PHILOSOPHY OF SCIENCE

The philosophy of science investigates various related philosophical questions that have to do with the enterprise of science. Among them are, for example, ontological, epistemological, ethical, and even political issues. In addition, there are linguistic problems like the question what important scientific terms mean. Experimental philosophers have joined the debate in the philosophy of science mainly to contribute to the latter sorts of issues and, specifically, to help analyse what scientific terms mean either to scientists or to scientifically untrained laypeople. Influential studies focused, for example, on the concepts of the *gene* (Stotz et al. 2004, Stotz & Griffiths 2004, Stotz 2009) and *innateness* (Griffiths et al. 2009; Khalidi 2016; Knobe & Samuels 2013; Linquist 2018) in the philosophy of biology specifically, as well as on *explanation* (Lombrozo 2006, 2009) in the general philosophy of science. For an early overview of the extant literature, see Griffiths et al. (2008) as well as Stotz (2009), and both Machery (2016) and Lombrozo (2016) for more recent discussions.

In addition, there have been many interesting developments in various areas that could be classed as belonging to the experimental and empirically informed philosophy of science. Studies in moral psychology are among them. Some researchers have discussed the moral convictions of scientists, for example, those of climate scientists (Bray & von Storch 2017). Others have examined scientific fields in view of its ethical challenges. See, for example, the recent study by Mittelstadt & Floridi (2016) on big data ethics in biomedical contexts.

A.4 LOGIC AND RATIONALITY

Experimental psychologists have investigated, for a number of decades, whether human subjects abide by the laws of logic when they reason. They have concluded, for the most part, that ordinary folk violate central norms of rationality very frequently. Two famous examples shall serve to illustrate this.

The first is Peter Wason's so-called selection task (Wason 1968). Wason gave his subjects a problem like this: There are four cards in front of you. Each has a letter on one side and a number on the other. You can only see the side of the card facing up. $Card_1$ has, say, the number 8 showing, $card_2$ the letter A, $card_3$ the letter C, and $card_4$ the number 5. Now consider the following rule: *If one side of the card shows a vowel, the other side shows an even number*. Which cards do you have to turn over to check whether all four cards obey this rule? Which ones are safe to ignore? Since a conditional like this is false if the antecedent is true and the consequent false, you have to turn over $card_2$ (true antecedent) to see if there is an uneven number on the other side (false consequent). You also have to check $card_4$ (false consequent) to see whether it has a vowel on it (true antecedent). Even though this is quite a simple task, most people tend to get it wrong. Instead, they most commonly flip over cards that the rule seems to talk about, that is, $card_2$ showing a vowel, which is correct, and $card_1$ showing an even number, which is incorrect. Most subjects leave card$_4$ untouched which, again, is a mistake. Interestingly, some tasks that are similar to Wason's in terms of their logical structure produce strikingly different results. Consider, for example, the "drinking age problem" (Griggs & Cox 1982). The rule is: *If somebody drinks alcohol, they must be of age*. When faced with this rule, people tend to determine, correctly, that they have to ask people who are drinking (true antecedent) their age and that they have to check whether underage people (false consequent) are drinking alcohol. Cosmides & Tooby (1992) have hypothesised that the difference in performance can be explained by the fact that humans do not possess a general reasoning capacity but several specialised problem-solving machineries. They are content-dependent and have evolved for specific purposes, for example, the policing of social norms.

The second example is the "Linda problem," (Tversky & Kahneman 1983) which is commonly interpreted as showing that ordinary folk commit an error in probabilistic reasoning known as the *conjunction fallacy*. Subjects are asked to imagine a person, Linda, who, as they are told, is 31 years old, single, outspoken, and very bright. She majored in philosophy in university, took part in antinuclear demonstrations, and has always been deeply concerned with social justice. After that, subjects are asked to rank statements about Linda in terms of likelihood – among them the following two: (1) "Linda is a bank teller." (2) "Linda is a bank teller and active in the feminist movement." Interestingly, people tend to rank (2) above (1). This violates the principle that the conjunction of two events cannot be more probable than either one of the conjuncts on their own. Tversky & Kahneman (1983) hypothesised that subjects who commit this error follow a mental shortcut: the *representativeness heuristic*. Instead of asking whether (1) or (2) is more likely, they ask which is more representative of the person described.

What do experimental philosophers have to contribute to the discussion about findings such as these? Here are three examples.

Firstly, they can make relevant distinctions between different interpretations of existing experiments. This can have dramatic effects on the interpretation of the experimental findings. Stephan Hartmann and colleagues have, for example, suggested in a number of publications (Bovens & Hartmann 2003, 85–88; Hartmann & Meijs 2012) that the judgements of Tversky's and Kahneman's participants in the Linda problem might have been entirely rational. To see this, consider the following comparison between two cases. In the first case, imagine, you ask Anna a question, Q_1, to which you do not know the answer. She gives you the answer A_1. How confident should you be that Anna's answer, A_1, is correct? What is the appropriate credence level, $Cr_1(A_1)$? In the second case, suppose once more, you ask Anna question Q_1. Again, you do not know the correct answer. She responds that the answer is A_1. Let us stipulate, however, that in this second case you ask her an additional question, Q_2, to which you do know the correct answer. It is A_2. Anna's answer is, in fact, A_2. How confident should you be that Anna's answers, A_1 and A_2, are correct? What should your credence level, $Cr_2(A_1\&A_2)$, be? And now compare the two cases. It does not seem irrational to ascribe a higher credence level to the conjunction $A_1\&A_2$ in the second case than to A_1 in the first, such that $Cr_2(A_1\&A_2) > Cr_1(A_1)$. After all, in the second case, Anna has proven to be a somewhat reliable source by answering Q_2 correctly. Perhaps, then, Tversky and Kahneman's subjects had something analogous in mind? Experimental philosophers are called upon to find out!

Secondly, experimental philosophers can follow the line of reasoning we examined in section 2.5. Prompted by empirical results such as the ones discussed earlier, they can investigate how the folk understand concepts that are central to psychological experiments. Pfeifer (2012), for example, examines how ordinary people understand conditionals, such as the following sentence (Adams 2005): *If Jones's first card will be an ace, then his second card will be too.* How sentences like these should be understood is important because, depending on the chosen interpretation, the likelihood of it being true is either very high or very low. If the sentence is understood as referring to a *conditional event*, the appropriate probability is $P(card_1$ is ace$|card_2$ is ace$) = 3/51 = 0.06$. If, instead, it is taken to refer to a *material conditional*, the probability is much higher. The material conditional is true if the antecedent is false or the consequent true. It is false otherwise. Accordingly, we have $P(card_1$ is ace $\supset card_2$ is ace$) = 1 - P(card_1$ is ace & $card_2$ is not ace$) = 1 - (4/52 \times 48/51) = 0.93$. Niki Pfeifer has tested empirically which interpretations of conditionals his subjects would endorse (Pfeifer & Kleiter 2010, 2011; Pfeifer 2012), concluding that people tend to interpret conditional statements as referring to conditional events.

Thirdly, x-phi researchers can engage with results about the reasoning of experimental subjects by discussing what we should, all things considered, conclude from them. An example of such an investigation is the contribution by Samuels & Stich (2004), who review findings as well as explanations given for them by different theorists. They note that authors who, following Kahneman and Tversky, work in the *heuristics-and-biases* tradition tend to arrive at a rather dim view of human rationality. In contrast, evolutionary psychologists think much more highly of it, holding that people often rely on evolved mental modules that help them navigate their world successfully. Samuels and Stich examine the various theses of the two camps, analyse how far they are compatible, and offer a resolution where they find persistent disagreement.

NOTE

1. For an overview, see Alfano & Loeb et al. (2018).

Appendix B

B.1 ONLINE RESOURCES

Experimental Philosophy Blog

http://philosophycommons.typepad.com/xphi

This is Thomas Nadelhoffer's x-phi blog. It started in 2004 and has 75 contributors from all over the world. Many of them are among the frontline researchers on whose contributions this book has mainly focused (their contact details are conveniently accessed by clicking on their name in the contributors' list on the left side). Overall, the blog has over 1,100 posts and more than 4,000 comments on all sorts of issues relating to x-phi. Content is bundled into categories (e.g. /action theory), which makes it easy to look for contributions relating to a particular topic. Unfortunately, Thomas Nadelhoffer closed the blog down in 2017. However, the archived content is still accessible and a valuable resource that is surely worth a visit!

Experimental Philosophy Page

http://experimental-philosophy.yale.edu/ExperimentalPhilosophy.html

The Experimental Philosophy Page is maintained by Jonathan Phillips and Christian Mott. It is based at Yale University. There are links to free web resources and books on x-phi. Furthermore, the blog links to various x-phi research groups and graduate programmes. It also allows one to search for x-phi literature sources (via a link to the PhilPapers database).

Experimental Philosophy (X-Phi) Facebook Group

https://www.facebook.com/groups/3040510972

The Experimental Philosophy (X-Phi) Facebook Group is moderated by Wes Anderson, Édouard Machery, and Thomas Nadelhoffer. This group is the place to be for anyone who wants to stay up to date about what is happening in the x-phi world. Postings include new findings and papers on x-phi, events (conferences, workshops, etc.), calls for papers, and so on.

PhilPapers

https://philpapers.org

PhilPapers is a bibliographic database of philosophical texts that is maintained by the general editors David Bourget and David Chalmers as well as numerous further area editors. There is a general area on x-phi and various subareas (https://philpapers.org/browse/experimental-philosophy) and various subareas.

Stanford Encyclopedia of Philosophy (SEP)

http://plato.stanford.edu

The SEP is an excellent (and quotable) online resource for peer-reviewed and open-access encyclopaedic articles on a large range of philosophical topics. In recent years, x-phi has increasingly been acknowledged by authors of the encyclopaedia. By now, it contains over 50 entries mentioning the term "experimental philosophy" (https://stanford.io/2Mx5u2l). The most noteworthy ones seem to be the entries "Experimental Philosophy" (https://stanford.io/2vZBxkC) by Knobe & Nichols (2017), "Experimental Moral Philosophy" (https://stanford.io/2vzrenQ) by Alfano & Loeb et al. (2018), and "Intuition" (https://stanford.io/2B05XJa) by Pust (2014).

Video Websites

http://www.philostv.com, http://www.bloggingheads.tv, http://www.meaningoflife.tv, http://www.youtube.com

Philosophy TV is a video website devoted to philosophical thinking maintained by managing editors David Killoren and Jonathan Lang. It features conversations between philosophers about various philosophical topics, including x-phi. Among the contributors are, for example, Mark Alfano, Joshua Knobe, Édouard Machery, Al Mele, Jennifer Nagel, Eddy Nahmias,

Jesse Prinz, Eric Schwitzgebel, Stephen Stich, and Justin Sytsma. Unfortunately, the website stopped posting new content in late 2016.

In contrast, Bloggingheads.tv and MeaningofLife.tv are still being updated. These two websites also offer conversations on various topics, including some on philosophical issues. Here, too, a number of experimental philosophers have made an appearance. Joshua Knobe, it seems, has practically moved in with Bloggingheads.tv. As of October 2018, he has appeared 25 times on the website.

Various conversations from Philosophy TV, Bloggingheads.tv, and MeaningofLife.tv also circulate on YouTube, as do many further talks and conversations related to x-phi and philosophy more broadly.

B.2 INTRODUCTORY TEXTS

There are, by now, many short papers that can serve as points-of-entry to x-phi. Among the early texts, Joshua Knobe's and Shaun Nichols' "Experimental Philosophy Manifesto" (2008) is, perhaps, the most noteworthy and most widely read. This introductory essay, which was published in the paper collection *Experimental Philosophy* (2008) edited by Knobe and Nichols, discusses basic metaphilosophical questions surrounding x-phi as well as its aims and methods. Also noteworthy is Joshua Knobe's early *Philosophy Compass* paper "Experimental Philosophy" (2007), where he introduces x-phi via examples from the experimental literature on reference, moral judgement, and free will. In it, he also addresses its philosophical significance. A few years later, Knobe et al. (2012) published a paper also entitled "Experimental Philosophy" in the *Annual Review of Psychology*. This text emphasises the interdisciplinary nature of x-phi as a collection of research programmes at the intersection of philosophy and psychology. It introduces x-phi research through a discussion of select x-phi contributions and with a focus on four fields of study where philosophers and psychologists have recently collaborated.

Apart from these general texts, there are many more specific discussions that can serve as introductory readings on specific problems about and within x-phi. Alexander et al. (2014), for example, discuss the contrast between positive experimental philosophy ($X-Phi_P$) and negative experimental philosophy ($X-Phi_N$) and offer a critical rejoinder to the pro $X-Phi_P$ stance of Nahmias et al. (2005, 2006). Williamson (2016) voices a number of fundamental concerns about x-phi and, specifically, $X-Phi_N$. Rose & Danks (2013) discuss the contrast between a narrow and a wide conception of x-phi, arguing decidedly for the latter. They are critical of the narrow view, later defended in Knobe (2016), that x-phi is simply the practice of cognitive science by philosophers. Furthermore, numerous papers on various thematic areas of x-phi have appeared in the past ten years, for example, Alexander's and Weinberg's

"Analytic Epistemology and Experimental Philosophy" (2007), Griffiths' and Stotz's "Experimental Philosophy of Science" (2008), and Sommers' "Experimental Philosophy and Free Will" (2010).

In addition, there are two introductory books on x-phi, namely, Joshua Alexander's *Experimental Philosophy – An Introduction* (2012) and Justin Sytsma's and Jonathan Livengood's *The Theory and Practice of Experimental Philosophy* (2016). Both are very instructive. The former touches upon many important themes, such as the role of intuitions in philosophical analysis and philosophical methodology more broadly, and it discusses x-phi research in various fields, for example, free will, ethics, epistemology, and the philosophy of language. In a closing chapter, it also offers a defence of x-phi against common criticisms. The latter book is rather different. Though it also discusses theoretical and principled aspects, the better part of Sytsma's and Livengood's book (chapters 5–14) is devoted to the practice of x-phi. It discusses, for example, how empirical research questions are developed, how appropriate research designs are determined, and how instruments are designed and administered. Above that, it offers a concise introduction to R, which is a widely used statistical software package (http://cran.r-project.org).

B.3 BOOKS

In the past few years, a number of important books on x-phi have been published. Knobe's and Nichols's *Experimental Philosophy* (2008) and *Experimental Philosophy – Volume 2* (2014) are two important paper collections. The papers are mostly reprints of influential contributions to x-phi. Later on, further book publications followed. Most of them are standalone titles: *Experimental Philosophy and Its Critics* (2012, ed. by Joachim Horvath and Thomas Grundmann), *Philosophy – Traditional and Experimental Readings* (2012, ed. by Fritz Allhoff, Ron Mallon, and Shaun Nichols), *Philosophical Methodology – The Armchair or the Laboratory?* (2013, ed. by Matthew Haug), *Current Controversies in Experimental Philosophy* (2014, ed. by Édouard Machery), *Experimental Ethics – Toward an Empirical Moral Philosophy* (ed. by Christoph Luetge, Hannes Rusch, and Matthias Uhl), and, perhaps most notably, the colossal 600-page *Blackwell Companion to Experimental Philosophy* (2016, ed. by Justin Sytsma and Wesley Buckwalter).

There are also notable series and multivolume works: In 2007, the first three volumes of *Moral Psychology* (ed. by Walter Sinnott-Armstrong) were published, followed by two more in 2014 and 2017. These five volumes touch upon many x-phi themes that are related to experimental ethics and folk morality. In 2015, Bloomsbury started *Advances in Experimental Philosophy*, which, as of October 2018, has eight installations and two announced titles. This includes volumes on innovative and recent developments, such as experimental work on logic and mathematics. *The Oxford Studies in Experimental Philosophy* series started in 2014 and consists of two volumes.

Appendix C

This book mainly focused on the historically most influential strand of x-phi, which investigates intuitions about philosophical issues and thought experiments. Hence, our discussion was confined to a number of experimental techniques that naturally suggest themselves in the empirical study of philosophical intuitions. However, if x-phi is construed more broadly, for example, as any "empirical work undertaken with the goal of contributing to a philosophical debate" (Stich & Tobia 2016, 5), then a number of additional methods may become relevant.[1] These are, among other things, bibliometrics, formal methods, tools from economics, evolutionary arguments, neuroscientific approaches, qualitative methods, and sting operations. In the following, I will give a very brief and selective overview of these methods. For a more comprehensive discussion, see the new volume *Methodological Advances in Experimental Philosophy* (2019) edited by Eugen Fischer and Mark Curtis.

C.1 BIBLIOMETRICS

Bibliometrics is the systematic statistical analysis of written texts. It can be used to test whether claims researchers make about a given field are plausible since these claims commonly allow empirically testable predictions about observable patterns in the literature. Here are two examples:

- Some philosophers of biology (e.g. Buller 2005) have claimed that the evolutionary behavioural sciences (esp. evolutionary psychology), which seek to explain behavioural traits in terms of evolutionary processes and adaptations, have a poor understanding of evolutionary theory and rely, as a result, on evidential standards that evolutionary biologists would reject.

According to these philosophers, evolutionary behavioural scientists rely mainly on outdated research on evolutionary biology from the 60s and 70s and ignore modern developments in the field.
- Philosophers (e.g. Williamson 2005) have claimed that philosophy is, at least according to the view prevalent in analytic philosophy, an armchair discipline whose practitioners seek to unearth a priori truths using deductive arguments. These arguments usually start with an intuition although, as Goldman has suggested, only the use of the term "intuition" is a new development. Great philosophers of times past have, he argues, always relied on intuitions though they did not call them by their modern name. In fact, "In the history of philosophy, and even in the early years of analytic philosophy," says Goldman, "the terminology of intuition is not to be found" (Goldman 2007, 2).

The philosophers who make such claims base them mainly on the *case-study method*. They rely, that is, on the analysis of specific contributions to the literature that they take to be of importance. This method undoubtedly has its strengths. For example, it allows the philosopher to go into considerable depth when he or she analyses the texts he or she has selected. However, it also has its drawbacks. Most importantly, the selection of texts that the philosopher works with can be biased (Machery 2016). She can choose to work only with texts that serve to make her point while ignoring other parts of the literature that countervail her conclusions. The various methods of bibliometric analysis allow experimental researchers to detect such bias.

The first of these methods is *citation analysis*. Machery & Cohen (2012) use this technique to test, among other things, whether the claim that evolutionary behavioural scientists rely mainly on outdated evolutionary science from the 1960s and 1970s is plausible. This thesis, after all, allows an empirically testable prediction, namely, that "the ratio of the number of citations from the 1970s to the number of citations from the 1990s should be substantially higher in biology than in psychology or anthropology (i.e. in the non-evolutionary behavioural sciences)" (Ibid., 188). Working with a three-year sample from the flagship journal *Evolution & Human Behavior*, Machery and Cohen report to have found "no evidence for a grossly distorted influence of the theories and findings in the evolutionary biology of the 1970s on the contemporary evolutionary behavioral sciences" (Ibid., 209).

The second method is an *indicator word search*. Andow (2015) uses this method to ascertain whether intuition talk has been on the increase in analytic philosophy (answer: yes) and whether this increase was markedly greater than in philosophy generally and in academia as a whole (answer: again, yes to both questions). To this end, he used articles from the journals *Mind* and *Philosophical Review*, which analytic philosophers view as two of their most acclaimed publication organs, and compared the rate of occurrence of indicator words for intuition talk (namely "intuit," "intuition," "intuitive," "intuitions," "counter-intuitive," "intuitively," and "counter-intuitively") with the rate of occurrence in other disciplines. Furthermore, Andow found evidence which contradicts Goldman's earlier mentioned claim that the terminology of intuition cannot be found in early analytic philosophy. As he states, "in both *Mind* and *Philosophical Review* intuition talk is common throughout the period surveyed [i.e. starting from 1900; NM]" (Andow 2015, 205; emphasis in the original, NM).

Ashton & Mizrahi (2018b) used the same method to test whether there is evidence for the view that philosophers mainly use deductive, rather than inductive, arguments. If that were true, they say, "we would expect philosophers to frame their arguments using mostly deductive indicators, such as 'necessarily,' 'certainly,' and 'conclusively,' rather than inductive indicators, such as 'probably,' 'plausibly,' and 'likely.'" (Ibid., 61) Using a sample from the JSTOR Data for Research corpus (http://dfr.jstor.org) from the years 1840 to 2012, they found that the percentage of articles using deductive indicator words was higher throughout most of this period. However, the percentages have converged over time so that "it looks like deductive arguments are gradually losing their status as the dominant form of argumentation in philosophy" (Ibid., 67).

The third method is a *categorisation approach* as used, for example, by Knobe (2015c). He wanted to know, among other things, whether the methods that philosophers nowadays employ differ from the methods they used to employ in the twentieth century. An indicator word search seems ill-suited to address this question because it is not entirely clear which methods would relate to which words. What is possible, though, is to categorise papers from different periods in terms of their methods, aggregate them, and compare the results. This is what Knobe did. He collected the most highly cited papers in the philosophy of mind from two periods: 1960–1999 and 2009–2013. Then, he categorised these papers in terms of their methods using the following categorisation system:

(a) Those that use only a priori reasoning and do not rely on results of empirical studies.
(b) Those that actually report original empirical results.
(c) Those that do not report original empirical results but do rely on the results of empirical studies published elsewhere (Knobe 2015c, 37).

He found that papers from period 1960–1999 largely employed only a priori methods (62.4 percent), while a smaller proportion relied on existing empirical findings (37.6 percent). No paper contained original empirical research results. In contrast, a majority of the papers from period 2009–2013 relied on empirical findings (61.8 percent), a sizable portion even contained original empirical results (26.8 percent), and a small fraction of articles used only a priori methods (11.5 percent).

Compared with the indicator word search, the categorisation approach has, of course, a number of downsides. Perhaps most importantly, it is more time-consuming and involves an element of subjectivity. However, it allows experimental researchers to approach more complex questions that require a certain degree of judgement in the categorisation of the material.

C.2 FORMAL METHODS

As I said in the conclusion of the book, x-phi and its methods are often seen as rivals of other traditions and techniques in philosophy. Experimental philosophers are partly to blame for this. As we have seen in section 1.6, proponents of X-Phi$_N$ have argued against the use of one very traditional method, namely, the MAP. This may have created the impression that experimental methods are generally incompatible with more traditional philosophical methods, for example, with formal approaches to philosophical problems. One such formal approach is Carnap's (1950/1962) method of *explication*, which, it seems, is often proposed as a methodological alternative to the data-driven approach of x-phi practitioners. As we have seen in section 3.2.4, Pinder (2017) argues for the method of explication to counter the experimental attacks on philosophical theories of reference (Machery et al. 2004; Mallon et al. 2009).

It seems reasonable to ask, however, why formal methods should be incompatible with formal methods in general and explication in particular. This is not very likely. Machery (2017, chap. 7) has recently made encouraging remarks about explication, a number of scholars have meanwhile embarked on experimental investigations of formal issues (Pfeifer 2012, 2014; Pfeifer & Douven 2014; Pfeifer et al. 2017; Pfeifer & Pankka 2017; Sanfilippo et al. 2018), and the recently published comprehensive *Blackwell Companion to Experimental Philosophy* (2016) contains a section on "Logic and Reasoning," where three authors explain how experimental and formal methods can be used symbiotically (Douven 2016; Ripley 2016; Schupbach 2016; see, also, appendix A.4). Also, some authors have recently explicitly defended a methodological combination of experimental investigation and Carnapian explication (Schupbach 2017; Shepherd & Justus 2015).

In fact, the argument suggests itself once we consider the notion of explication in a bit more detail. To Carnap, explication is the method of replacing a vague folk concept (e.g. warmth), which he calls the "explicandum," with a more precise scientific concept (e.g. temperature), which he refers to as the "explicatum." As he explains, an explication is successful to the extent that the explicatum fulfils a number of criteria, namely, "(1) similarity to the explicandum, (2) exactness, (3) fruitfulness, (4) simplicity" (Carnap 1950/62, 5). As Schupbach (2017) argues, experimental inquiry can help us to ascertain whether a given explication fulfils the first criterion, that is, the similarity to the explicandum. The degree of similarity that an explicated (or engineered) concept bears with the pre-theoretic folk concepts is usually judged by relying on one's own intuitions. Since these intuitions are, as we know, not necessarily representative of a language community as a whole (see chapter 3 of this volume), it seems preferable to conduct systematic studies to assess what the characteristics of a given explicandum really are. In other words, it is preferable to use the methods that proponents of x-phi have developed. In addition, x-phi research about folk concepts may provide information that bears on the degree of similarity that a given explication can reasonably be required to deliver. If it turns out that a given folk concept is ambiguous or excessively vague, then this may be used as a justification for eliminating it or for replacing the explicandum with a rather dissimilar explicatum (Machery 2017). This, after all, seems justified, on Carnap's view of explication, if empirical information shows that it is impossible to find a more similar concept that is also sufficiently exact for scientific purposes.

These considerations show, I believe, that formal methods can be fruitfully supplemented with experimental research techniques. It may be asked, however, whether there is also reason to believe that experimental researchers in philosophy should also care about formal methods and, in particular, about explication. I think there are at least two reasons. Firstly, the literature on concept explications can be a valuable research heuristic for experimental philosophers who are interested in finding questions to study. Before the advent of x-phi, philosophers and scientists have, after all, proposed numerous explicata in various fields, and these are practically waiting to be studied by experimental researchers. Secondly, it may be that the combination of Carnapian explication makes for a more defensible version of experimental philosophy overall. Schupbach (2017), at any rate, has recently defended this claim. As he argues, some of the arguments against x-phi that we considered in chapter 4 can be effectively rebutted by combining X-Phi$_p$ and Carnapian explication. A common argument against studying folk judgements is that we cannot expect to gain any philosophically relevant insights from them because, at the end of the day, the folk are just laypeople. So why should their judgements matter? As Schupbach points out, however, when we combine Carnapian explication with experimental research we are "not interested in what non-philosophers think about our philosophical questions." Rather, "we are taking an important step toward ensuring that the explicatum that we proceed to examine – with all of our philosophical expertise – connects to the proper object of study," namely, the object of study that we, philosophers and non-philosophers alike, care about. (In other words, Schupbach's point is that we practice a kind of experimental philosophy that is sanctioned by what we called the argument from relevance, as discussed in section 2.5.)

C.3 TOOLS FROM ECONOMICS

Philosophers have used various tools from economics to study philosophical problems empirically. They have, for example, used game theory to study the logic of human interactions. This method is most relevant, of course, to practical philosophy and, more specifically, to political philosophy and ethics. In addition, there are applications in other areas of philosophy, such as social epistemology.

The philosopher who is mostly credited with having introduced game theoretic considerations to the analysis of societal problems is Thomas Hobbes (1651/1995). He argued for the justification of a tyrannical ruler: the Leviathan. The logic he used was, roughly, the following. Imagine we lived in a "state of nature" with no government. In conflicts over scarce resources, each of us would then be judge, jury, and executioner at the same time since there would be no higher authority to turn to. Because we would constantly be afraid that others might abuse their absolute power, we would try to beat them to the punch and apply force pre-emptively. This, in turn, would lead to a spiral of violence that would make all our lives, as Hobbes famously put it, "solitary, poore, nasty, brutish, and short" (Hobbes 1651/1995, 84). In that situation, we would be better off with an all-powerful dictator who strikes down conflicts as soon as they arise. This, after all, would stop the spiral of violence. In other words, tyrannical state power would be better for all of us compared to the baseline case of a potentially nasty state of nature. Therefore, it would be justified.

As citizens of modern liberal democracies we would, of course, object to Hobbes's argument for tyranny. This is not to say, however, that he was not on to something. There are aspects of it we can learn from, as modern political philosophers have recognised. To illustrate, consider, for example, the modern debate about public health insurance. The existence of such an arrangement seems desirable because citizens should, it seems, be willing to pay a premium to exclude the risk of not being able to afford treatment for a serious illness. However, there is a problem with any such system, and this problem is analogous to the one that Hobbes diagnosed about his state of nature. If every treatment citizens demand is paid for by the health care system, this will incentivise exploitative behaviour. Out of fear that other people will abuse the system to pay for things they do not really need, you and me will do so, too. This, in turn, will raise costs for society as a whole. Of course, this does not mean that public health care systems are unjustifiable. It does mean, however, that we have to project the likely empirical consequences of any specific system and consider them in the argument. It has long been recognised that game theory is perhaps the most important empirical research tool for doing this (Alfano & Rusch et al. 2018; Braithwaite 1955). For this reason, it is commonly used by political philosophers and ethicists to empirically analyse the problems they study (Luetge & Mukerji 2016).

As I said earlier, game theory can also be used outside of practical philosophy (de Bruin 2005, 2010), for example, in social epistemology. Philosophers who work in this area study epistemic aspects of social systems, for example, science and democracy. One of the issues debated here is the production and sharing of knowledge across society with the help of scientific experts. From an epistemological perspective, the problem is to explain how the transfer of knowledge from an expert in a scientific field to society at large is even possible. For, as we have seen in section 3.1.1, knowledge seems to require justified true belief (in addition to whatever else it requires). A person who merely acquires a true belief without a suitable justification for it does not really know it. Now, crucially, when we consult experts, they normally do not give us detailed justifications for their beliefs. They simply tell us what they think because we, as non-experts, would probably not even understand their reasoning in its entirety. Accordingly, it is a conundrum how we can gain knowledge from them. One way to explain this is to say that we can treat their status as experts as a justification for believing what they say. But why should we do that? For all we know, the experts might lie to us. To fill this gap in the argument, we can appeal to game theory, as Blais (1987) has proposed we do. He argues that once we analyse, with game theoretical techniques, the empirical properties of the "knowledge game," we understand that it is, generally speaking, not in the self-interest of experts to lie to us. Science, after all, is a self-policing enterprise. Participants who can be proven to lie or misrepresent the facts have their careers and reputations ruined. At least, that is the argument. Whether it is sound with respect to any specific area of science will, of course, depend on the specific empirical properties of the knowledge game that is played there. Some areas, it may be argued, are corrupt. For more information on how this might be determined empirically, see section C.7.

A second set of tools from economics that philosophers can use comes from *experimental economics* whose methodology differs in various respects from the methodology that research in x-phi has mostly followed. As our discussion of influential x-phi studies has made clear, most of them rely on experimental research practices that are borrowed from experimental psychology, the most common ones being vignettes and questionnaires (e.g. Knobe 2003a; Machery et al. 2004; Nahmias et al. 2005, 2006; Weinberg et al. 2001). Typically, a philosophical case or problem is presented to a group of subjects, and they are asked to answer questions about it. Though they are usually compensated for their participation, the compensation is a fixed amount that does not depend on the way they behave in the experiment. In contrast, and this is the first methodological difference, participants in an experimental economics study must be compensated, and the amount they receive must depend on their performance. A second difference is that in psychological studies subjects are frequently deceived by experimenters. Furthermore, a third salient difference is that researchers in experimental economics often keep a pool of participants over a longer period to study how the behaviour they exhibit in experiments changes over time. In contrast, researchers in psychology hardly ever proceed in that way.[2]

To illustrate how the methodology of experimental economics can contribute to the discussion of a philosophical issue, consider the following claim: People behave more ethically when others can observe what they do. This idea has been a philosophical commonplace throughout the ages. It underlies, for example, the famous thought experiment of the Ring of Gyges that Glaucon proposes to Socrates (Plato 1997, 360b–d). It also figures in Justice Brandeis's famous remark that "sunlight is said to be the best of disinfectants" (Brandeis 1914, 92). Is it true, though? And do ordinary folk believe it? To find out, we could simply ask test subjects whether they act more unethically in private and whether they believe people generally behave more ethically in public. Apart from the obvious problem that people often misjudge their own psychology and behavioural tendencies, such an experiment would have an additional flaw. People tend to report behaviour they think is socially desirable.[3] This is one of the problems experimental economics is supposed to neutralise by fiddling with participants' incentives. Ostermaier & Uhl (2017) used it to test whether individuals do, in fact, behave more ethically when others can observe what they do. They were specifically interested in the case of lying. To this end, they told participants to roll a die and record the result. Subjects were informed that they would be paid according to the outcome of the roll (2€ x number of eyes). Individuals could cheat without risk (e.g. by recording 5 instead of 2) because nobody checked the result of their role and every outcome is equally likely. However, it is possible, using statistics, to infer the prevalence of cheating at the group level. Ostermaier and Uhl used this fact to compare two experimental conditions. In the public condition, subjects knew that they would have to report the outcome of their role "in public," that is, facing the other participants. In the private condition, they did not have to do this, and they knew it. In addition to this reporting task, there was a guessing task. Before subjects had even rolled their die, they had to estimate the average outcome reported at the group level. Their performance was, again, incentivised. They received €12 for the correct number and €2 less per 0.1 deviation. After the experiment, all participants were given a trolley case.

They had to judge whether it is permissible to divert a trolley that threatens to kill five persons to another track where it will kill only one. Ostermaier and Uhl used participants' answers to categorise them as "outcome-minded" (if they answered affirmatively) or "rule-minded" (otherwise).

The experiment yielded two basic insights. Firstly, participants seemed to expect unethical behaviour in both groups, but a little more in the private condition. If everybody had expected truthful reporting, the guesses should have averaged to 3.5. Instead, the results were 4.18 (private condition) and 4.27 (public condition), respectively, which was not a statistically significant difference. Interestingly, then, ordinary folk do not seem so convinced that sunlight is, indeed, the best disinfectant. Secondly, test subjects were wrong. The level of honesty was indeed significantly higher in public than in private, with subjects' reports averaging 4.38 (public condition) and 4.91 (private condition), respectively. This result, however, seemed to be driven almost entirely by the behaviour of outcome-minded people who conformed significantly more to their expectations of others' behaviour in the public condition. No significant difference was found for the rule-minded folks. Ostermaier's and Uhl's results suggest, therefore, that public scrutiny might, indeed, have positive effects if people tend to be outcome-minded and if they expect others to be more honest than they really are. This type of finding could not have been unearthed using a traditional vignette experiment. It illustrates why x-phi researchers are well advised increasingly to use the methodology of experimental economics.

Finally, a third tool from economics is *cliometrics*. Pointing to some promising research in the experimental philosophy of science, Machery (2016) suggests that it may be fruitfully applied in x-phi research. Cliometric research methods are quantitative techniques designed to find regularities in social and economic variables over time. As such, they have commonly been used in the study of social and economic history. However, they may, as Machery argues, drawing on work by Paul Meehl, also be used to analyse problems in the philosophy of science. Specifically, Meehl (1992, 2002, 2004) proposed to apply cliometrics to analyse which properties of a scientific theory (e.g. simplicity, explanatory power, and rigour) make it successful, that is, guide it to the truth (or verisimilitude). Since the relationship is, plausibly, probabilistic such that certain properties will make theory success more likely than others (but not inevitable), statistical methods seem to be called for to solve the problem. To apply them, it is necessary, in a first step, to identify and formalise various properties of theories and to metricise the predictive power of theories. Then, it is possible to analyse historical theories statistically and to explain their comparative success in terms of their properties. If successful, such a research programme could conceivably reveal the properties of successful theories more reliably than researchers' judgements such that one could identify the winner theory in a scientific dispute considerably earlier. This, in turn, might allow the scientific community to allocate resources more efficiently. X-phi researchers, it seems therefore, should consider cliometrics as a research tool when it is applicable.

C.4 GENEALOGICAL ARGUMENTS

Genealogical arguments have long been popular in philosophy. They aim to "explain away," as it were, particular philosophical theses by analysing the historical origin and development of belief in them, that is, their genealogy. Friedrich Nietzsche, for example, famously suggested a genealogical explanation for religious belief (Nietzsche 1878/1986). So did David Hume (Hume 1757/2007). Both are sometimes cited as forefathers of x-phi (Knobe & Nichols 2008).

Nowadays, perhaps the most popular form of the genealogical argument is the *evolutionary debunking argument* (EDA) which, arguably, goes back to Charles Darwin's own ideas (Jong & Visala 2014). It relies on empirical inputs from the evolutionary sciences and, in particular, the evolutionary behavioural sciences (esp. evolutionary psychology). The EDA is applicable to various fields, among them ethics (e.g. Singer 2005), metaethics (e.g. Joyce 2006a, 2006b), and the philosophy of religion (e.g. Goodnick 2016). In all these areas, it serves the purpose of undermining credence in a particular claim by establishing that belief in it is (or can be explained by) an evolutionary adaptation that is not truth-tracking. Accordingly, to be sound, evolutionary arguments have to establish, firstly, that a given belief is (or is based on) an adaptation and, secondly, that it is not truth-tracking.

By design, EDAs run the risk of committing the "genetic fallacy," (Jong 2012) which is the error of dismissing a belief based on its origin though plausible reasons for its truth exist. Accordingly, it is plausible to suspect, as some authors have argued (e.g. Nichols 2014; Wilkins & Griffiths 2013), that the plausibility of EDAs differs depending on their domain of application. Furthermore, the scepticism they raise about a particular belief can infect many other beliefs, giving rise to an unattractive form of global scepticism (Kahane 2010). Perhaps the most contested versions of the EDA have been proposed in ethics.

C.5 NEUROSCIENTIFIC APPROACHES

Within philosophy, neuroscientific approaches have been applied predominantly to ethics and the free will debate, using various methods.[4]

Based on evidence from fMRI studies, Greene (2008, 2014) has famously argued that deontological theories should be regarded as mere rationalisations of emotional responses to philosophical thought experiments (see appendix A.1). His reason for claiming this is that characteristically deontological judgements can be shown to correlate with increased brain activity in areas that are associated with emotional processing.[5] Depending on the methods employed and the nature of the reasoning in which neuroscientific input is used, such arguments can be more or less controversial. Like the EDAs we discussed in the previous section, Greene's neuroscientific approach, for example, runs the risk of committing the genetic fallacy. After all, he claims, roughly, that a given philosophical thesis is unreliable if it can be traced back to an unreliable causal origin. Deontologists can, it seems, reject this argument as irrelevant by providing an argument of their own which does not draw on the intuitions Greene seeks to debunk.[6]

However, not all applications of neuroscience to philosophical questions invite this type of critical response. We have already seen this when we discussed the x-phi of free will (in section 3.4).[7] Nichols & Knobe (2007), recall, proposed that individuals who judge that an agent in a deterministic scenario acts freely commit an affective performance error. Emotional processes, claim Nichols and Knobe, interfere with people's judgement. As we discussed, Cova et al. (2012) employed a neuroscientific approach to test this hypothesis. They used individuals with frontotemporal dementia as test subjects because we know from neuroscience that this condition leads to a reduced ability to process emotional information. Accordingly, on Nichols' and Knobe's hypothesis, subjects with frontotemporal dementia should choose the compatibilist option in thought experiments significantly less. Cova et al. (2012), however, did not confirm this prediction, thus casting doubt on the affective performance error model.[8] For a similar study regarding the Knobe effect, see Young et al. (2006).

That said, neuroscientific approaches certainly hold great promise but have been comparatively rare in x-phi studies. This certainly has to do with the degree of specialisation that is required to do neuroscientific investigations (Bickle 2018). In addition, tremendous costs can be involved, at least in the case of fMRI experiments.

C.6 QUALITATIVE METHODS

So far experimental philosophers have almost exclusively employed quantitative statistics-based research methods. As we have seen in our discussion of the most influential x-phi studies, they have offered their participants thought experiments with a limited set of alternatives for answers. Subjects could respond, for example, by saying "yes" or "no" or by choosing a point value on a Likert scale. The data were then translated into a given metric format. This approach has many advantages. It allows researchers, for example, to analyse vast swaths of data in a fairly straightforward and standardised way. However, the quantitative approach also has its downsides. One important downside is that it requires testable hypotheses to start with, for example, "Do the intuitions of ordinary folk agree with the descriptivist theory of reference for proper names?" If researchers are unsure, however, which hypothesis to pursue, they cannot rely on quantitative methods. In that case, they might be better off asking participants open-ended questions. This is the qualitative approach. Its methods comprise interviews, focus groups, which are little discussion groups, and so-called "think aloud studies", in which participants are given a standard x-phi questionnaire and asked to think aloud while answering it. What participants say is recorded, transcribed, and coded using a coding manual, which instructs coders what to look for (e.g. apparent contradictions, specific concepts, patterns of thought, and so on). Quantitative methods such as an indicator word search (see section C.1) can assist in the analysis.[9]

Recently, a number of x-phi researchers have proposed, called for, or employed qualitative methods (e.g. Andow 2016; de Curz 2018; Feltz & Millan 2015; Lim & Chen 2018; Nichols & Bruno 2010). To illustrate how such research might be conducted, consider Devitt (2015), who has proposed that qualitative techniques from linguists might help us to test theories of reference for proper names. Rather than handing out vignettes and asking the participants whether (or to which extent) they agree with given statements about them, we may proceed as follows. In a first step, we find participants who are "experts" on, say, a particular pop star, for example, Beyoncé. These participants, we may reasonably assume, refer to Beyoncé when they use the name "Beyoncé." Then, we give them one of two vignettes to read. In both of them, a person uses the name "Beyoncé" and makes a statement about the person she refers to using that name. In the first case, she has a description in mind that identifies Beyoncé correctly, while, in the second case, she has a false description in mind, which does not identify Beyoncé. After that, we ask our participants to explain what happens in the vignettes they read. Russell's descriptivist theory of reference for proper names (see section 3.2) would seem to allow a prediction for both cases. In the first, where the person associates the correct description with "Beyoncé," participants should be significantly more willing to say that the person in the vignette made a statement referring to Beyoncé. In the second, where she has a false description in mind, our participants should be unwilling to say that she referred to Beyoncé. Though Devitt ultimately rejects this experimental approach, it illustrates the possibility of conducting experiments in philosophy about topics such as reference without relying on the conventional vignette approach. The particular approach he describes has some advantages over the latter. For one thing, we are not after people's intuitive judgements about the reference of proper names. Rather, we examine how they use them. Since some philosophers think intuitions are irrelevant to philosophical questions (see section 4.3.5), this approach might strike them as less controversial. Also, if ordinary people do not use "Beyoncé" in a way that confirms the descriptivist theory, we can still use our data to come up with new hypotheses. We can do this because the data we have collected is much richer in information than the data that is commonly collected in standard vignette studies. To sum up then, x-phi researchers are well advised to consider qualitative methods to supplement their toolbox.

C.7 STING OPERATIONS

As we have seen under section C.1, researchers are sometimes interested to examine a general empirical hypothesis about an entire field of study. Machery & Cohen (2012), for example, used the method of citation analysis to investigate whether evolutionary behavioural scientists rely, by and large, on outdated evolutionary theory. However, citation analysis (and bibliometrics more generally) is not the only empirical method which can be used to assess entire scientific fields. Another one is the sting operation. It is applied to gauge the quality controls that are applied in a particular area.

In a recent study published in *Nature*, Sorokowski et al. (2017) report on a sting operation they conducted to assess the practices and procedures of open-access journals. Given the recent proliferation of predatory open-access journals, which publish articles of poor quality for a fee, researchers were interested to find out whether blacklisted open-access journals were comparatively more willing than whitelisted journals to accept fake scientists as editors.[10] They created a profile of a fictitious scientist named "Anna O. Szust" and used it to apply to 360 open-access journals for the position of editor. "The profile," they explain, "was dismally inadequate for a role as editor. Szust's 'work' had never been indexed in the Web of Science or Scopus databases, nor did she have a single citation in any literature database." (Above that, the name contained an "Easter egg:" The word "oszust" means *fraud* in Polish.) Researchers found that of the blacklisted journals about a third accepted the application, while only very few of the whitelisted journals, most of which have by now been kicked off those whitelists, did accept the application.

In the humanities, such sting operations have been conducted, too. The most well-known one is certainly the infamous *Sokal hoax*. Concerned about the abuse of mathematical and scientific concepts in the writings of postmodern thinkers (e.g. Lacan, Kristeva, Irigaray, Baudrillard, and Deleuze), the physicist Alan Sokal wrote a parody paper (Sokal 1996), which mimicked the sophisticated style of these authors' writings but was, as he puts it, "chockfull of absurdities and blatant non-sequiturs" (Sokal & Bricmont 1998, 1–2). He submitted it to *Social Text*, a well-reputed and fashionable journal in the area of cultural studies, which accepted and published it. What does this show? Admittedly, not too much. As Sokal himself said later on, "the mere fact the parody was published proves little in itself; at most it reveals something about the intellectual standards of *one* trendy journal" (Sokal & Bricmont 1998, 3; emphasis in the original).

Recently, Pluckrose et al. (2018) conducted a more systematic sting operation, which has become known in social media circles as #sokalsquared. They wrote 20 fake papers and submitted them to journals in fields they collectively refer to as "grievance studies," among them cultural studies, gender studies, and race studies. Pluckrose et al. (2018) did this, they explain, to test their suspicion that these areas of study are corrupt in various ways. Specifically, they wanted to test whether reputed journals in these fields will publish papers that are methodologically and ethically suspect, contain assertions that might be dangerous if taken seriously, or consist simply of "rambling nonsense." One paper argued, for example, that men should be trained like dogs to counteract rape culture. Another proposed to ask white male students to sit on the floor in chains during class so that they could "experience reparations." Yet another advised straight males to self-penetrate anally in order to decrease transphobia. When the study ended, seven out of the 20 papers had been accepted, seven more were "still in play," as the authors put it, and the remaining six had been retired due to fatal flaws. Pluckrose et al. (2018) argue, therefore, that "there are excellent reasons to doubt the rigor of some of the scholarship within the fields of identity studies that we have called 'grievance studies.'" Whether this conclusion is warranted remains to be seen, of course. The debate is still in its early stages.

Suffice it to say that, in the brief time since the publication of this sting operation, some scholars have voiced concerns of various kinds. Pluckrose et al. (2018), for example, evidently seek to argue that the fields they targeted are especially problematic in comparison to other fields. They provide, however, only partial evidence for this conclusion since they do not engage in a comparative study with other fields. In addition, some scholars have pointed out that issues concerning research ethics might be at stake.[11] Sting operations are certainly controversial empirical research tools whose usage should be considered carefully.

NOTES

1. Note, however, that this encompassing understanding of x-phi would be more in line with E-Phi (see section 1.4) and with what Rose & Danks (2013) have called a "broad conception of experimental philosophy."

2. See Hertwig & Ortmann (2001) on the methodological differences between experimental psychology and experimental economics. For a plea in favour of the experimental economics methodology in ethics research, see Jauernig (2017).

3. This is the well-known *social desirability bias* (Edwards 1953).

4. A further important area in which philosophers draw on insights from neuroscience is, of course, the debate about consciousness, which I set aside for reasons of space.

5. Greene also uses *reaction-time measurements* to provide further support for his thesis that characteristically deontological responses are the product of emotional processes. Reaction times are relevant because Greene's thesis makes a prediction about them. People who respond based on emotion should be quicker in their judgements than people who override their emotion and give a reasoned response. For another study that uses reaction-time measurements, see Arico et al. (2011).

6. I do not intend to adjudicate the debate about Greene's argument here. For fuller discussions of the points touched on here, see Kumar & Campbell (2012) and Königs (2018).

7. A further celebrated application of neuroscience to the debate about free will is, of course, the contribution by Benjamin Libet (2002).

8. Similar approaches have been used in the debate about theory of mind (see Tsoi 2016).

9. For a fuller description of the qualitative approach as it relates to x-phi, see Andow (2016).

10. The blacklist Sorokowski et al. (2017) used was the well-known "Beall's list" compiled by University of Colorado librarian Jeffrey Beall. The whitelists were those of the Journal Citation Reports (JCR) and the Directory of Open Access Journals (DOAJ).

11. Sorokowski et al. (2017), for example, report having consulted an ethics review board prior to conducting their study. In contrast, Pluckrose et al. (2018) did not consult a review board. For this reason, Portland State University (PSU) has meanwhile investigated one of the hoaxsters, namely, Peter Boghossian, who is an assistant professor at PSU. It was concluded that, by participating in the hoax, Boghossian violated the university's ethical guidelines for human-subjects research. (Mangan 2019)

Index

abstractness, 51, 77, 110–11
action: intentional action, 87–103; philosophical theory of action, 87–90.
adaptation, 203, 212
adversarial cooperation, 142
affect, 95, 111–13
affective performance error, 111–12, 124n55, 144, 213
agent causality, 105
Alexander, Joshua, 16, 18, 20, 67, 165n8, 199–200
Alfano, Mark, 192, 196n1, 198, 209
alternate possibilities, 106, 117, 158
American Supreme Court, 100
analogy: between empirical and philosophical observation, 34–39; between intuition and vision, 20–21, 37–38. *See also* argument, from analogy
analytic philosophy (A-Phi), 4–8, 18, 22–26, 31, 42, 51, 70, 73–74, 85, 134, 136, 155–56, 159, 169, 204–5. *See also* method, method of analytic philosophy
Andow, James, 6, 75–76, 116–17, 120, 124n51, 124n55, 204–5, 214, 217
anger, 96
Anscombe, Gertrude E. M., 90

a posteriori, 2–3, 8–9, 13–16, 22–27, 31, 54
Appiah, Kwame A., 28n9, 86
a priori, 2–5, 8–9, 13–16, 22–27, 31, 127, 149, 162, 164, 204–6
argument: from agreement, 41–44, 147, 161; from analogy, 55n1, 57n30; from disagreement, 43–44, 66, 82, 161; from expertise, 160; from framing effects, 49–51, 67, 146; from intercultural variation, 66, 82; from irrelevant factors, 45–47, 66–67, 72, 82; from majority opinion, 146–47; from reference, 86, 122n19; from relevance, 129, 208; from reliability, 39, 128; from socioeconomic variation, 66–67, 71–72; transcendental argument, 4. *See also* experimentally informed argument
armchair philosophy (AC-Phi), 1–4, 8–10, 13–15, 22–26, 52, 144, 149, 169
Asperger syndrome, 92
attitudes, 97–101
autism spectrum disorder, 92

Bat-and-Ball problem, 44
Bealer, George, 35, 153, 155

Bear, Adam, 87, 124n51, 125n60
Bedeutung, 78
Beebe, James, 83
belief. *See* doxastic voluntarism *vs.* involuntarism; knowledge, standard analysis of; reliabilism
bias, 95, 122n18, 133, 142, 144, 160, 167n40, 204. *See also* experimenter bias; heuristics-and-biases tradition; social desirability bias
biased questionnaire/vignette, 122n18, 142
biased sample, 133, 163
bibliometrics, 6, 203–6, 215
big data ethics, 194
blame. *See* praise and blame
blinding, 138–42, 166n16
blind review, 139, 166n13
blind spots, 38
Bonferroni correction, 168n42
Bonjour, Laurence, 155
brain, 14–15; and emotional information, 113; implant case, 116; and information processing, 95, 191, 213; rewiring case, 68; surgery case, 62
Bratman, Michael, 90
British empiricists, 5
Buckwalter, Wesley, 43, 132, 200
burden of proof, 17, 93, 103, 106, 116, 120, 149, 155
business ethics, 192
bypassing, 113–17, 120, 124n55

Cappelen, Herman, 6, 27n4, 27n6, 87, 131, 154–55, 159–61, 164n2, 167n30
Carnap, Rudolf, 57n29, 86–87, 122nn20–21, 122n23, 206–7
case-study method, 204
categorisation approach, 205–6
causal-historical theory of reference. *See* reference, causal-historical theory of
causation, 193. *See also* agent causality; event causality
Chalmers, David, 27n8, 167n32, 198
charity. *See* principle, of charity
Chomsky, Noam, 166n15

circularity. *See* vicious circularity
citation analysis, 204
classical philosophical question, xvii, 3, 6, 10–11, 13–17, 19, 21–26, 31–32, 51–52, 75, 127–28, 148, 151, 154
cliometrics, 211–12
coding manual, 214
cogito argument, 4
cognitive error, 139, 144, 164
cognitive process, 10, 25–26, 40, 64, 74, 147
cognitive science, 52, 135, 199
Colaço, David, 27n4, 28n14, 43, 167n33, 168n43
collectivism, 103
compatibilism, 17–18, 42, 51, 103–18, 123n46, 128, 139. *See also* free will; incompatibilism; source compatibilism
computer-based study, 140
conceptual analysis, 19
conceptual engineering, 86, 207
conceptual inventory, 53
concreteness, 109–11
conflict of interest, 160
confounder. *See* internal validity
conjunction fallacy, 195–96
consciousness, 165n12, 217n4
consequentialism, 40, 56n13, 144, 165n11, 191. *See also* epistemic consequentialism
constitutional law, 100–101
context effect, 49–50. *See also* framing effect
context of discovery *vs.* justification, 159–60, 167n39
contradiction, 137, 165n10, 214
control: actual *vs.* regulative, 116–17
counter-example, 33–34, 36, 55n8, 61–62, 79, 155
counterfactual dependency, 193
counter-intuitiveness, 40, 55n7, 103, 105, 107, 155, 160, 168n42, 205;
cultural studies, 216
culture, 63–64, 73, 76, 82–83, 85, 92, 118–19, 123n42, 132

Index

data collection. *See* validity
deception, 210
deductive *vs.* inductive arguments, 205
definite descriptions, 78–79, 119, 156
dementia, 113, 165n7, 213
democracy, 209
Dennett, Daniel, 4, 56n24, 106, 123n47
deontology, 40–41, 55n12, 56n13, 191, 213, 217n5
Descartes, René, 3–4, 8–9, 13–14, 74, 76
descriptions. *See* definite descriptions
desire, 113, 115, 123n36
determinism, 16–17, 41, 51, 104–20, 124n55, 125n60, 142, 144, 213; hard determinism, 123n45. *See also* free will
Deutsch, Max, 6, 27n4, 71, 84, 87, 122n17, 143, 146, 154–61, 165n8, 167nn30–39
Devitt, Michael, 87, 122n18, 142, 214
dialetheism, 165n10
disagreement, 41–45, 56n15, 56n16, 66, 70, 82, 134–35, 150, 161
disgust, 46–47, 64
dispute. *See* verbal dispute
diversity, 160
doctrine of double effect, 101
Doris, John, 71, 136, 192
doxastic voluntarism *vs.* involuntarism, 74–75
dualism. *See* metaphysical dualism

East Asians, 20, 64–65
economics, 135; tools from economics, 208–12. *See also* experimental economics
education, 65, 72, 134, 163
effect size, 50
eliminativism, 122n19. *See also* race, race eliminativism
emotions, 40, 46–47, 64, 95, 108–13, 139–40, 191, 213, 217n5
empirically informed philosophy (E-Phi), 12–15, 22–26, 31, 39
epistemic consequentialism, 75–76
epistemic permissibility, 76

epistemology. *See* knowledge
error theory, 45, 93–96, 108, 113, 115, 124n50, 140, 144; types of error theories, 124n55
ethics, 40, 55n12, 75, 101, 191–92
ethnicity, 20, 42, 65–66, 72, 143
event causality, 105
evolution, 53, 195–96, 203–4
evolutionary debunking argument, 212
evolutionary psychology, 203–4
experimental economics, 101, 135, 209–11
experimentally informed argument, 31–57; force of, 40
experimental philosophy: as cognitive science (X-Phi$_C$), 8–12, 15, 17, 21–26, 31, 74–75, 92–93, 118–19, 127–28, 130–31, 150–51, 164, 169, 199; indirect role of, 159–61; as metaphilosophical critique (X-Phi$_N$), 19–26, 31, 39, 54, 63, 67, 70, 75–76, 80, 85, 93, 118–19, 127–31, 136, 150–55, 159, 161–62, 169, 206; as philosophical methodology (X-Phi$_P$), 15–19, 21–26, 31, 39, 54, 75–66, 92–93, 101, 103, 107, 115, 119, 127–31, 134, 150–55, 159, 161–62, 169, 207
experimenter bias/demand, 73, 121n5, 138–40, 142, 145, 163
expertise defence/expertise reply, 136–37, 163, 165nn8–9
explanation, 194
explication, 57n29, 122n20, 206–7; explication defence, 86–87
extension, 121n11
external validity, 131–37, 144–45, 163

facts: basic facts, 53; facts and observations, 33–36; philosophical facts, 35–36
fallacy, 47. *See also* conjunction fallacy; genetic fallacy; naturalistic fallacy
fatalism, 115–17, 124n57
fMRI study, 191, 213
folk concept, 52, 87, 93, 95–96, 107, 119, 121n8, 122n25

folk judgement, 28n13, 75–76, 113, 136, 144, 146, 194–96
folk psychology, 73, 103
framing effect, 47–50, 67, 70, 146, 165n12, 193
Frankfurt, Harry, 124n58, 156–58, 167n36
Frankfurt case, 124n58, 156–58
free will, 2, 10, 15–17, 41–42, 51–53, 103–18, 213; conditions for free will, 105–6
Frege, Gottlob, 77–78
frontotemporal dementia. *See* dementia
fruitfulness, 122n21, 207

game theory, 208–9
gender, 132
gender studies, 216
gene, 194
genealogy, 212
genetic fallacy, 160, 212–13
Gettier, Edmund, 8, 55n8, 61–62
Gettier case, 55n8, 61–62, 73, 76, 151–52, 155
Gettier intuition. *See* intuition, Gettier intuition
Glock, Hanjo, 5, 27n5, 171n2
Gödel, Kurt, 79
Gödel case, 79–87, 119, 122n18
Goldman, Alvin, 6, 155, 165n8, 204–5
group agency, 102–3
Grundmann, Thomas, 167n29, 200

Hacker, Peter, 149
Haidt, Jonathan, 46, 64
Hales, Steven, 16, 165n8, 166n26
harm principle, 56n19
Hartman, Stephan, 195–96
health insurance, 208–9
heuristic, 195–96, 207
heuristics-and-biases tradition, 196
Hobbes, Thomas, 123n46, 208
honesty. *See* lying
hopelessness, 19, 153
Hume, David, 33, 123n46, 212
hypothetical scenario, 151–52

Ichikawa, Jonathan, 121n15, 167n29
identity. *See* personal identity
illusion. *See* optical illusion
implicature, 121n16
incentives. *See* experimental economics
incompatibilism, 16–17, 41–42, 104–20, 142, 144, 155. *See also* compatibilism; free will
indifference, 94, 100–101, 123n37
individualism, 103
innateness, 194
intension, 121n11
intention: in the action, 88–90; motivating intention, 89–90; prior intention, 89
intentional action, 87–103
internal validity, 137–44
interview, 118, 214
intuition, 4, 39, 41–47, 49–50, 63, 66–67, 79, 82, 86, 128, 136, 147; appeal to intuition, 5–6, 40, 87, 146, 153; concept of intuition, 35–36, 149–51; consequentialist intuition, 40–41, 55n12, 144; deontological intuition, 40–41, 55n12, 144; epistemic intuition, 63–76; faculty of intuition, 20; "free will no matter what" intuition, 115–17; Gettier intuition, 73, 76; independent confirmation of intuition, 21, 153; moral intuition, 46–47; in philosophical argument, 5–6, 154–61, 204–5; referential intuition, 80–87; trustworthiness of, 20, 54, 63. *See also* method, method of analytic philosophy
intuition-driven romanticism, 63
intuition mongering, 40, 55n12
intuition pump, 4
intuitive plausibility, 5, 8, 17–19, 42
involuntarism. *See* doxastic voluntarism *vs.* involuntarism
Is-Ought-dichotomy, 166n22

Jackson, Frank, 19, 51–52, 56n25, 155
jargon. *See* philosophical jargon

jealousy, 159–60
judgement asymmetry, 123n36. *See also* Knobe effect
judgement scepticism, 152–54, 161

Kahneman, Daniel, 44, 47–48, 195–96
Kane, Robert, 41, 106
Kant, Immanuel, xvii, 27n1, 191
Knobe, Joshua, 9–11, 25, 28n9, 73–74, 83, 87, 90–103, 109–14, 117, 119, 121n4, 121n6, 122nn28–30, 123nn32–38, 124nn50–54, 125n60, 133, 139, 141–42, 146, 166n16, 166n19, 193–94, 198–200, 205–6, 209, 212–13
Knobe effect, 11, 83, 87–103, 119, 122n30, 123n36, 124n50, 213
knowledge, 3, 6–8, 34–36, 42, 50, 59–76, 151–52, 155, 209; foundation for, 3–4, 13; standard analysis of, 6, 35, 151, 155. *See also* cogito argument
Kripke, Saul, 79–83, 87, 119, 122n24, 155–56

language: naïve view of, 77; philosophy of, 76–87
language communities, 76, 82, 207
law, 100–101
libertarianism, 105–6. *See also* free will; incompatibilism
lifeworld, xix, 28n13, 51, 92, 106, 128
Linda problem, 195–96
linguistic competence *vs.* performance, 166n15
linguistic turn, 77
Locke, John, 6, 123n46, 192
logic and rationality, 194–96
lying, 122n25, 152, 210–11

meaning, 78, 139, 151. *See also* reference; semantic *vs.* speaker meaning
mental module, 196
mental shortcut, 195

mental state, 74, 113, 115–17, 141, 150, 166n24
metametaphilosophy, 21–26
metaphilosophy, 19, 21–26, 85, 93, 119, 127, 199
metaphysical dualism, 14
metaphysics, 192–93
method: method of analytic philosophy (MAP), 5–8, 10, 18, 18–24, 34, 51, 60, 63–64, 70, 80, 93, 151, 154, 159, 161–62, 167n33, 206; method of cases, 27n4. *See also* explication; metaphilosophy
methodology of philosophy, 1–29
Mill, John Stuart, 123n46, 124n57
mind *vs.* body. *See* metaphysical dualism
moral judgement, 45–46, 103, 199
moral psychology, 194, 200
moral responsibility. *See* responsibility
motivated reasoning, 167n40
Mukerji, Nikil, xx, 36, 55n1, 55n11, 56nn13–16, 121n9, 123n37, 166n22, 169, 192, 209, 219
Müller-Lyer illusion, *37*

Nadelhoffer, Thomas, 17, 21, 95, 123n32, 124n52, 134, 197–98
Nado, Jennifer, 28n16, 55n6, 136, 150, 155, 167n29
Nagel, Jennifer, 11, 29n21, 50, 55n5, 72, 121n4, 121n7, 198
Nahmias, Eddy, 16–18, 21, 42, 56n26, 107–10, 113–18, 123n44, 124n51, 124nn54–55, 134, 139–40, 142, 144, 146, 155, 199, 209
naturalism, 122n19, 166n20
naturalistic fallacy, 166n22
natural kind concept, 87, 122n24
natural laws, 15, 104, 115. *See also* determinism
natural sciences, 2, 15, 28n17, 166n13
Nazi Germany, 98–99
neuroscience, 40, 52, 106, 113, 212–13
Nida-Rümelin, Julian, 40, 56n13
Nietzsche, Friedrich, 212

Nisbett, Richard, 64
normality, 87, 193
normative ethics. *See* ethics
nudging, 192

objections to x-phi, 127–68; methodological objections, 131–45; philosophical objections, 145–62; scope of, 127–31
observations: empirical observations, 32–34, 38; philosophical observations, 35–36, 38; reliability of, 36–39
online study, 140–42
opportunity sample. *See* sample
optical illusion, 37–38
order effect, 49, 69–70, 73. *See also* framing effect
order ethics, 192
ought implies can, 192
overgeneralisation, 133–34, 136–37

paradox, 36
performance error, 93, 101, 109, 111, 119, 124n53, 213. *See also* affective performance error
personal identity, 53, 192–93
personality, 43, 133, 165n5, 192
phenomenal state, 141
philosophical jargon, 139
philosophy: of action, 90–103; of biology, 193, 203–4; of knowledge, 3, 6–8, 34–36, 59–76; of language, 76–87; of law, 100–101; methodology of, 1–29, 31, 63, 73, 121n7, 152, 170; of mind, 103–18, 122n19; nature of, xvii, xix, 1, 9, 13–14, 21–22, 147–49; political philosophy, 208; of race, 86–87; of religion, 212; of science, 122n19, 193–94; views of, 21–26. *See also* metaphilosophy
philpapers, 125n60, 197–98
physical continuity, 193
physics, 15, 148, 171n1

pineal gland, 14
placebo, 138–39
Plato, 6, 61, 210
postmodernism, 216
pragmatics, 85, 94–95, 121n16, 139
praise and blame, 94–96, 102–3, 157
predatory journals, 215
prince-cobbler case, 6, 192
principle: of asymmetry, 34, 36; of charity, 146; of falsification, 33, 36
Prinz, Jesse, 16, 28n16, 137, 141–42, 199
problem of induction, 33
proper names, 77, 79–80; geographical *vs.* personal, 122n17
psychoanalytic argument, 160
psychological continuity, 192–93
psychology, 15; cognitive psychology, 32, 38, 44, 54; experimental psychology, 71, 163, 209; perceptual psychology, 38, 54; social psychology, 138, 192
Pust, Joel, 35, 56n14, 155, 198

qualitative research, 56n26, 118, 125n59, 164n1, 213–15, 217n9
quasi-experiment, 165n4
question. *See* classical philosophical question
Quine, Willard Van Orman, 166n20

race: race eliminativism, 86; race realism, 86–87; race studies, 216
randomisation, 69, 133, 138, 165n4
rationalisation, 40, 191, 213
rationality. *See* logic and rationality
Rawls, John, 19
reaction-time measurement, 217
realism, 122n19
reality, 27n1, 37, 45, 192
real-life case, 152
reason, 13, 25, 63, 191
reference, 76–87; argument from, 86, 122n19; causal-historical theory of, 79–80; descriptivist theory of, 79, 214
relativism, 165n10

reliabilism, 62–63, 67
religion, 212
relocation problem, 156, 159
replication, 71–72, 82–84, 92, 117–19, 121n4, 135, 141
#repligate, 71
representativeness heuristic, 195
representative sample: sample research ethics, 216
responsibility, 51, 113, 156–58. *See also* free will
rights, 100–101
Ring of Gyges, 210
Russell, Bertrand, 62, 77–81, 136–37, 156, 214

sample, 132–38; opportunity sample, 134–35; random sample, 133; representative sample, 132–38; sample size, 135, 165n7
scepticism, 130, 166n26, 212. *See also* judgement scepticism
Schwitzgebel, Eric, 137, 165n12, 199
Searle, John, 53, 88–89
self. *See* personal identity
self-interest, 160, 209
self-selection problem, 132–33
semantic *vs.* speaker meaning, 84–85, 121n16, 122n17
side-effect effect. *See* Knobe effect
simple view, 90–92, 95, 101
simplicity, 122n21, 207, 211
singular terms, 77, 79
Sinn, 78
social desirability bias, 210, 217n3
social epistemology, 209
social norms, 99, 195
social ontology, 103
socioeconomic status, 20, 42, 64–66, 71–72, 132–33
Socrates, 210
Sokal, Alan, 216
Sokal hoax, 216
#sokalsquared, 216
Sosa, Ernest, 20, 166n27
soul, 14, 212
source compatibilism, 116–17. *See also* compatibilism
speaker meaning. *See* semantic *vs.* speaker meaning
standard analysis of knowledge. *See* knowledge
statistics, 167n42, 210, 213
Stich, Stephen, 6, 11, 43, 63–64, 73, 76, 118, 132, 134, 165n6, 196, 199, 203
sting operation, 215–16
Sytsma, Justin, 8, 83–85, 121n15, 140, 143, 165n3, 166n18, 199–200

theory of mind, 217n8
thinking, 1–2, 47; analytic *vs.* holistic thinking, 64; everyday thinking, 52, 94
Thomson, Judith Jarvis, 147–48
thought experiment. *See* method, method of analytic philosophy
token causation. *See* causation
trolley case, 55n12, 210–11
truth, 211; of determinism, 105, 120; necessary truth, 4; truth value, 33, 78–79
Truth Fairy case, 75
two-worlds paradigm, 93

Uhl, Matthias, 200, 210–11

validity, 131–45. *See also* external validity; internal validity
ventromedial prefrontal cortex, 95
verbal dispute, 12, 27n8, 45
verbal framing. *See* framing effect
vicious circularity. *See* circularity
Vienna Circle, 77
virtue ethics, 191–92
visual sense, 20–21, 37, 39, 153
voluntarism. *See* doxastic voluntarism *vs.* involuntarism

Weinberg, Jonathan, 18–20, 42, 63–67, 70–74, 80, 82, 118, 121n4, 122n28, 132, 135, 142–43, 153, 166n28, 167n29, 199, 209

WEIRD, 134
well-being, 166n21
Westerners, 20, 64–65, 81–82, 84
Williams, Bernard, 192
Williamson, Timothy, 1–2, 27n1, 149–54, 165n8, 166n26, 167n29, 169, 199, 204

Wittgenstein, xix, 5, 52, 77, 88, 121n10, 148–49
Woolfolk, Robert, 134, 138, 140, 142, 166n16

x-phi. *See* experimental philosophy
X-Phi Replicability Project (XRP), 71

About the Author

Nikil Mukerji is a postdoctoral researcher in philosophy at Ludwig-Maximilians-Universität München (Munich, Germany) and academic director of the executive master's programme Philosophie Politik Wirtschaft (PPW), also at LMU. His interests include moral and political philosophy, informal logic, and experimental philosophy. He is the author of four monographs (*Das Differenzprinzip und seine Realisierungsbedingungen*, 2009, German; *Einführung in die experimentelle Philosophie*, 2016, German; *The Case Against Consequentialism Reconsidered*, 2016; *Die 10 Gebote des gesunden Menschenverstands*, 2017, German) and co-editor of two volumes (*Rethinking Responsibility in Science and Technology*, 2014; *Order Ethics – An Ethical Framework for the Social Market Economy*, 2016).

https://philpeople.org/profiles/nikil-s-mukerji

www.ingramcontent.com/pod-product-compliance
Lightning Source LLC
Chambersburg PA
CBHW021824300426
44114CB00009BA/316